NORTH SEA

HOLSTEIN

Hamburg

R. Elbe

HANOVER

Ber

R. Rhine

SAXONY

N'LANDS

Dresden

WEST-
PHALIA

Frankfurt

Pragu

BOHEMIA

BAVARIA

FRANCE

Munich

HAPSBURG

SWITZERLAND

ALTIC SEA

R. Oder

Danzig

PRUSSIA

RUSSIA

R. Vistula

Warsaw

SILESIA

POLAND

EMPIRE

HUNGARY

Vienna

R. Danube

Budapest

THE GERMAN
CONFEDERATION
in 1815

━┿━┿━ The Confederation
- - - - Country borders
.... State borders

GEIST DER KOCHKUNST

THE ESSENCE OF COOKERY

by

Baron von Rumohr

THE ESSENCE OF COOKERY

Geist der Kochkunst

by

Baron von Rumohr

now for the first time
translated into English

by

BARBARA YEOMANS

PROSPECT BOOKS
LONDON
1993

A catalogue record for this book is available
from the British Library

© English translation Barbara Yeomans

Published by Prospect Books, 45 Lamont Road, London SW10 0HU
Typeset by Serif Typesetting Ltd, Leeds

Printed and bound by Henry Ling Ltd, Dorchester

ISBN 0 907325 49 1

Contents

Translator's Introduction

Walter Bickel, writing in 1965, said, 'It is not easy to limit one's praise of this exceptional work.' Karl Friedrich Freiherr von Rumohr laid down the basic ground work upon which the true art of cookery is constructed. His official biographer, G. Poel, said in his article in the *Allgemeine Deutsche Biographie*, published in 1889, that Rumohr's *Geist der Kochkunst* exuded a certain feeling of ease and contentment and had achieved a tour de force in combining the art of living sensibly and well with the art of eating sensibly and well.

Rumohr's work is important for numerous reasons. Perhaps the primary reason is that it stands alone in giving us an accurate picture of eating throughout Germany in the early nineteenth century. Although Karl Friedrich Freiherr (Baron) von Rumohr was a nobleman, his interest was in good quality, everyday food and the traditional dishes of his country. He did not wish to indulge the fancies of the rich and was opposed to artifice of every kind. His principle was that one should be able to taste what one is eating.

He was the first in Germany to insist on making the best of natural raw materials, using art to bring out the good qualities of each foodstuff, not destroy them. He was constantly concerned that cooks should not destroy the individual flavour, colour and nutrients of foods by overcooking them or by cooking them in the wrong way, and in unsuitable combinations.

Rumohr wrote his book out of a genuine interest in cookery and eating, 'aus Leidenschaft für das Gute und Echte' (from a passion for what is good and authentic), in the words of Wolfgang Koeppen. For an amateur, he has an amazing knowledge of cookery styles and techniques, both ancient and modern, based upon his extensive reading and study, together with close observation. Being blessed with financial independence, he travelled a great deal during his lifetime, and this obviously increased his practical familiarity with foreign cuisines.

Rumohr's approach is philanthropic. He regards it as his mission to show his fellow countrymen and, particularly, women, how to

7

make the optimum use of the products of German agriculture at a time when the raw materials are undervalued due to over-production, the closing of certain foreign markets and imports of new products from other countries. His work is scientific, well ordered and practical. It is a book from which one really can cook and, for its time, is unusual in the precision of its instructions.

Rumohr's knowledge of and attitude to matters of nutrition, diet and hygiene are far in advance of his contemporaries. He tells us frequently that excessive washing and cooking will destroy, or at least impair the nutritional content of foods, and knows that different foods suit different people. Foods which are excellent eaten individually may not be good when combined, and dishes which are left standing around for too long will not be wholesome. He advises that all kitchen equipment be kept scrupulously clean and instructs cooks and servants to be fastidious in their personal habits.

Finally, besides giving us a clear view of contemporary German eating, the book offers a wealth of minutely observed cultural details. We can learn a great deal about German housekeeping, trade, attitudes and fashions. Rumohr is not pretentious. He simply believes wholeheartedly in his subject.

Although the book obviously achieved a measure of success in the nineteenth century, it has been somewhat forgotten since then. It does not deserve this neglect. It first appeared at a time when French cookery writers were particularly prolific and its honest approach stands in fine contrast to the airs and graces of the bulk of the French books. Walter Bickel points out that Rumohr was a contemporary of well-known French gastronomes such as Brillat-Savarin and Grimod de la Reynière and believes firmly that the German was their superior in terms of the depth and scope of his knowledge. Bickel agrees with the view of other experts that Rumohr's lack of success is largely due to the fact that he was not French and did not live in Paris.

By the end of the French revolution, social boundaries in that country had changed beyond all recognition. The nouveaux riches, many with purses enlarged by profits from the wars Napoleon was waging, thronged drawing rooms that formerly would have been closed to them. Nobles who had fled the revolution as emigrés and had returned to a penniless existence found themselves on the same social footing with commissaries who sold provisions and goods to the army. Men who had lived precariously by bartering were now successful financiers. It was the day of the self-made man, eager to elevate himself socially and to enjoy the life of the privileged, presenting the evidence of this success to the world. A logical way of achieving this was by establishing a reputation as a lavish and sparkling host.

The revolution saw a noticeable hiatus in the production of cookery books in France. The new order under Napoleon, together with the scientific advances in cooking stoves, increased interest in the properties of individual foodstuffs and the introduction of new products, such as the tomato which was by now being grown in Provence, soon gave birth to a number of books which have become famous in culinary history.

In 1803, Grimod de la Reynière began publishing his *Almanach des Gourmands*, to which Rumohr refers. This was not a cookbook, but rather a manual of advice, and it continued to be published until 1812. Grimod de la Reynière was an eccentric character, born into a wealthy family and cruelly fond of playing pranks on his fellow men. In post revolutionary France he saw his chance to assist the nouveaux riches in becoming splendid hosts and the Almanach discussed subjects such as foods in season, new culinary ideas and behaviour at table. It recommended suppliers, chosen by a Jury de Gustateurs organised by Grimod from among his friends in the arts, and discussed the restaurants springing up all over Paris and the establishments where ready-cooked entrées and pastries could be bought. In 1807, Grimod published a more elaborate work to guide his readers, the *Manuel des Amphitryons*, covering everything a host needed to know for the management of a distinguished table.

While Grimod de la Reynière was giving out advice, the great cookbooks of the new classic French cuisine were beginning to appear. The first was *Le Cuisinier Impérial* by A. Viard in 1806. The work was named for the Emperor whose taste for classicism gave the new cuisine its name. Its title subsequently changed according to whoever was in power in France, the fourth and final change being for the Third Republic in 1871, when it became Le Cuisinier National. This was a true cookery book, presenting most of the basic sauces of the new cuisine along with soufflés, sautés and recipes using the new tomatoes and potatoes. The author did not pretend to cover all cuisine, but hoped to provide simple explanations of cooking operations.

One of the pioneers of the new French cuisine was Antoine Beauvilliers, a chef who had been in the service of the Comte de Provence. His 'Grande Taverne de Londres' had been one of the first real Paris restaurants. As indicated by the name of his establishment,

Beauvilliers admired English ways and his two-volume *L'art du Cuisinier*, published in 1814, reflected this. He offered 'the best of English cooking which I have had the advantage of being the first to transplant to France'. Interestingly, Beauvilliers granted that English beef was superior to French, but said that German beef was even tastier if it travelled to France on the hoof – by the time the animals ended their long journey, they were so fatigued that their fat had been incorporated into their flesh, thereby tenderising it.

Rumohr tells us that the French were influenced by the English, particularly in respect of the superior English style of roasting, and informs us that this was a two-way traffic. He mentions two English cookery books which contain French recipes. One of these is *A New System of Domestic Cookery*, by Mrs Maria Rundell, first published in 1806. This was one of the best selling cookbooks of the period, offering rather ordinary recipes to English housewives, with emphasis upon economy and the avoidance of wasteful expenditure. It was popular during most of the nineteenth century, in America as well as in England.

The books of Beauvilliers represented largely 'la cuisine bourgeoise' in France, which Rumohr is prepared to praise. However, in 1815, the separation of French cuisine into two streams, haute and bourgeoise, became more apparent with the publication of the first book of Marie Antoine (Antonin) Carême, *Le Pâtissier Royal*. Of this book, Rumohr says that it is 'most instructive, but gets itself lost in the idle amusements of an outrageously luxurious lifestyle'. Indeed, Carême himself warned housewives away from his pages, saying 'Bourgeois kitchens of limited means would be wise to follow simple methods and not try to imitate the ways of the grandes.'

Carême was born in 1784 into a large, poor family and, at the age of seven, was obliged to find shelter and work in a cookshop. By 1801 he had progressed to the pastry shop of M. Bailly, where he remained for several years and learned the basics of fine pastry making. This subject formed the main substance of his first book. Carême soon attracted the attention of Talleyrand, who was famed for his strategic use of the dinner table as an arena of diplomacy, a topical subject mentioned by Rumohr. Carême became chef to the English Prince Regent, Czar Alexander I of Russia and Baron de Rothschild, and continued to exert a great influence upon 'la grande cuisine' beyond his death in 1833, by which time he had published, in addition to *Le Pâtissier*, *Le Pâtissier Pittoresque* (1815), *Le Maître d'Hotel Français* (1822) and *Le Cuisinier Parisien* (1828). His final work, *L'Art de la*

Cuisine au Dix-Neuvième Siècle, which set out to codify the grande or haute cuisine of France, was unfinished and had to be completed by Armand Plumerey from Carême's notes.

In December 1825, there appeared in France a book which remains much quoted as, in the words of the Penguin translation of 1970, it 'has a timeless appeal – being wise, witty and anecdotal, containing some of the best recipes for food and some of the most satisfactory observations on life'. This book is *La Physiologie du Goût* by Jean-Anthelme Brillat-Savarin and Rumohr's second edition, published in 1832, offers a short comment on it. It 'contains some important tips' and is 'an ingenious book', says Rumohr.

Brillat-Savarin was born on 2nd April, 1755, into a family of lawyers in Belley, the chief town of the region of Bugey, an area famed for its food and drink. He completed law studies and obtained a post as magistrate in Belley, being elected Mayor in 1793. The outbreak of the revolution drove him abroad, first to Cologne and then to Switzerland, whence he proceeded to the United States where he 'found refuge, work and peace', giving French lessons and playing the violin in a theatre orchestra. He returned to France in 1796 and, in 1808, Napoleon made him a Chevalier de l'Empire in recognition of the courage and humanity he had shown as Mayor of Belley at the height of the revolution. Living now peacefully in Paris, Brillat-Savarin performed his judicial functions conscientiously, entertained his friends and played the violin, spending two months of each year back in his home town of Belley. His Paris dinners were famed for their excellence. A favourite leisure occupation was writing, and Brillat-Savarin spent many evenings writing and revising what he called his 'gastronomical meditations'. He would occasionally read extracts to a few friends after dinner and was finally encouraged to publish *La Physiologie du Goût* at his own expense in 1825, but without his name on it. Despite this precaution, all Paris soon knew who had written the remarkable work everyone was talking about, but Brillat-Savarin did not enjoy fame for long. He died of pneumonia on 2nd February, 1826. His book was recognised in France as without precedent, 'a unique combination of recipes and aphorisms, reflections and reminiscences, history and philosophy, which raised gastronomy to the level of an art'. How well these words describe the lesser known German volume which had been published three years earlier! Brillat-Savarin's 'Tell me what you eat: I will tell you what you are' has become proverbial. It is a great pity that the wisdom of Karl Friedrich von Rumohr is not similarly remembered.

Rumohr himself had a generally low opinion of other cookery books, and of German cookery books in particular. At the end of his second book, he tells the aspiring young cook that he 'should read my book and no other'. Germany's protracted internal and external wars left her well behind other European countries in matters of culture, and major influences from abroad were apparent in food technology and in the refinement of table manners. In Rumohr's time, many of the cookery books which had recently appeared were translations of French and English works, while others were collections which did not reveal their source but could not belie their foreign origin. Rumohr calls them 'haphazard accumulations of recipes of all kinds, many of which are quite absurd'. He regrets that they are tending to suppress the valuable national and provincial dishes of Germany and says that, as most German cookery books are 'no more than imitations of the French books', it is better to refer back to the original French source, 'because that information will always be more pure, simple and relevant than the twaddle offered by the rabble of imitators'. He has already referred to the German books as 'little incubators of gluttony which rarely supply the information required by the good housewife or by anyone else running a household', and it is clear that he fervently hoped to fill this gap which he perceived in the culture of his country. He strove to meet a need which he considered to be urgent. Certain sentences in his book indicate that he was well aware of the magnitude of the task he was taking on. Little comments like 'I have tried in vain to improve the ways of German cooking women' have a ring of sadness and disappointment. Optimistically however, he believes that 'the art of cookery is beginning to assert itself while the theory is developing apace'. Walther Rehm, pointing out that Rumohr displays 'the modesty of a man of the world', says that in his book, the art of cookery *has* asserted itself, the theory *is* developed. Appropriately, Rehm quotes Goethe's maxim that 'there is a subtle empiricism which gets to the heart of a subject, thus becoming a theory in its own right. Such a mental leap can only occur where the standard of education is superlative'. Rumohr proves this.

Karl Friedrich Ludwig Felix von Rumohr, author of *Geist der Kochkunst*, was born on 6th January, 1785, on his parents' estate, Reinhardsgrimma, near Dresden. He was the younger son of Henning von Rumohr and his second wife, Wilhelmine Caroline von Fersen. The family was titled and wealthy and had held extensive lands in the Duchies of Schleswig and Holstein for generations. Soon after Karl's birth, his parents returned from Saxony to their estates near Lübeck, where the boy spent most of his childhood.

His father, a local government official (*Landrat*) in Holstein, was a large, passionate and intelligent man, while his mother is said to have been a very beautiful and attractive woman, who sparkled in local society. Their home was frequently full of visitors and this generous entertaining is bound to have influenced the growing boy. He was a lively child, keen to learn, and was soon dissatisfied by the education initially offered to him. As was customary, this was supplied by impoverished theology students who were easily intimidated by their sophisticated, arrogant young pupils. Boredom caused Karl to become inattentive and naughty, and he began to spend long periods shut up in his father's extensive library.

One day, in his thirteenth year, one of Karl's sisters encountered him leaving home with a bundle of belongings. He explained that he was going to try to find a place where he could study in peace. At this, his parents sent him to Abbot Wehland in Holzminden, in the Duchy of Brunswick. He remained dissatisfied, however, finding no stimulus in the Abbot's teaching, although his new surroundings did encourage his instinctive feeling for works of art. At the age of fifteen, he saw his first art collection in the home of Count Brombeck, and recorded the profound impression this made in his book of memoirs, *Drei Reisen nach Italien* (Three Trips to Italy).

Fate then took a hand in Karl's education. In 1803, his father died, and the young man inherited the family estates in the Duchy of Lauenburg, together with a considerable income. This rendered him financially independent and aided his decision not to follow in his father's footsteps and enter the Civil Service. He had recently entered the University of Göttingen where, besides studying languages and history, he took drawing lessons under Domenico Fiorillo, having now decided to dedicate himself to the history and development of art. He became friendly with the artistic Riepenhausen family, who possessed a fine collection of copperplate engravings. Their influence led Karl to begin his own collection of drawings and engravings which later graced his home at Rothenhausen, near Lübeck. He visited the famous art gallery in Kassel and studied the art treasures in Dresden and, during this period, became a convert to the Catholic Church. We are told that this conversion took place in order to facilitate his study of Italian art treasures, but Karl himself never made any comment about it, and we are led to believe that he was not a religious man.

Having completed his studies in Heidelberg, Rumohr wished to travel to Italy to study that country's art treasures. He set out early in 1805, stopping on the way in Munich, where he met the young poet, Ludwig Tieck, who became a close friend. From Munich he wrote to a friend that April 'We . . . eat extremely well here. We write our own menus and our appetites never flag as we bathe every day. What a world! What a climate! I eat enough for four and drink all the right wines too.' We have here our first indications of Rumohr's lifelong interest in food and dining. Like his father, he was a big man who obviously enjoyed a considerable appetite, comparing the stout figure of Falstaff with his own. He did, however, suffer problems with his health, and this probably increased his awareness of the varying qualities of foodstuffs with regard to nutritional value and digestibility. He was also a man with a mercurial temper who appears to have had a great aptitude for making himself unpopular, even with his close friends. Ludwig Tieck wrote that he was 'an unpredictable character . . . He would let himself become totally preoccupied by a single thought or feeling'. He was 'good natured, lovable, devoted. Then, all of a sudden, cold, strange, forbidding', not the same man at all. He loved contrasts in life and exhibited many in himself. Tieck's biographer, Rudolph Kopke, gives us further details: 'An enthusiastic man, whose feelings and opinions changed rapidly, he was always being pulled in opposite directions, not because he was irresolute, but rather because he became over-excited.' Rumohr seems to have been capable of being everything at once. He was modest and overbearing, compliant and arrogant, fickle and obstinate, a cynic and follower of fashion, a democrat and an aristocrat.

Having viewed and appreciated Munich's art treasures, Rumohr travelled on with Tieck and other young friends to Italy. He visited Verona, Mantua, Florence and Siena before finally settling in Rome. He soon came to regard Italy as paradise on earth and his view of Florence and Siena was coloured by the works of the old masters. The medieval atmosphere and friendliness of the people of Siena tempted him to settle there permanently and he would have loved to have seen Rome in all the unruly glory of its antique ruins, as depicted by Piranesi. He arrived too late, however. The armies of the invading French had tidied up the city and had sterilised and classified the ruins, reducing them to empty tourist attractions. Thieves and homeless people no longer lived among the once weed-infested heaps of stones and there were no more herdsmen with their white cattle, sheep and goats in the Forum. Rumohr would have revelled in the conviviality of the ancient world. He had read many of the classical authors and might have imagined that the sun and moon over the ruins of Rome were the stars of Hellas, the herdsmen straight from Homer. He loved the Italian way of life and praised the Italians as the forerunners in all modern intellectual development, including the art of cookery. In Rome, he ate at Palmaroli's. This man was regarded by his guests as the 'King of Fettucine'.

In Rome, Rumohr became friendly with Joseph Anton Koch and Johannes Christian Reinhart, painters and engravers, and often visited the home of Wilhelm von Humboldt, where he also got to know the latter's brother, Alexander. This man's inspired descriptions of natural phenomena encouraged a deeper appreciation of the forms of nature in the young Rumohr, and he later quoted Alexander's accounts of the tubers and roots cultivated in the Americas in his cookery book.

Leaving Rome finally, Rumohr moved on to Naples, where he was delighted by the traditional comedies enacted in the theatres. With Tieck, of whom he was very fond, he then returned northwards, visiting Rome, Florence, Parma and Milan before stopping for a spell in Munich to conduct research into the Bavarian style of cookery. After a two year stay abroad, Rumohr returned to his property, Rothenhausen, near Lübeck, which he shared with his sister, Friederike von Rumohr, a bright and intelligent companion. He devoted himself to his studies when not travelling, but often had yound artists and writers sharing his roof. One of these, Hinrich Steffen, recorded how he and his host only met each other at meal times, each being otherwise absorbed in his intellectual efforts. Steffen tells us that Rumohr always took a great interest in meals. His friend Tieck, and Novalis, were also interested in the culture of the table and Novalis wrote 'Dinner time is the most significant point in the day. It seems to form the day's purpose, its flowering. Breakfast is the flower bud.'

Rumohr certainly believed in this view and arranged his life accordingly. Many people were wont to criticise him. Alexander von Ungern-Sternberg, a nobleman from the Baltic coast who was then a very fashionable writer, met Rumohr in Tieck's house and wrote, 'I met Baron von Rumohr, the art specialist . . . He was a man who carried his wisdom in a dry and disagreeable way but who was much sought after on account of his originality.' Heinrich Laube, whose work, 'Reisenovellen' was a distasteful imitation of Heine's

'Reisebilder', devoted an entire chapter to his encounter with Rumohr in the Hotel de Bavière in Leipzig. He relates how, as macaroni had just been served, he told his table companion that he was on his way to Italy. The companion, no other than Rumohr, 'just nodded his head. He was absorbed in eating a fricassee and was interested in nothing else'. Laube continues 'He was a large fat man in grubby clothes, who was making a great thing of eating his lunch. He had an obscure expression and his jacket was impregnated with reddish snuff. During the pauses in the meal, he stuffed this nasty, unseemly tobacco into a soft and shapeless nose. The only trace of nobility in his heavy face, which was upholstered with dry flesh, was an expression of cultivated cunning and finely tuned gourmanderie.' When Rumohr spoke, his small eyes smiled with pleasure 'as if he had a mouthful of jam . . . his forehead crept right up over his half bald head and you could read there all the fine and sophisticated thoughts which appear in Rumohr's writings'.

Rumohr tolerated this criticism, which came from his female acquaintance also. Caroline Schelling-Schlegel wrote two earnest letters to him during 1808 and, poking malicious fun at Rumohr's name, told her friend Luise Gotter 'bei Lichte besehen, rumore es in diesem jungen Mann ziemlich ohne Zweck und Ziel' (if you watch him closely, this young man rumbles about with little apparent purpose or goal). She continues that his greedy enjoyment of food is so well developed that there is no arguing with him on the subject of cookery, and finds it quite disgusting that a man should be able to talk of a crab with as much fervour as of Jesus.

Rumohr never married but, beside his sister, he did have one female associate who regarded him as 'a good soul'. This was Bettina von Arnim und Schelling, who was almost the same age as he. They went for walks together in the Englischer Garten in Munich and Rumohr visited Bettina at home, debated with her and painted land-scapes over a warming glass of schnaps. The pair seem to have enjoyed a warm and rewarding relationship.

The people of Lübeck were horrified at the occupation of their town by Bernadotte and, in 1808, Rumohr's home became the focus of gatherings of local men who shared a profound hatred of the French. This led Rumohr to attend the Congress of Erfurt and he narrowly escaped being arrested by French police on suspicion of conspiracy. He fled through Bohemia to Vienna, where he lived until 1810 when, spending some time in Munich, he met Crown Prince Ludwig of Bavaria. It is interesting to speculate whether Rumohr attended the Prince's marriage celebrations in Munich on 12th October of that year. This great event, which included wagon races among teamsters from the local breweries, was the forerunner of the famous Bavarian Oktoberfest which now disrupts Munich life for two weeks every autumn.

It was during 1810 that Rumohr was finally given permission to return to his Lübeck home and he remained there, under police surveillance, until the fall of the first French Empire. He published his first writing, a commentary on the work of a Mr Jacobs on the subject of the art treasures of Greece, that same year.

In letters to his Munich friend, Robert von Langer, Rumohr spoke of his homesickness for Bavaria, his research and writings on the subject of archaeology and art history, his own attempts at painting and engraving and of his growing collection of works of art and books, including European cookery books dating back to antiquity. We know that Rumohr did not simply collect these books. It is evident from his own work that he both read and studied them.

Rumohr did not feel happy in the North. He felt restricted by the Northern narrowness of spirit. In the autumn of 1816, he left for Italy again, accompanied by a young painter named Franz Horny. This trip was to last until 1822, and Rumohr made three subsequent trips, in 1828, 1837 and 1840. His literary output during these years was considerable. It included a four-volume novel, *Deutsche Denkwürdigkeiten aus alten Papieren* (Reminiscences of Germany, drawn from old records), which depicted German, and French, life in the middle of the eighteenth century, two collections of short stories, various travel books and commentaries on art history, as well as assorted translations. The work for which he was most praised during his lifetime, both for its scholarly and extensively researched content and for the fine quality of the actual prose, was the three volume *Italienische Forschungen* (Italian Investigations). Another book, *Die Besitzlosigkeit der Kolonen in Toscana* (literally The Lack of Property of the People of Tuscany), offered clear evidence of the depth of Rumohr's own observations, combined with thorough research. In it he demonstrated the link between the abandonment of an established agricultural tradition and industrialisation, together with the capitalist strivings of former times. In yet another work, *Die Schule der Höflichkeit, für Alt und Jung* (The School of Etiquette for Old and Young), Rumohr offered humorous advice to everyone, from beggars upwards, as to how they should behave in accordance with their station in life.

Today, however, it is not for these works that Karl Friedrich von Rumohr is remembered. He returned from Italy in 1822, having been robbed near Olevano and suffered the trauma of the death of young Horny; and in that same year published the book which was to render him immortal. The first edition, which appeared under the auspices of Cotta's bookshop at Stuttgart and Tübingen, was entitled *Geist der Kochkunst von Joseph König. Überarbeitet und herausgegeben von C.F. von Rumohr* (Edited and published by . . .). It bore a quotation from Pliny, 'Maximum hinc opus naturae ordiemur et cibos suos homini narrabimus –. Nemo id parvum ac modicum existimaverit, nominum vilitate deceptus'.

Joseph König was Rumohr's personal cook, his 'Mundkoch', who had accompanied him faithfully on his Italian travels. The profession of 'Mundkoch' was an esteemed one, dating back to times when influential noblemen lived in fear of being poisoned and employed a trusted protector to cook and taste all their food. Marx Rumpolt, whose comprehensive *Ein new Kochbuch* was first published in Frankfurt in 1587, had a great deal to say about the responsibilities of the 'Mundkoch'. He wrote, 'The personal cook is one of the most important and trusted servants . . . he stands closer to his master than all the others; he is familiar with his tastes in food and his eating habits. It is the personal cook's task to entertain and feed his master to the very best of his ability.' He must also supervise the other servants who are concerned with kitchen and cellar.

It is interesting that Rumohr chose to publish his cookery book under another man's name. Walther Rehm, in his Späte Studien, refers to 'the nobleman's ancient aversion to publishing anything, least of all under his own name'. Rumohr himself explains that the art of cookery was held in very low esteem in Germany in the early nineteenth century. He was, however, eminently qualified to write such a book. His indifferent state of health had sharpened his awareness of the suitability of different foodstuffs and combinations of ingredients. His comfortable financial circumstances enabled him to sample whatever he fancied, without undue concern about the cost. His knowledge of ancient eating habits, and of contemporary styles, was derived from intensive study of ancient and modern history, combined with extensive travel and lengthy stays in foreign cities. Being also naturally greedy, fond of convivial eating and concerned for the welfare of mankind, it is logical that Rumohr should have wished to share his knowledge and enthusiasm with as wide an audience as possible.

The first review of the book appeared in the *Allgemeine Literaturzeitung* of Halle, and the reviewer expressed his regret that 'the author of a book written with such a conscientious, scientific and philanthropic approach to the subject of mankind's most basic needs should have hidden his identity behind the name of a servant'. The book received wide acclaim and, when the second edition was published in 1832, with additions and improvements, Rumohr felt so confident about his progeny that he admitted its true authorship, which had long been suspected. The actual title of the book remained unchanged, however. Rumohr attempted to justify himself in his 'Preface to the Second Edition' by explaining that the work had been intended to assist the said Joseph König, who needed money for the education of his two growing sons.

It is important to remember at this juncture that Brillat-Savarin's famous *Physiologie du Goût*, which is accorded a place of such significance in culinary history, was first published three years after Rumohr's first edition. One specialist has commented, 'Had Rumohr been French, there would probably have been much less fuss about Brillat-Savarin.' The two men did not know each other – Rumohr never visited France, although Brillat-Savarin did spend a short time in Germany – and it is likely that they would not have found any great pleasure in each other's company.

Although he was never attracted to France, Rumohr never lost his love for Italy, or for travel for its own sake. Staying in Florence and Siena during his third trip, he had the honour of showing the art treasures of those cities to Friedrich Wilhelm, then Crown Prince of Prussia, later to become Friedrich Wilhelm IV of Prussia. The two became quite friendly. Rumohr's relationship with the Prince of Denmark, who became King Christian VIII in 1839, was even closer, and he occupied the position of gentleman-in-waiting to Christian between 1835 and 1836. In Dresden, Rumohr spent time with Tieck until their comradeship was ruined by various outspoken remarks and opinions which Rumohr did not hesitate to express in his novels. C. G. Carus, the famous doctor, Count Baudissin and Baron Stackelberg, renowned for his travels in Greece, also moved within Rumohr's sphere. He became increasingly difficult to be with, suffering from an unhealthy sense of his own importance. This often made him quite unreasonable, subject to fits of intense anger, and it eventually led to a break with his sister Friederike, the constant companion of his family home. He sold the Rothenhausen estate and, in 1842, settled in the town of Lübeck itself. Rumohr's comfortable home was filled with the splendid collection of art treasures which he had collected over the years and he continued to entertain a wide circle of influential friends to sumptuous dinners, although his health was not good. Invited by Friedrich Wilhelm to visit him in Berlin to discuss artistic matters, Rumohr was overcome by the unmistakable symptoms of dropsy and was obliged to return to Lübeck. He hoped that bathing in mineral waters might cure him and, early in the summer of 1843, set out for Bohemia to achieve this aim. By the time he reached Dresden, he was weak and discouraged and consulted Doctor Carus, who forbade further travel. Rumohr's death was worthy of a great gourmet. He was sitting at breakfast, 'in the bud of the day', on 25th July, 1843, when he suffered a fatal heart attack and sank into the arms of his servants with the words 'Kinder, betet für mich!' (Pray for me, children!). He was buried in the cemetery in the new district of Dresden and his royal friend Christian VIII arranged for the erection of a marble memorial praising Rumohr as a gifted writer of history, initiator of detailed studies of medieval art history, and as an expert on established art, as well as promoter of the new.

Rumohr never got around to writing an autobiography, nor did he leave many letters, always a good source of biographical information. There are, however, many details to be gleaned from his own writings, and from the writings of those who knew him. The most important of these is *Karl Friedrich Rumohr, sein Leben und seine Schriften*, published in Leipzig in 1844 by Heinrich Wilhelm Schulz. The conclusion to the book was written by Doctor Carus, who speaks of Rumohr's physical constitution, the shape of his skull, and his last illness. It is Carus' belief that Rumohr suffered abnormalities of the brain. [Obituaries which appeared in the *Altonaer Merkur* and the *Allgemeine Zeitung* placed great emphasis on Rumohr's importance as an art historian without paying much attention to his other achievements.]

Karl Friedrich Freiherr von Rumohr lived through turbulent times in the history of Europe and the world. The United States of America, having won independence from British rule, were in the process of establishing themselves and were receiving numerous immigrants from Europe, Germany included. Indeed, in the early 1840s, German emigration numbered over a hundred thousand a year. The French nation lived through revolution and the rise and fall of Napoleon. They overran parts of Germany and were hated and feared by many. Germany itself did not exist as we know it today, being divided into numerous small duchies and principalities with the greater powers of Prussia and Austria vying for supremacy. Italy was similarly fragmented, while Denmark was looking to include the German Duchies of Schleswig and Holstein within its own borders.

Although Rumohr speaks frequently of 'Germany' and 'German' people, at the time of his birth, the Germans had made less progress towards national unity than the other peoples of Western Europe. The Reformation, which ultimately helped to knit the English nation more closely together, had the opposite effect in Germany. The Peace of Augsburg in 1555 had allowed each ruler to decide whether Catholicism or Lutheranism was to prevail in his dominions and the Peace of Westphalia in 1648, which concluded the Thirty Years' War, furthered the process of disintegration by weakening the only surviving symbol of unity, the Holy Roman Empire. It undermined Imperial authority by recognising the sovereignty of the member states, which were now permitted to conclude treaties with foreign powers. When Rumohr was born in 1785, Germany remained a mosaic of more than one thousand eight hundred political entities, ranging in size and influence from the seventy-seven major secular principalities down to the fifty-one Imperial cities, forty-five Imperial villages and 1,475 territories ruled by Imperial knights. The very debility of the Empire proved an obstacle to unity, inviting self-aggrandisement on the part of the princes. Its rulers, the Hapsburgs, were more concerned with their own Austrian domains than with the broader interests of the Empire and their example encouraged the particularist tendencies of the smaller German courts. Also, the Hapsburgs were Catholics, and this created immediate antipathies between them and the Protestant North. Rumohr himself, having converted to the Catholic religion, wrote that he experienced hostility in his home area of Lübeck. However, the great literary and intellectual revival of the 'Aufklärung' (Enlightenment), together with the ensuing 'Sturm und Drang' (Storm and Stress) and Romantic periods which, taken together, roughly span the years of Goethe's lifetime (1749-1832), contributed decisively to the creation of a German cultural nation. The intellectuals regarded politics as something distasteful but were nevertheless taking an important step in the evolution of the modern German state. Rumohr himself was influenced by Goethe and his contemporaries. The contrast between the classical lifestyle, with its harmonious organisation and adherence to established, well ordered rules and the modern, romantic style with its perpetual tendency to chaos, engendering new and wonderful creations, appealed to Rumohr. Such contrasts could be applied to cookery. Walther Rehm writes 'The polarised tensions of the Goethe period actually exercised a controlling influence over every sphere of intellectual interest.' 'Original' cookery was as opposed to 'stewed' cookery as classic and romantic, termination and infinity, healthy and ill, substantiality and artificiality. Rumohr definitely stood for classical tradition, upholding the essential good qualities of raw materials and uncomplicated methods, decrying overcooking and excessive complexity in dishes.

When Rumohr was born in 1785, Prussia was still under the rule of her third King of the Hohenzollern line, Frederick the Great (1740-86). His entire reign had been a period of great conflict with the Hapsburgs. Frederick's passion was the army, and he raised the Prussian force to a permanent number of 150,000 men, which led Mirabeau to observe that Prussia was not a country which had an army, but an army which had a country. Frederick's predecessors had done much to improve Prussia's economy and administrative systems, and this enabled him to use his superb military machine to raise Prussia, a country with no natural frontiers, to the rank of a first-rate European power. Had Frederick lived a little longer, it is thought that he might have challenged the Hapsburgs not only for immediate military supremacy, but for the permanent political leadership of Germany also.

The collapse of the old order in France brought sweeping changes on both sides of the Rhine. Prussia entered the War of the First Coalition in 1792 and withdrew in the Treaty of Basel in 1795. This brought the French into possession of the Prussian territories of Mors, Cleves and Upper Guelders west of the Rhine. Rumohr mentions Basel in his 'Preface to the Second Edition', saying that, following this treaty, the Northern part of Germany remained at peace until 1806. In 1797, France and Austria made peace at Campo Formio, leading to the surrender by the Hapsburgs of their Rhenish possessions, along with the Austrian Netherlands and Milan. France had now annexed all German territory west of the Rhine. The War of the Second Coalition led to the defeat of Austria at Marengo and Hohenlinden in 1800, resulting in the Treaty of Luneville in 1801. Napoleon now dictated that the German Diet should secularise the ecclesiastical principalities and mediatise the Imperial cities, suppressing some 112 of the smaller entities in favour of the larger states like Bavaria, Baden and Württemberg. The War of the Third Coalition led, after the defeat of Austria at Austerlitz in December 1805, to the separation of the West German states from the Holy

Roman Empire, to the constitution under French tutelage of the Confederation of the Rhine (17th July, 1806), which brought the number of German states down to forty, and to the final demise of the Holy Roman Empire itself, three weeks later. Finally, the defeat of Prussia at Jena on 14th October, 1806, followed by the crushing Treaty of Tilsit (July 1807) reduced the Hohenzollern possessions to about half their previous size by annexing to the new Kingdom of Westphalia the Prussian territories to the West of the Elbe. The new Grand Duchy of Warsaw was given all the land that Prussia had acquired by the second and third partitions of Poland in 1793 and 1795.

Prussia's prostration by Napoleon proved to be her opportunity for recovery. After August 1807, her First Minister, Stein, undertook extensive administrative and social reforms. The Emancipating Edict of 9th October, 1807, abolished serfdom in principle, preparing the way for social reconstruction, while the Municipal Act laid the foundations of a modern system of local government. The years 1806-15 witnessed the beginnings of a genuine popular awakening, and the reforms enjoyed the support of intellectuals and the middle classes, even if they did not reach down to the peasants and artisans and failed to find favour with some of the nobility who felt their privileges threatened. The 'emancipation' of the peasants meant, in fact, that they were freed not only from feudal burdens, but from the land itself. The Prussian term for this was 'Bauernliegen' (laying the peasants flat) and the movement was comparable to the clearing of the Scottish Highlands in the eighteenth century. Rumohr mentions, and praises, the Highland Clearances in Chapter 19 of his first book. He appears to believe that the English were right to use the land so gained for the raising of fine beef cattle.

The Hohenzollern policy of toleration drew a remarkable group of non-Prussian scholars to Berlin. Among these was the philosopher, Johann Gottlieb Fichte who, between 13th December, 1807, and 20th March, 1808, delivered his famous 'Reden an die Deutsche Nation', in which he spoke 'to Germans only, and of Germans only', pointing to a 'system of national education' as the way out of Prussia's difficulties. His ideas profoundly influenced the Minister of Instruction, Rumohr's friend Wilhelm von Humboldt, who was the author of many enlightened reforms, including the founding of the National University of Berlin in 1809-10.

The disastrous French retreat from Moscow in 1812 made possible the war of liberation in which Prussia stood out as the natural leader after she joined the war following the Treaty of Kalisch on 28th February, 1813. Six months later, Austria joined the Allies and, by March 1814, they had entered Paris itself. Napoleon abdicated on 11th April and his attempt at recovery in March 1815 was defeated at the Battle of Waterloo on 18th June, 1815.

In 1815, the victorious Allies met at the Congress of Vienna, at which, incidentally, we learn that the great Carême was chef, summoned by Talleyrand. The Congress gave Germany a new political form which was embodied in the Federal Act of that year. The new German Confederation replaced the old Holy Roman Empire, with the Austrian Emperor as its permanent president. The Emperor was, however, too clearly seen to be concerned with maintaining the integrity of his extensive non-German possessions to be accepted easily as the leader of a 'German' state. In the Vienna settlement, he recovered his Italian lands, adding Lombardy to them, in return for giving up all claim to the Southern Netherlands. Thus, having only a relatively small German base in the Ostmark, he ruled over more Czechs, Hungarians, Poles, Serbs, Croats and Italians than over Germans.

Austria's constant rival, Prussia, strengthened her claims to German leadership by her new acquisitions. Although she lost the more easterly parts of her Polish territories to Russia, she gained the purely German Rhineland and Westphalia, rich in mineral resources, as well as important for their control of the Rhine and for the culture and intelligence of their people. These factors, together with the efficiency and integrity of Prussia's Civil Service, combined with the strength of her army, gave her a great advantage over Austria in her bid for the leadership of the German nation in the nineteenth century. (See the map at the beginning of the book.) The Federal Act of 1815 constructed an organisation which made little provision for united national action. It was too reminiscent of the old Holy Roman Empire. Ordinary people still relied upon the authority of the ruling dynasty, and of the state, as the principle of their internal unity. Personal loyalty to the monarch and obedience to the law administered by his officials could be demanded of all subjects, regardless of nationality. In both states, it was easy for the nobles and upper classes in particular, who clung to the privileges they had inherited from the past and provided the army officers and higher civil servants, to give such loyalty. The Prussian Junkers, masters of the once Slav estates to the East of the Elbe, played a vital part in nineteenth century Germany. They believed that the existing

Prussian state would best serve their agrarian interests and therefore did not support German unity. The middle class was beginning to develop both in numbers and in wealth, however, although it remained bound to the existing social order. Town populations had become sharply stratified and power in local government was in the hands of wealthy, hereditary oligarchies. In the countryside, where three quarters of the German population still lived in 1815, society remained, over wide areas, in the feudal stage. Serfdom was not abolished in Austria and Bavaria until 1848 and even then the process of emancipation was far from complete. The influence of the courts and the nobility remained predominant.

The extremely limited provision for united action by all the German states made by the Federal Act did arouse protest, particularly amongst the younger generation. In 1815, some of the students of Jena founded an association of university students called the 'Burschenschaft', of which the aims were both patriotic and, at first, liberal. The organisation grew, becoming the General German Students Association in 1817, and soon began to arouse hostility, particularly from Metternich, the Austrian Chancellor. Frederick William III of Prussia was also beginning to regret former liberalism and, together with Hardenberg, Chancellor of Prussia, Metternich soon took measures to prevent the spread of revolutionary doctrines and practices in Germany. It is very likely that Rumohr is referring to the Burschenschaft movement when he speaks disapprovingly of secret societies formed by students. The Carlsbad Decrees of August 1819 sealed the spirit of repression and reaction in Germany for the next thirty years and, until Frederick William III's death in 1840, Prussia almost ceased to count as a great power, so subservient was her policy to that of Austria. In 1830, revolutions broke out in France and Parma but, throughout the German Confederation, Austria and Prussia, the machinery of repression was, if anything, strengthened.

From 1840 onwards, a change set in, however. Frederick William III was succeeded in Prussia by his erratic son, Frederick William IV, whom Rumohr knew. The change created an atmosphere of expectancy in Prussia. At the same time, German nationalism received a double stimulus. The French seemed to be threatening the Rhineland and Christian VIII of Denmark, also Rumohr's friend, who had come to the throne in 1839, wished to press the Duchies of Schleswig and Holstein into complete unification within the Danish state. The chief internal force making for national unity at this time was the growth of an educated middle class engaged in the free professions and in industry and commerce, to whom the divisions of Germany, both political and social, were at once a logical absurdity and a serious hindrance to their activities. The rise of the Zollverein (Customs Union) under Prussian leadership, from 1834 onwards, contributed to the desire for still greater national unity, and the minds of Germans who desired this unity began to turn towards Prussia as their natural leader.

At the close of the Napoleonic wars, Germany showed few signs of her future economic greatness. Both agriculture and industry suffered from geographical difficulties. Much of the North German plain was infertile, while important mineral resources lay on the periphery of the country and could not be exploited until improved transport was available. Germany's chief coastline was on the Baltic, the trade routes of which were of minor importance, and in the days of sailing ships her North Sea ports of Hamburg and Bremen were unable to compete successfully on the Atlantic trade routes with the more favourably placed British and Dutch ports. Communications were poor within Germany, there was a lack of capital for investment in industry, medieval social institutions survived both in the countryside and towns, and political divisions created trade barriers. Like the other German states, Prussia suffered severe economic depression after 1815 and took active steps to ameliorate matters. The most important step was the enactment of Maassen's Tariff Law of 1818. This abolished many internal dues and decreed that customs duties should now be collected at the frontiers, facilitating trade between Prussia's two separate groups of provinces. Other small enclaves were soon absorbed into the Prussian customs system and larger states created similar customs unions. In 1834, Bavaria and Württemberg formed a customs union with Prussia and the Hesse states. This union, the Zollverein, had an area of 162,870 square miles and a population of 23.5 millions. Within eight years it had been joined by Baden, Nassau, Frankfurt-am-Main and Luxemburg, although some states, and the three Hanse towns, Hamburg, Bremen and Lübeck, remained outside it.

The development of the Zollverein had an important influence on the genesis of the German industrial revolution. The improvement in communications was also important. In the 1820s, Prussia embarked on a huge road building programme to foster industry and trade. River traffic grew on the Rhine, Elbe, Weser and Danube. The first river steamers carried passengers, but subsequently the transport of goods, such as coal from the Ruhr, became more important. It was, however, the railways which really shook the nation out of its economic stagnation, completing what the Zollverein had begun. The first German railways were short suburban lines, but in 1839, Dresden, the capital of Saxony, was joined by rail to Leipzig, the chief commercial centre of the kingdom, 70 miles away. By the end of 1846, over 2,000 miles of railways were open. German shipping was also growing. Most important was the rise of the shipping of Hamburg and Bremen in the Atlantic trades. Between twenty and thirty German vessels were bringing sugar and coffee from Brazil in the early 1830s. Bremen constructed the outport of Bremerhaven in 1827 and became the principal port from which emigrants left for the New World, while Hamburg became a great commercial centre.

The provision of capital, together with the exploitation of Germany's coal and lignite resources and the gradual development of her iron, steel and allied industries, now laid the foundations of her industrial expansion. The ironworks of Silesia and the Siegerland, the steelworks of Solingen and the silver mines of the Harz were small concerns run on the handcraft system, but, by the time of Rumohr's death in 1843, a few large scale iron, steel, engineering and machine-making establishments had already been set up. Most textile factories remained small and primitive, although mechanisation was proceeding, particularly in cotton and silk manufacturing, where the raw materials were imported. Rumohr refers to increasing industrial mechanisation in the first chapter of his second book, mentioning that it was, of course, unpopular with the people.

There was substantial progess in agriculture during Rumohr's lifetime, and he makes repeated references to the improvements. He explains in his 'Preface to the Second Edition' how, in the early part of the nineteenth century, the doubling of agricultural output, together with the closing of some foreign markets and the introduction of new imports, led to a collapse in the prices of agricultural commodities, with widespread effects for the German people. He mentions improved methods of flour bolting, resulting in finer flour for bread making, and to the raising of fatter animals for slaughter. A relatively recent appearance in the German world of vegetables was the potato, and Rumohr gives detailed instructions regarding its preparation. Before the Thirty Years' War, the potato had been grown only in gardens, and was a curiosity in the kitchen. After the war, however, it was reintroduced to the North of Germany via England and Holland, and quickly became popular there, fitting in well with the established diet of vegetables, fish and meat. It was less well received in the South, however, as the traditional diet there was based on flour, milk and egg dishes, i.e. porridge, pancakes, dumplings, pasta, etc. The use of the potato did not in fact become widespread in the South until the famine of the 1770s, when Frederick the Great personally promoted it.

Rumohr also refers to improved methods of beer production, along the lines of the Bavarian system. Munich beer was first mentioned on 2nd October, 1815, in the household accounts of the religious chapter of Freising and, since 1487, had been subject to the 'Reinheitsgebot' (Purity Order) promulgated by Duke Albrecht IV. This stated that its sole ingredients were to be malt, hops, yeast and water, conditions which still apply today.

Rumohr's fellow Germans leaned towards robust conviviality, and they developed a whole hierarchy of eating and drinking places, ranging from the ordinary 'Wirtshaus', the common man's tavern, through the 'Gasthof', or country inn, where the standard of welcome varied enormously, to the 'Keller' or 'Brauhaus', which was often attached to a brewery, serving hearty food with the drink. The 'Weinstube' was a similar establishment, specialising in wines. Along steep slopes above the Rhine and Moselle, and on favoured hillsides of the Palatinate, German landowners had made advances in the cultivation of their fragrant white wines. Great care was taken over the years to refine growths and differentiate them by accurate place names of origin, as well as by year of vintage. The first dated wine in Europe appears to have been bottled in the commune of Hochheim on the Rhine in 1711 and it was at Johannisberg that the method of leaving the grapes of a fine growth on the vine well after normal harvest time was developed.

For the middle classes, the Kaffee-Konditorei, serving coffee, tea and hot chocolate along with substantial cakes, came into fashion. Rumohr is most disparaging about these, accusing them of hastening the demise of household baking traditions and making people ill with their outlandish and excessive combinations of ingredients. The municipal dignitaries in the more prosperous German towns assembled in the Ratskeller, located in the cellar of the town hall. Here, each group would sit at its 'Stammtisch', its traditional table, to enjoy roast and boiled meats, Rhenish wine, puddings and cheeses.

The Germans were generally looked down upon by the English and French for their boorish and unrestrained ways at the table, and for their excessive consumption of alcohol. Rumohr himself bewails his countrymen's lack of culture, saying that they should never attempt to discuss metaphysics or mathematics at the table as they are not even capable of expressing themselves clearly on matters of domestic and public life. The diet of ordinary people remained very limited in range, although Rumohr makes it quite clear that wide variety was available to those who could afford it. Most green vegetables were not raised commercially before the time of Rumohr's death, and middle and lower class families relied on their own gardens and, if appropriate, vineyards. Only staples such as rye, wheat, cabbage and root crops were sold in the market place. Herds of beef cattle were uncommon, and most of the meat eaten was pork. Superior, thick jowelled hogs were raised in Westphalia, and Rumohr praises the quality of the ham produced there. Local sausage specialities abounded throughout Germany, and there was a considerable variety of soups which, until shortly before Rumohr's birth, had been an important constituent of almost every meal. Slowly, however, the traditional morning meal of a hot and very thick soup was replaced by one of the new, hot beverages, eaten with buttered slices of bread. As Rumohr explains, the art of cookery was not highly regarded in Germany at the time when he wrote and published his book. He laments Homeric times 'when men were spiritually free and accustomed to speaking out freely, and the art of cookery was treated without any shame or fear, just like any other subject which affects the well-being of mankind'. He questions the point of improvements in agriculture and increase in variety of available raw materials, if people do not know how best to utilise them. Comparing the art of cookery with other artistic disciplines, he stresses its fundamental simplicity – 'The basic rule could not be easier to grasp: make the best of every edible substance', but regrets our inability to appreciate this fact and learn from it.

Rumohr was influenced by Benjamin Thompson, the American-born Englishman from Salem, Massachusetts, who did a great deal of scientific and philanthropic work in Bavaria. In recognition of his efforts, Thompson was given a title by the Holy Roman Empire and is thus better known as Count Rumford. Besides inventing a nutritious soup to feed prisoners and poor people, Rumford is credited with inventing the first kitchen range with an enclosed flue. He criticised the enormous quantity of fuel which was consumed in the large, open grates, in which the fire remained open to the chimney, so that a great deal of heat went straight upwards without serving any purpose. These open ranges usually had an oven to one side and often a water boiler on the other side, or, in the case of a very wide grate, at the back. The heating of both oven and boiler tended to be very uneven, and attempts were made to control this by building flues, controlled by sliding or pivoted metal plates, or dampers, around them. The dampers could be opened by hand to draw the hot air through the flue, or closed to shut it off. Pots and kettles were suspended over the fire by means of a chimney crane. They might also be placed on a trivet, attached to the side of the grate and swung out over the fire, or on the fall bar, the top front bar of the grate which could be folded down when a deep fire was not required. The top of the side oven served as a hob area also. Meat was roasted on spits which were turned by smoke jacks. These were tin plated vanes placed in the chimney above the fire and rotated by the draught. A series of gears, pulleys and chains transmitted the motion to the spit. The restricted width of grates in smaller ranges made it necessary to roast on a vertical axis and clockwork bottle jacks were introduced to suspend the meat and turn it in front of the fire.

When Rumford first encountered a smoke jack, he was extremely outspoken in his criticism. He was far in advance of most of his contemporaries in his understanding and scientific application of the principles of thermodynamics and calculated that less than one thousandth part of the fuel necessary to be burned in order to provide enough power for a smoke jack to turn a loaded spit would be sufficient to power a small steam engine. He went on to advocate an enclosed stove in which every cooking vessel would have its own separate fireplace, so that no more fuel than was absolutely necessary would be burnt, but this was a complicated design and was not widely adopted. His principles were, however, incorporated in the closed ranges, the principal development during Rumohr's lifetime. The closed range had a smaller grate, covered with a cast iron plate which prevented the heat ascending the chimney until it had passed through the flues surrounding the oven and boiler. As the iron cover was heated, it acted as a hot plate for cooking. The large fires of open ranges had really been suitable only for roasting and in some houses the range had been supplemented by a brick stove burning charcoal, which provided a gentler heat for stewing. However, stews could simmer gently over the fire of a closed range, as the hot plate protected them from too intense a heat. For fast boiling, circular holes with removable lids were provided which exposed the vessels to a higher temperature. Chimney cranes and trivets were therefore no longer needed. The closed range was also much cleaner. As the smoke passed through flues under the hot plate, the chimney opening above the range was closed off by a register door. Food was no longer in contact with the grime of the fire and pots and pans were no longer blackened by soot. Being protected from the fiercest heat, they lasted longer. Rumford had also shown how meat could be roasted inside an oven, providing that there was a current of hot air, so roasting ovens were provided with a ventilator at the front and an outlet at the back to provide the requisite circulation.

In Chapters III and IV of Book One, Rumohr gives many details on the subjects of cooking stoves, types of fuel and kitchen equipment. It is obvious from his words that open ranges were still widely used in Germany in the early part of the nineteenth century, and he mentions the detrimental effect of the smoke upon the health of the cook [in the days of down-hearth cookery, hearth death was second only to childbirth as the most common cause of death in women] and upon the flavour of the food. He speaks of the new 'economy stoves and ovens' as recommended in Count Rumford's book, and of the problems of roasting meat in closed ranges. On the subject of kitchen equipment, he is aware of the problems of lead glaze poisoning and praises the quality of English stoneware. He is also aware of the danger of verdigris poisoning from unclean copper vessels and advises that they should be kept scrupulously clean. Rumohr is unusual among his contemporaries in giving such details of the kitchen, and we are grateful to him for a vivid and valuable picture of the early nineteenth century kitchen in Germany.

Rumohr is remarkable in his attitudes to the health-giving properties of foods and to the suitability of different foodstuffs for different people. He is aware that although two separate foodstuffs may be excellent if consumed individually, they may not be good when combined, the reverse also being true. We know that his own health was not good, and this would have increased his awareness of the relative suitability and digestibility of foods. In his chapter on meat stock Rumohr, writing as if in the words of his cook, Joseph König, says 'on the instructions of my lord and master, whose delicate disposition was unable to tolerate the heavy Roman style of cooking, I used to place in this pot each day: a small piece of bacon, two pounds of beef, one pound of veal, a young chicken and a young pigeon'. Roots, herbs and fine vegetables were added to the meat, and the dish was later served garnished with anchovies, fresh butter, radishes, cucumber salad and similar dishes. This does not itself sound like light food, but he goes on to say that the 'quantities served would have been enough for several people'.

Rumohr believes that the 'entire art of cookery would be just a use-less contrivance if it did not succeed in promoting and maintaining a feeling of healthy well-being'. He agrees that man should eat, in order to live, not live, in order to eat, and says that 'man is no more than what he eats'. 'He should have the conviction to eat moderately and the prudence to eat well.' Rumohr is aware of gaps in current knowledge of nutrition. 'If we had more precise knowledge of the properties of individual foodstuffs we should be able to envisage a meal structure in which a perfect balance of nutritious items was achieved each time. The suitability of a meal is affected not only by the properties of the foodstuffs but also by the digestive abilities of the individual consumers.' His attitude to nutrition, dietetics and hygiene in the kitchen is very modern, although he is still slightly influenced by the old ideas of the humours with regard to digestion, saying, 'if ingredients are skillfully combined in a dish . . . each food type can encourage and assist the breakdown of the others, for dry foods and moist foods will help each other, as will fat and lean, cold and hot'. The digestibility of different foods is very important to Rumohr and seems to have been something of an obsession at the time when he was writing. Maybe it was exacerbated by the German tendency to overeat. A page taken from a contemporary Westphalian cookbook gives precise details of the time taken by a healthy stomach to digest various foods. For example, pork requires five hours fifteen minutes while apples require only two hours.

Rumohr's views are particularly noticeable in his chapters on vegetables. Young peas and beans are 'difficult to digest because of their skins'. Turnips are good combined with meat, but 'those who have weak digestive systems will not find this dish beneficial'. Cucumbers are 'coarse textured and indigestible and held by Southerners to be fever inducing', while garlic 'is bad for the breath. Its fibres are indigestible and cause belching', although Southern people 'regard garlic juice as a prophylactic against fevers'. Rumohr has a particular aversion to almonds. He points out that they are often added to sweet pastries and puddings but render them heavy and indigestible. He says 'People who eat quantities of marzipan and almond confections find that their teeth are ruined. Whole communities have been known to inflict the most serious damage to their entire digestive systems by the consumption of almond pastries and cakes. I have even heard of one woman who killed herself by eating marzipan.' He recommends that almonds, and raisins, be left out of pilaus and criticises the North Germans for adding them to all sorts of dishes, a practice left over from medieval cooking habits.

Rumohr's approach to the art of cookery is well ordered, scientific and, again, remarkably modern. He starts the first book by defining the art of cookery itself. It is 'to develop, with the aid of heat, water and salt, the nutritional, refreshing and delectable qualities of those natural substances which are so suitable for the nourishment or restoration of mankind'. He goes on to discuss each of the basic elements, heat, water and salt, paying great attention to the quality and efficiency of each of the types available. Book One then deals with the processes of cookery, roasting, boiling, stewing and so on, and with each new topic we are given a succinct, accurate definition of the process in question. Boiling, for example, is 'rendering an item edible, or at least more edible, by the use of water maintained at boiling point'. Book Two then tells us how to cook a wide range of foodstuffs from the plant kingdom whilst Book Three deals, with some humour, with behaviour at table and the nature and suitability of different meals, both for normal households and for festive occasions. The final chapter, added when the book's second edition was published in 1832, deals with cookery for the ill and convalescent.

Throughout the work, Rumohr insists that the cook should always try to make the very best of the raw materials available, and should not destroy valuable nutrients, flavour and colour by overcooking. He is opposed to all contrived cooking, saying 'Wherever artifice is used, there is something essentially lacking.' As already mentioned, Rumohr's knowledge of ancient cuisines is extensive and he is highly critical of the Roman style of cookery as represented by Apicius. In his view, there was no longer any trace of an appreciation of the essential good qualities characteristic of every foodstuff. 'The height of achievement appeared to be the annihilation of the character of any dish by blending and over-processing.' He does, however, praise the Romans for the organisation of their fish farms and for their introduction of new species to Italian shores.

Chapter II in Book One deals specifically with the characteristics of the edible natural substances and informs us that 'The nutritional element should under no circumstances be suppressed or eliminated by overcontrived preparation . . . we should always strive to preserve it, to develop and increase it.' There are repeated references to the dangers of overcooking vegetables in Book Two. Of asparagus, Rumohr says 'the Germans cook it too much . . . Asparagus should certainly be tender to eat but its valuable salts should not be dissolved and boiled away by overcooking'. He heartily dislikes a German method of cooking spinach. 'In German kitchens, I have seen spinach boiled in water and then wrung out with the hands so that it could not possibly retain any flavour or juice. After this treatment it was chopped up with raw onions and returned to the fire with some butter or stock. No-one will be surprised to hear that this tasted like a green onion purée, its colour alone being reminiscent of spinach.'

In addition to his scholarly knowledge of classical cuisine, Rumohr is, of course, very familiar with Italian cuisine and clearly has a good knowledge of British, French and Spanish cookery. He has heard about the flavouring essences used in Indonesia and, from reading the accounts of travellers, has comments to make on subjects as diverse as the diet of North American fur trappers and South Sea Island methods of cooking on heated stones or in heated trenches.

The Italians are frequently mentioned and receive credit for having been the leaders in all matters of modern intellectual development, including the art of cookery. Rumohr points out that, in the sixteenth century, Italian cookery was already highly refined. In contemporary Italy, however, he believes that 'only the popular style of cookery is worthy of praise. Wherever people have pretensions to refined cooking, there is a conflict between stinginess and excess'.

The French are conceded the honour of having invented meat stock, 'the basis for all moist concoctions . . . creating innumerable healthy and tasty dishes'. Rumohr praises the pot au feu, the traditional French household soup, but regrets that contemporary French haute cuisine, like the Italian, is tending towards over refinement, complication and excess.

Rumohr is impressed with the quality of British beef and explains that pudding is a dish of English origins, being made of a flour and water batter and eaten with roast beef, particularly in the days before potatoes became widespread. He says 'This dish has now been developed to such an extent that it may be regarded as one of the best foods for toothless gourmets . . . Recently the English plum pudding has become the most popular variant.'

In his chapter on behaviour at table, Rumohr praises the English way of holding cutlery, with the knife in the right hand and the fork in the left. He considers that this is much more efficient and graceful than the European style of putting down the knife after cutting off a morsel of food so that the fork can then be taken in the right hand to transport the food to the mouth. Such details as these afford us a rare insight into social habits in the early nineteenth century. Rumohr's precise instructions regarding the laying of tables of different shapes provide another valuable example.

Rumohr dedicated his book to six German noblewomen and says at the end of the Introduction that he hopes 'that it may go some way towards replacing the national tradition of cookery which has been lost in some parts of Germany. My work is . . . dedicated to the sort of women who are the head of their households or who do take an intellectual interest in the running of their establishments'. He is forthright in his belief that it is more important to have a decent and appetising meal every day than to have splendid and opulent dinner parties now and then, and regrets the demise of many everyday, regional dishes. How much influence did his book have when it was first published and why have so few people heard of it today?

The publishing of an improved and extended second edition, in which Rumohr admits the true authorship of the book, indicates that it was successful initially. He carefully explains his aims in writing the book and reflects upon whether he has fulfilled them. Speaking of the increasing emancipation of women, he feels that many saw the first edition 'partly as an encroachment on their authority and partly as an onerous and unwelcome harking back to antiquated, forgotten duties'. He says 'Most kind reader, I now offer you this book for a second time . . . enlarged and improved. I trust that this edition may influence your lifestyle more than the first . . . was able to.' The fact that *Geist der Kochkunst* was subsequently published in 'Reclams Universal-Bibliothek' provides evidence of its continuing popularity. The Reclam edition combined it with two of Grimod de la Reynière's pieces and was edited by Robert Habs, who praised the combination of a fine literary style, depth of knowledge and observation with humour also. Walter Bickel informs us that the last known new edition of Rumohr's work was published in 1922 at the Georg Müller Press in Munich. It was edited by Carl Georg von Maasen, himself an important gourmand and cook and author of *Die Weisheit des Essens* (The Wisdom of Eating). The edition edited by Bickel was published in 1965 by the Arne Press in Hamburg, and the König Press in Munich brought out an edition soon afterwards, in which it referred to Rumohr as 'ein zu Unrecht Vergessener' (a man who should not have been forgotten). The edition from which the translation is taken is a copy of the second edition of 1832, published in 1966 by the Insel Press, Frankfurt-am-Main, with an introduction by Wolfgang

Den edlen Deutschen Frauen:

Frau Gräfin von Arco, gebornen Gräfin
von Seinzheim.

Frau Gräfin von Arco, gebornen Gräfin
Trauner.

Frau Gräfin von Lerchenfeld, gebornen
Freyin von Grosschlag.

Frau Gräfin von Seinzheim, gebornen
Freyin von Frankenstein.

Frau Gräfin de la Perouse, gebornen
Gräfin von Arco.

Der Freyfrau von Veningen, gebornen
Freyin von Dalberg.

The dedication in the first edition of Geist der Kochkunst.

Koeppen. In 1978, the Olms Press in Hildesheim published a facsimile of the first edition, praising it for the true German character of its recipes. Karl Friedrich von Rumohr would undoubtedly have been pleased to see this revival of interest in his work. He cared deeply about his subject and his opinions and advice remain as fresh today as they were when he wrote them. He has given us an invaluable picture of cookery and domestic life in Germany at the beginning of the nineteenth century and offers us a philosophy of life and its simple pleasures which is at once honest, attractive and heart-warming. If, when learning to cook, we were to take his advice and read his book and no other, we would gain an excellent knowledge of all the basic processes involved. He would have succeeded in his aim of providing a strong, but flexible structure upon which, with the help of our imaginations, we could then build.

Barbara Yeomans, 1993

* The text in the translation between the { } brackets is taken from the second edition published in 1832.

Acknowledgements

First of all, my gratitude is due to Alan Davidson for introducing me to *Geist der Kochkunst* and its author, Karl Friedrich von Rumohr.

Thomas Flögel supplied vital background information, and Russell Harris found answers to my most obscure queries whilst encouraging me with his enthusiasm. Finally my husband, Neil Mitchell, was my consultant and assistant in translating Rumohr's more archaic phrases. My thanks to all.

Books Consulted

Esther B. Aresty: *The Delectable Past:* George Allen and Unwin, 1965

Brillat-Savarin: *The Philosopher in the Kitchen:* Penguin, 1970

Ann Drayton: *The Exquisite Table:* George Allen and Unwin, 1980

David Eveleigh: *Firegrates and Kitchen Ranges:* Shire, 1983

Rachael Field: *Irons in the Fire:* Crowood, 1984

M. F. K. Fisher: *Brillat-Savarin, The Physiology of Taste:* Harvest/ Harcourt Brace Jovanovich, 1978

William Harlan Hale: *The Horizon Cookbook:* American Heritage Publishing, 1968

Molly Harrison: *The Kitchen in History:* Osprey, 1972

E. J. Passant: *A Short History of Germany:* Cambridge, 1971

Renate Peiler: 'Unvergessene Küche', *Essen & Trinken:* Gruner & Jahr, 1979

Uta Schumacher-Voelker: 'German Cookery Books, 1485-1800', *Petits Propos Culinaires* 6: Prospect Books, 1980

Ursula Stiller: *Köstliches aus der alten Westfälischen Küche:* Hans-Peter Kock, 1990

Tom Stobart: *Herbs, Spices and Flavourings:* Penguin, 1977

A. J. P. Taylor: *The Course of German History:* Cambridge, 1971

The Cook's Encyclopaedia: Batsford, 1980

Geist der Kochkunst
The Essence of Cookery

Geist der Kochkunst

von

Joseph König.

———

Ueberarbeitet und herausgegeben

von

C. F. von Rumohr.

———

Maximum hinc opus naturae ordiemur et cibos suos homini
narrabimus —. Nemo id parvum ac modicum existimaverit, nominum vilitate deceptus.

C. Plinii Sec. nat. hist. prooem. lib. XX.

Stuttgardt und Tübingen,
in der Cotta'schen Buchhandlung,
1822.

Publisher's Preface

The author of this book posesses an unusual knowledge of his subject. Beside great skill, he has the ability to make connections, and this has enabled him to elucidate the general principles of a subject which appears to be purely practical.

Some people will find the very earnestness and almost scientific severity of our author somewhat strange and alienating. Recent interpretations of the art of cookery have rarely been comprehensive and have not taken full account of its influence on physical and spiritual wellbeing. People have been trying for ages to establish a scientific framework for agriculture and animal husbandry. Even the poets have not been above enthusing over farming. There is daily competition between political economists and philanthropists to further the cause of distributing all the species and varieties of food plants and animals throughout the world. As so often happens however, we have halted in mid-stream. Those scientific, poetic and economic rumblings have so far met with a shamefaced silence on reaching the matter of cooking or processing the very raw materials people were so keen to possess. Those fine philanthropists hardly wish to appear as the inventors of soups for the poor. In these times of depressing overproduction such inventions would not represent any material improvement in social welfare. The philanthropists are so confoundedly soppy that they are ashamed to admit that people are working so zealously and economically to improve the standard of our bread and raise fatter meat animals. Indeed, they would rather give the impression that farming improvements are aimed only at stimulating trade or encouraging the circulation of money. They are loath to admit to themselves or others that there is any importance in trying to improve peoples' diets.

I am not, however, about to mistake the noble shame which the majority of our contemporaries exhibit at the mention of cooking and eating as a tender feeling for human dignity. I am happy to agree with the well-known proverb, that man eats, in order to live, and does not live, in order to eat. Surely it is then logical for man to eat sensibly and to exercise his judgement in the choice and preparation of his meals, as in all other matters?

He should certainly be health conscious in his eating. He should have the conviction to eat moderately and the prudence to eat well; it is quite pointless for us to try to convince ourselves that the tendency to neglect eating is the result of stoic wisdom. It is caused by pure laziness.

Whilst attempting to be the first to defend a philosophy of life which contrasts with contemporary prejudices, I cannot help looking back to classical times with some wistfulness. Those were healthy times, when men were spiritually free and accustomed to speaking out freely, and the art of cookery was treated without any shame or fear, just like any other subject which affects the wellbeing of mankind. The songs of Homer depict for us the feasts of the heroes and there is evident pleasure in the succulent food, ideally suited to nourish the mighty race of men. Later on, dinner parties provide the background for philosophical investigations. Finally, philosophical doctors and scientists, Hippocrates[1] and Galen in particular, become interested in the characteristics and effects of foodstuffs. From time immemorial, all doctors[2] who cared at all about the health of the human race have considered that the choice and preparation of foods is important. When important vegetable plants were introduced in ancient Rome, they acquired the nicknames of famous men: Lentulus, Piso and Cicero. Roman literature was full of the most wonderful details of the culinary history of the ancients and our modern archaeologists would do well to make much more use of this information.

Most modern writers behave quite differently and, although they themselves may be less dignified, they make considerably more claims for the dignity of their subject. The occasional short pastoral poem has ventured to mention a repast of bread and milk and men have also sung the praises of the potato, doubtless in contemplation of its rounded shapes which delight the sense of beauty. I must not forget to mention the travel writers, who have made an exception here by doing themselves proud in their expression of commendable appetite and persistent attention to anything fit to eat. It is possible that they do not merit quite such elevated praise because land and sea voyages do tend to sharpen the appetite[3] and hunger is indeed the best seasoning. It might in fact be reasonable to assume that their alluring descriptions of various foods and meals have no scientific or philanthropic purpose. They are pure outpourings of the heart.

It should, however, be clear to all that I do not count our mounting numbers of cookery books and recipe collections as great intellectual works, nor do I acknowledge them as proof that our contemporaries have an intelligent and worthy interest in cookery. These books – those which are of some value, and particularly the mass of totally useless volumes – are either the products of flat, unreflecting experience, or they are straight compilations[4] which are therefore devoid of any scientific ideals. I shall refrain from making any further comments on this subject and refer the reader to the relevant remarks of our author during the course of his book. It would in any case be unfair to him to compare his work with those other cookery books. Admittedly, it too is not strictly scientific in form, as well as in the way in which it does not fully utilise all the advantages of natural science, chemistry and mechanics which might benefit the art of cookery. The book does, however, contain some true basic principles. It is full of relevant remarks and useful suggestions and we can at least see that the art of cookery is beginning to assert itself while the theory is developing apace.

The little observations towards the end of the book on the serving and arrangement of meals and the moral factors which might improve or reduce the enjoyment of a meal, or favour or hinder its digestion, were very probably picked up from the servant's standpoint. People sitting around a table normally have little conception of how closely they are observed from behind.

My part in the preparation of this work has been quite insignificant. I have been concerned only with the style and occasional notes and therefore make no bones about publishing the above words with the book and, in my humble opinion, launching it upon the world with a very restrained degree of praise.

Introduction

I was formerly in service and, as a result, had the opportunity to travel. I am also reasonably familiar with the written works, both ancient and modern, which deal with, or merely touch upon my favourite subject. These factors have convinced me that the art of cookery is closely linked to national character and to the intellectual development of separate races. In short, it has a bearing upon the most general and the most elevated interests of the human race. I need hardly say how much this realisation encouraged my enthusiasm for the art and the scientific consideration thereof.

It is not safe to maintain that the level of civilisation of a race can always be ascertained from the degree of good sense and understanding which it appears to have applied historically to the choice and preparation of its everyday foods. There are innumerable intermediate stages between the repulsive diet of an Eskimo or nomadic tribesman and the pure, flavoursome frugality of a civilised, but not over-civilised, race. If we were to take the trouble to observe these stages carefully, they would correspond precisely to the stage of mental and moral development of the people concerned. Dull witted, brooding people love to stuff themselves with quantities of heavy food, just like animals for fattening. Bubbly, intellectual people love foods which stimulate the taste buds without overloading the belly. Profound, meditative people prefer neutral foods which do not have an assertive flavour and are not difficult to digest, and therefore do not demand too much attention.

The task of tracing all the various different levels and shades of meaning would be worthy of the finest historical researcher. We are much more concerned with protecting our work against the suspicion of indulging the whims of the rich. This is because, whenever cooking is mentioned, we are only too ready to think of delicacies. In contrast with the Greenlanders' habit of eating whale meat and other similarly crude and loathsome customs, a certain over-refinement of the art of cookery is tending to appear among civilised people. This usually accompanies an affected taste in literature and art.[5] And as every extreme soon engenders its counterpart, this over-refinement is always accompanied by the most disgraceful carelessness. Two camps are establishing themselves simultaneously in the field of cookery and, like the Stoics and Epicureans, they are equally powerful for the moment. This very contrast gives rise to two monstrous vices however, gluttony and eating between meals. The latter is much more harmful because it is more widespread. It is my intention to use my book to counteract these offshoots rather than encourage them.

By gluttony, I mean a level of wasteful greediness or greedy wastefulness which tends to be a characteristic of the type of rich people who owe their wealth and possessions to a cold, calculating self-interest. These people are quite incapable of utilising their superfluous resources in a benevolent and magnanimous manner for the general good.[6] Gluttony is manifested by a desire for expensive food of any kind together with a total disregard for quality, even if better food is readily available and costs less. A further characteristic of gluttony is the stimulation of the appetite by means of the rarest delicacies and by constant change and variety. The digestion is also assisted by various artificial means. The ancient Romans left for posterity a fine example of such caprice and artifice and it is highly unlikely that their degree of folly or their scale of consumption will ever be surpassed. We can at least say that there has not been another such accumulation of unbridled wealth since the fall of the Roman Empire, nor has any such excess been dissipated by such depraved men. Rome was quite obviously the natural focus of all the culinary delicacies of the ancient world. It also demonstrates more clearly than anywhere else in the ancient or modern world that all the treasures and delicacies of the earth will not suffice to provide a healthy and tasty diet for the glutton himself, or for the nation which propagates the creeping vine of greed. A distorted view of cookery will instantaneously cancel out all the advantages offered by a well stocked market. At the time when Horace was writing,[7] natural edible products were already being misused in Roman cookery, which was lapsing into a series of rigid, uninspired preparations. Two centuries later, when Coelius Apicius wrote the book which has served as the model, both in form and content, for all modern cookery books, there was no longer any trace of an appreciation of the essential good qualities characteristic of every foodstuff. The height of achievement appeared to be the annihilation of the character of any dish by blending and over-processing. Compared with Apicius' over-seasoned broths and creations, the turnips, baked in hot ashes, which the great Curius was eating when the deputies of Samnium came upon him must have seemed a very tasty dish to an unjaded palate.

The following is an example of Apicius' destructive style of cookery.[8]

'Roast some pig's liver and then remove any membranes from it; before this, however, pound together some pepper, rue and fish essence,[9] add the liver and work the mixture together just as for meatballs. Shape the mixture into balls[10] and wrap them, with individual bay leaves,[11] in caul fat, then smoke these for as long as you like. When you wish to eat them, remove them from the smoke and roast them again. Put them into a dry mortar, add pepper, lovage, marjoram and pound the mixture. Pour in a little fish essence; add some cooked brains and work thoroughly, making sure that there are no lumps. Add five egg yolks and blend well, so that the mixture amalgamates; moisten it with fish essence, drop it into a brass pan and cook it. When it is done, turn it out onto a clean table and cut it into small dice. Grind some pepper, lovage and marjoram together in a mortar. Mix everything together in a stewpot and heat it up. When it is hot, take it off the heat, work it, bind it and tip it into a dish. Sprinkle pepper over and serve it up.'

Even allowing for the fact that my quick translation may well not give a strict interpretation of the text, which is difficult and is actually damaged, we still cannot fail to recognise that the food has been dried up and overseasoned so much that it has been mummified.

The structure of Roman cookery must of course have been quite different at the time when Cato was including recipes for domestic cereal and vegetable dishes in his book of agriculture. Even Horace[12] was still able to declaim:

- Necdum omnis abacta
Pauperies epulis regum.

On the other hand Athenaeus[13] is ashamed to compare his own style of cookery with the pure simplicity of the Homeric style, although, compared with the methods of Apicius, the Greek's ways are themselves very straightforward. Apicius therefore affords us no knowledge of the golden age of Romano-Greek cookery. The revelries of Helagabal – described by Lampridius – afford us even less. It is therefore a mistake to make judgements based on these sources. This has already happened. There have been attempts to cook in the Apician style and Smollet mocks them most wittily in 'Peregrine Pickle'. The experiments have been unsuccessful, not only because of the basic absurdity of the late Roman style of cookery, but also because of the lack of those strong essences and liquids, derived from sea creatures, which the Romans used in their cooking. An aromatic plant juice which was much used by the Romans was not known to our modern researchers and the third and principal cause of failure has been the most unlikely assumption that this juice was the unpopular asafoetida used by our chemists.

With all their abundance of food, the later Romans did retain some sense of the basic qualities and good flavours of the edible natural substances. Apicius himself tells us that vegetables should still be bright green when boiled and the Italians still excel in this art today. Athenaeus roasts his onions in hot ashes in time-honoured fashion. Italians still maintain the tradition of baking their onions, beetroot, pumpkins and tomatoes in the oven, after the bread.

Whatever objections we may raise to the later Roman theory of cookery, we cannot deny the value of the measures taken by the Romans towards the end of the Republic and during the first centuries of the Empire to fill their kitchens and cellars with all the earth's delicacies. They built enclosures[14] in which fish from all the known waters were raised and fattened; their methods of introducing foreign species to Italian shores might well raise a blush from our softies. Our fashionable oyster and pie shops can hardly bear comparison with those storehouses of live fish. A pie which has stood around for too long, or a green, stinking oyster can claim to be a delicacy only because – like the roasts of Scharaffenland [the mythical land of plenty and fools' paradise depicted in Peter Breughel's painting] – it has been procured from a hundred miles away. Just because our modern habits of gluttony have remained, somewhat reluctantly, more reasonable than those of the ancient Romans, being much more restricted and petty, they seem, for all their small scale, to be all the more favoured, encouraged and practised. After all, the most ordinary and homely of our numerous cookery books are no more than little incubators of gluttony which rarely supply the information required by the good housewife or by anyone else running a household. They are crammed with all kinds of strange mixtures,[15] substitutions and disguises which are in themselves quite superfluous and which should naturally be left to the realms of fantasy and the tastes of individuals. The honest, motherly aspect of the German cookery books, with their heavily concealed, almost Apician streak of depravity is actually suggestive of our current spate of novels and tragicomedies. Like the cookery books, these seek to disguise their inner immorality beneath a screen of sentiment and apparent frankness.

The national and provincial dishes have their foundations in the local characteristics, both of people and country, and are almost always tasty and nutritious. They tend to become suppressed[16] by these cookery books, or rather by these haphazard accumulations of recipes of all kinds, many of which are quite absurd. Unfortunately most of the modern German cookery books are no more than imitations of the French books. Their barbaric and unnecessary use of French names proves this. Even the best German cookery books will offer only a few useful instructions for preparing true regional and popular dishes, which will be likely to come from the author's home area. Infinitely superior versions of the rest of their subject matter will be found in the old French cookery manuals. Even if they did not discover them in the first place, the French are responsible for the spread of all chopped and mixed dishes. Anyone who is fond of them should refer back to the source because that information will always be more pure, simple and relevant than the twaddle offered by the rabble of imitators.

I should now like to include a short commentary on French cookery literature.

I ought first to point out that the Italians, the leaders in all matters of modern intellectual development, also excelled in the art of cookery before ever the French did. In the sixteenth century, Italian cookery was already highly refined. We have some indications, mainly contained in novellas, that this refinement may date back even further. The Italians wholeheartedly applied their love of art and their sense of beauty to the table. We can see this in the great artists' banquets of the Golden Age (see the Osservatore Fiorentino) and in the heraldic designs which were painted on jelly. The envoys of Pius II were nearly poisoned by such jellies in Siena (see Senesi's novella). Around 1570, Bart. Scappi,[17] head cook to the holy Pius V, published an excellent and informative cookery book, some details of which are quite valuable, although contemporary tastes were already becoming somewhat affected. In Italy today, only the popular style of cookery is worthy of praise. Wherever people have pretensions to refined cooking, there is a conflict between stinginess and excess.

The Medici princesses brought the aesthetic refinement of the traditional Italian cooking to the French court. They also brought the taste for art and fruitless imitations of Italian and Spanish poetry.

The refinement soon reached Germany from France. We have proof of this in the cookery books printed in Frankfurt around 1600,[18] and in the provisions lists of the Kommandant von Hanau in Simplicissimus, an incomparable portrait of life during the Thirty Years' War. In the North, the barbaric inclination to gluttony stood in the way of a complete assimilation of more refined cooking methods. People who are obliged to be moderate in their eating habits will still not fully abandon gluttony, and excessive heavy drinking will also damage the stomach. If the digestive system is unhealthy, any refinement of the palate is quite inconceivable.

No matter how much the Italians may have influenced French cookery in the past, it fell to the French to develop meat stocks, using them as the basis for all moist concoctions and thereby creating innumerable healthy and tasty dishes. The Italians had not used meat stocks in the past and still did not do so.[13] The Greeks and Romans possessed quantities of olive oil of various qualities and this was universally used to lubricate liquid and moist dishes. As in Southern Europe today, it also led to an excessive use of hot seasonings, to which Pliny[20] was already objecting. Where olive oil did not provide enough flavour, people turned to liquamen, the liquid essences. These had formerly been prepared from ingredients such as salted pears but were increasingly made only from expensive fish. This is the case in the East today. Apicius gives us ample descriptions of jura and juscula, which were used just like strong meat stocks. They were mixtures of oil, acids, seasonings and plant juices which were designed to tickle the palate.

In the North, however, the place of oil in cookery had long been occupied by butter, clarified butter and other animal fats. Only the French, who produce good oil only along their southernmost coast, and a little butter only in the extreme North of the country, found themselves obliged to find a substitute for the fats they needed. As so often happens, this pressure drove them to utilise meat stocks, with delicious results, opening a new era in world history. The majority of Europeans are now so accustomed to the use of meat stocks that they are horrified by the ancients' contrived style of cookery. The cookery of the Spanish, Italians and Greeks of today, still bearing some resemblance to the style of the ancients, also outrages them.

I possess the original household accounts, dated 1756, of Louis XV and these clearly show that the diet of the royal family was quite frugal at that time. Only eight or nine dishes were served. Two thirds of the meat utilised in the kitchen was converted into strong stock in which the remaining third was cooked. Quantities such as these can obviously only be handled in royal kitchens but we can clearly discern the trend of the modern style of cookery. It is perhaps less distinct in another much quoted book of the same period, *Les Dons de Comus*, which, apart from covering the true French method of cooking with meat stocks, also illustrates my recent remarks by including numerous contrived little dishes in the Italian style. It is sufficient to look at the chapter entitled Divers Entrements, which includes all the rôties (little pieces of bread, garnished, and crustini) which are still used most effectively to ornament Italian meals.

The rise to power of the ordinary people in the French Revolution raised the pot au feu, the traditional French household soup, to a position of great honour. It was quite rightly the pride of the French nation. Tastes were gradually weaned off the strong seasonings and again became more refined and sensitive. Due in part to the efforts of the French, the new way of cooking became more and more widespread. At the same time, the French people's preference for the English, particularly for those who were starting a new life as North Americans, brought with it the influence of the English style of roasting. French cookery was sorely in need of this. It was certainly approaching my ideal of perfection at the time. The recent trends of the Parisian 'cuisine bourgeoise' still show traces of this approach. After a short, heady spell of political manoeuvering, the hyperactive spirit of the French was forced by a powerful hand to apply the sharpness of its wits to less important matters. The art of cookery was in the firing line, with the result that more wit and ingenuity has been lavished upon it in the last few decades than has been spent upon all the other branches of modern French literature. These works have a tendency to over-refinement[21] and I would advise prospective cooks to be wary of them.

French cookery is currently becoming far too complicated again, just as it did in the past. However, if we compare French cookery books with the majority of German cookery books, the latter are much more overdone than their French models. No matter what subject is involved, when uninspired people try to imitate others, there always seems to be a tendency for them to exaggerate the more perverse aspects of the model. It would actually be quite difficult to find an equivalent to certain German recipes in the better French books. The German concoctions taste like a chemist's shop. An example is provided by the *Wienerisches Kochbuch*, in which I found a creation made of mushrooms, shallots, lemon peel and basil, all mixed

51

together with other, less assertive seasonings. Any man who has not dulled his taste buds with frequent smoking, or is not quite devoid of imagination, would shudder at this combination of the delightful and the unpleasant with the bitter and astringent.

Unfortunately the habit of eating fussy snacks has already established itself in more than one part of Germany. It happens in areas where the national dishes have been displaced, or at least debased, by senseless concoctions of weird and wonderful ingredients, and where the food on middle-class tables is ceasing to be sufficient or appropriate. Eating between meals arises from an erratic craving for random stimulation of the palate. It tops up the current account of the stomach which is finding that the traditional local provisions are no longer sufficient for its needs. The spectre of eating between meals will knock in vain on the doors of moderately prosperous, professional citizens if their families are contented and united by a diet which is sufficient, nourishing and delectable and in total harmony with the local style. As long as he is sure of receiving good, regular meals, a family man will not dream of ruining his appetite by consuming insubstantial snacks. If, however, a tasteless, inappropriate and disorganised meal regularly awaits him at home, he will fall into the habit of leaving his office in the middle of the morning in order to fetch some sour and salty morsels from some grubby Italian cellar shop. These snacks will fill the gap left by the lack of proper food only because they are so indigestible that they completely destroy the healthy appetite. As there are great differences in culture and customs from one part of Germany to another, the habit of eating between meals, with its characteristic 'fast food shops' has so far established itself in a few provinces only. It is most entrenched in Upper Saxony.

I recommend the unhappy victims of the vicious spectre of eating between meals to review the chain of events which have gradually reduced them to their incurable condition. The respectable, virtuous wife[22] does not understand how to prepare and arrange the meals. This may be because she has not inherited a traditional style of cookery based upon the sensible use and preparation of local products. It may be because she has a horror of cooking (this is not always connected with a lack of interest in eating), or it may be because, having no spontaneous skill of her own, she is forced to resort to the soul-destroying cookery books with their ridiculous recipes. This will result in some discontent in the household. The meal time, hitherto a point when all the family members happily came together after their diverse occupations of the day, becomes the focus of all kinds of foolish annoyances which could easily be avoided. In no time at all, a neighbour will only have to breathe a word and the head of the family, such a diligent man until now, will be off to the market, the drug store or to any other purveyor of witches' brews. Thus the bad habit begins and the family's health and contentment, and even its common livelihood, will rapidly descend the path to total ruin.

Eating between meals at home may be confined to the individual, or it may be a social activity. The individual nibbler maintains a constant contact with kitchen, cellar and larder; he can be recognised immediately by his decaying teeth, swollen eyes and dreamy appearance. Social eating between meals revolves around the newly fashionable suppers known as *thé dansant* or *thé dégoutant*, etc. A state of impoverished gentility has brought them to popularity. These customs and institutions will certainly not foster intellectual life as do healthy, robust meals which are well thought out but swiftly eaten.

The more noticeable snack consumption of German grammar school pupils and university students has much more serious consequences. Because of this, raisins and almonds, so insignificant in themselves, have earned the nickname of 'students' fodder'. Admittedly, the students eat snacks out of sheer necessity. They sometimes have to make do with so-called horse feed. This is because no philanthropist has as yet taken it upon himself to organise a thorough modernisation of the drinking and eating facilities in German universities. The abnormal state of degeneration of these facilities does, of course, force the students to resort to all kinds of confectionery and sweets. This is why our young people are tending to leave school and university with fundamental damage to their digestive systems so that, later on, they are unable to lead healthy and contented lives, despite taking the waters or going horse riding to improve their constitutions. Who would deny that we have here the root cause of all literary feuds, disagreements and party squabbles?

Future generations would clearly be spared some annoyance if the German student body would follow my advice and take to eating in a mess, twenty to forty people together, in the manner of English Army officers. It goes without saying that this should not lead to the formation of any secret societies, or hetaera.[23]

Observing such needs around me, and wishing to take my part in alleviating the evils of our times, I was encouraged to get to the roots of the art of cookery, taking it right back to basics. My own master and tutor made me a decent cook by itemising and upholding the basic principles of cookery and this taught me that you cannot be a practical cook without having a good basic grounding. One of his maxims was that the interpretation of the general instructions which he used to proclaim, and especially all the little nuances and shades of culinary invention, should be left to the imagination of the individual cook. I hope that my interpretation and presentation of his principles has been accurate and effective and that it may go some way towards replacing the national tradition of cookery which has been lost in some parts of Germany. My work is therefore dedicated to the sort of women who are the head of their households or who actually take an intellectual interest in the running of their establishments. These women have graciously taken upon themselves the protection and patronage of my little book against all its merits.

Preface to the Second Edition

Kind reader! Although I know from experience that prefaces are never read, I also know that they have their place in the structure of literature and are obligatory trimmings for all books. The preface to each edition of a book will be different from the others. The preface to the first edition apologises for the audacity and impudence of the author in his paradoxical assumption that he has a better understanding of something than his predecessors. The preface does, however, betray a certain degree of confidence in the future. It is presumed that the reader has already been won over and that his opinion is already favourable; the author therefore considers himself an important person and that the public should be made aware of every little detail which has led to the writing of his book. The public should enjoy, even crave, this information. Having made this assumption, kind reader, I shall now take the liberty of explaining briefly to you how I came to write this book.

The greatest mountains often grow from very little molehills. A slap in the face, or relaxing in an armchair, for example, may lead to something big. Why then should I be ashamed to admit to you that my book also began as a few chapters which set out, without bitterness, to mock at certain aesthetic truisms and sayings by applying them to a little respected art form. These general maxims were used daily in such an unrestricted, vague and fickle way that they appeared to me to be as suitable for one art form as they were for the next. The two sides did at least gain equal profit.

It happened that my cook at that time, the well known Joseph König, was begging me most urgently and repeatedly to make a greater contribution to the up-bringing of his growing sons than was actually convenient for me. After various attempts to sort the matter out, I had no choice but to bring my creation to its necessary conclusion. I made it into a book which the doting father could sell for the benefit of his family. He found a publisher. This work is thus a charity production in the truest sense. It will not aid its author, but will benefit the artist who undertakes the actual practical work.

Apart from this objective, which is a noble one by normal German standards, I had a second, perhaps more exalted and certainly more general, mission. This was to make the paying public aware of the chronic lack of value of all agricultural produce at that time, and of the cheapest ways of utilising this produce, or at least of making the very best of it.

We know that Northern Germany was at peace from the Treaty of Basel in 1794 until 1806. During this period, agricultural production continued to supply those nations which were at war and the demand caused prices to remain high and steady. These prices were more effective than ever art and science could be in encouraging a doubling of agricultural output.

The increase in volume of output continues but the general state of peace has led to a closing of foreign markets, and to the introduction of new imports. The Mediterranean area is supplied by Egypt, Southern Russia and, recently, by Sardinia, which had been ignored for years. The West Indies are supplied by the Western States of North America. Goods come from countries where soils are fertile and where the use of compulsory slave labour allows the growth of crops without cash input. Their produce can therefore be sold at the prevailing prices and still make some profit.

With conditions changing in some places and not in others, the German market soon became dangerously saturated. This caused a reduction in the prices of the primary products of agriculture and the new low prices were soon insufficient to cover production costs. Disregarding the complaints of the country people, it has sometimes been said that the distress caused by this imbalance affected only the owners and leaseholders of agricultural land. Its effects were, however, much more general. When landowners and leaseholders are unable to pay their taxes regularly, when they are obliged to cut out any expense which is not absolutely essential and when they are occasionally unable even to fulfill obligations entered into, then there will be hickups in other branches of business and food production – and who will deny that my predictions have been correct? We then find that, in the midst of nature's bounty, governments are forced to provide financial subsidies for entire provinces, just as apple trees must be supported in a glut year when the weight of their crop of apples is too great.

I do cherish great respect for the acumen of mankind, but in recent years people have not had the wit to make any sort of use of nature's great bounty. The only solution which was attempted with any seriousness was stockpiling, and this came to a sticky end. A co-operative society was planned to work hand in hand with the agricultural and horticultural unions but this project collapsed before it ever got off its feet. This was due to a total lack of enthusiasm and to ignorance of current conditions and requirements. Some ten years ago, an extraordinary man suggested that the rotting cereal crops be converted into corn shares. I do not know if he was serious about this, but the plan might have succeeded. For our contemporaries bear many resemblances to the multitude who were drawn to the edge of the abyss by the world famous Mr Law, with his Mississippi shares, just as a false Messiah lured thirty thousand Jews into the Aegean Sea in Byzantine times. Both men were subsequently considered to be devils in disguise but we cannot be sure whether the people themselves realised what deluded simpletons they had been.

I would not be bothering to express my disapproval of these predicaments if there were not a well-known rule of economics, which is both agreed and accepted, stating that, if products can no longer be profitably marketed in their raw state, it is absolutely necessary that they should be further refined into processed goods. It should then be possible to export these goods or to utilise them in the home country, or to make them serve both purposes. Taking wool as an example, no-one would find it strange if, in conditions of decreasing demand, production were either cut back, or utilised in the manufacture of fabrics and carpets. Thus flax and hemp are converted into linen and sailcloth and the mining industry goes over to iron and steelworks. It was therefore logical to apply this accepted and irrefutable principle to those foodstuffs where excess production was causing such serious problems. This fact remains quite certain: improved methods of agriculture will favour artificial price rises, but when these price rises cease, agricultural production must be cut back unless it is assured of a steady and invariable market by a general improvement in the diet of the population.

I have a hunch that the existing grain mountains could be reduced by measures such as an improvement in the important methods of beer production, probably along the lines of the exemplary old Bavarian system, or by increased use of more finely bolted flour, or by getting people used to better fed, fattier meat and poultry. In good years, the effects of an image of inexhaustible surplus, together with the resulting low prices, are not so very great. If it were possible to control this surplus, to make use of it, then demand would be rejuvenated and trading aroused, no longer deterred. Such a revival is always sufficient to raise average prices, and these are the only rises to be encouraged because they have an equalising effect and benefit everyone to the same degree. This excellent book aims most earnestly to foster the above-mentioned views in a discreet and tactful manner. At the same time it attempts to encourage the intelligent and quick-witted Germans to make full use of their agricultural produce, both for the pleasures of the table, which are short-lived, admittedly, and for the more long-lasting benefit of a well maintained state of health. Most kind reader, I now offer you this book for a second time. It has been enlarged and improved. I trust that this edition may influence your lifestyle more than the first edition was able to. May you derive great pleasure from the fine aroma of readily available herbs and the good quality and management of your regional produce. You would be making a contribution to an important branch of artistic skill in Germany and you would almost certainly feel much healthier for it too.

Now, have I fulfilled some, or all, of my various aims, or none at all? It certainly requires more than one blow to make a block of iron assume the shape we want. In any case, the sale of my book has certainly helped the offspring of my cook, so this particular aim has at least been fulfilled. On the other hand, I am embarrassed to admit that my work has not had the slightest influence on the views of the political economists. The notion that 'foodstuffs are the most abundant objects of domestic trade' is certainly a subtle one. How can we keep track of the fragmented small-scale trade between our farms and the markets and kitchens of our towns? How can we accurately measure the annual turnover of this trade? It is an important question because, if we look at the accounts of orderly households in our towns, and compare the amount spent annually on food and drink with the amount spent on clothing, equipment and other necessities, we see that the amount spent on food and drink constitutes a good half of the overall total. In poorer households the percentage is much greater. I must, however, admit that our political economists, who are extremely numerous, do not consider foodstuffs as worthy objects of trade until they have been converted into stores and cargoes for our warehouses and ships. They must regard the English with some contempt, these rich people! Despite their wealth, however, they pay close attention to the trade in foodstuffs and behave as if they held this to be the most important branch of interior commerce.

After this detailed account, it remains only for me to mention the peculiar, very personal situation in which I have found myself, quite against my will, as a result of this book. I must tell the story right from the beginning.

Who can forget that it is not long since women, even in Germany, were held in a position of subordination and servility. It was their official duty to be responsible for the running of household and kitchen, their special department. Some time ago, this ceased to be the case, thank goodness. Now one never hears those rough admonitions, those stern reprimands, bordering on reproaches, which often used to bring tears to the eyes of gentle women. However, although women no longer recognise an absolute duty to care for household and kitchen, they are still unwilling to give up their exclusive right to control this important area. They are behaving like the men who also like to hang on to their lines of business, even taking on new duties, when they have neither the time, nor the will, nor the ability to deal with them properly. This is why many women saw the earlier edition of this book partly as an encroachment on their authority and partly as an onerous and unwelcome harking back to antiquated and forgotten duties.

Is it then an encroachment? This would mean that women fully accept that it is their duty to run the household. If, on the other hand, it is a reminder of hated duties which were cast off long ago, then it cannot simultaneously be seen as an encroachment. What more can I do? Our women, who do not like having to deal with fine distinctions and logical consequences, have absolutely no basis for their arguments on this subject.

All this should prove that my book has sprung from thoroughly ethical, philanthropic and patriotic roots, sentiments which show my character in an honourable light but will not earn any favours for the work itself. It is fashionable to attribute a little devilry to today's works of art and this is why I was happy to hear that people were expecting to find a certain degree of ambiguity in it. We have to admit that something which is universally true must logically hold good for all and sundry.

Wachwitz, 17th April, 1832.

Book One :
The Elements of Cookery
Animal Foodstuffs

I   The Concept of Cookery

The art of cooking is to develop, with the aid of heat, water and salt, the nutritional, refreshing and delectable qualities of those natural substances which are suitable for the nourishment or restoration of mankind. We should therefore apply Horace's famous epithet, 'Mix usefulness with grace', exclusively to the art of cookery. This has so often been thought of only in terms of the totally useless and completely biased arts of poetry and painting.

The art of cookery is useful in its unswerving dedication to mankind's lasting need for food, nourishment and refreshment. It has two ways of bringing out food's delectable qualities however; firstly by fulfilling the purposes already listed, as nourishing and healthy foodstuffs almost always taste good; and secondly, by the process of adding an appropriate seasoning to the plain but nourishing dishes and foodstuffs, and by giving them a pleasant appearance.

In the course of history incidentally, the art of cookery has at times been dominated by the first of these characteristics and at times by the second, and it would therefore be quite appropriate to adopt a style of cookery which is as strictly defined, graceful and outstanding, as other artistic disciplines.

Many examples of true national dishes have been preserved for us today by a strict style of cookery. One example is the roast beef of the English which is a memorial to those ancient times depicted in the songs of Homer. The ancient Chinese who, like the English, are an insular, solitary people who stick to the old ways, are also fond of succulent, roast meat. The pilau, that tasty rice dish, has been preserved for thousands of years in the same way in all cultures from China to Italy where rice is the chief crop. In a pilau[24] the grains of rice are boiled until partially cooked and then cooled. They are then mixed with animal products and returned to the fire, seasoning added and the cooking completed. This method of cooking preserves the starches and sugars which occur in such abundance in this excellent grain; the Northern peoples however, to whom rice has been brought from far afield, are in the habit of cooking these beneficial elements right away, and of contenting themselves with the remaining fibres, now devoid of any substance or flavour.

It is the height of achievement to cook with grace and combine appeal and ornamentation with nutrition. The achievement is not easy to maintain. I intend to concern myself primarily with this style of cooking. It is 'le genre mâle et élégant', as the excellent Carême[25] puts it.

Cooking with grace gives rise, however, to a state of over-refinement and exaggeration, where ornamentation and decoration are stressed to the detriment of nourishment and content. The Greeks reached this stage very early; the Romans experienced it later, most specifically at the time when Apicius was compiling the forerunner of all modern cookery books. His book is noteworthy for more than one reason. Firstly because it does contain, here and there, some Roman household rules which remain useful today. We can complete the details of these by referring to the writers on agriculture. Secondly, as already observed, because it also represents the greatest corruption imaginable of the art of cookery; we can learn from it to what extent man can accustom himself to strange flavours when he, without reflection or restraint, allows himself to become obsessed by novelty. He will strive to maintain the freshness of the new by constant experimentation.

II General Characteristics of the Edible Natural Substances

With regard to their general relationship with man, the edible substances can be categorised into those which simply nourish, those which simply season, and those which combine both properties.

The nutritional element should under no circumstances be suppressed or eliminated by over-contrived preparation, as does unfortunately happen all too often. On the contrary, we should always strive to preserve it, to develop and increase it. It is therefore imperative that the nutritional quality of a raw material should not be reduced before it is even prepared for eating. This occurs, for example, when meat and fish are washed excessively, as Germans tend to do, or when they are simply left for long periods in cold water. Water dissolves the glutin[26] and leaches the goodness from both fish and meat. In order to prove this, two pieces of the same fish should be boiled; one piece after it has been lying in water for a quarter of an hour and the other piece immediately after being cut up. Both pieces should then be tasted. In most cases the so-called blanching of foods is also a pointless practice which always reduces the nutritional quality. Blanching is often undertaken with the sole purpose of giving the food a better appearance, a purpose which cannot be achieved. The nutritional quality and good flavour of a food should not be sacrificed simply for a good appearance. Decoration is really only desirable when it is directly related to the character[27] of the food.

We should also beware of washing out the seasoning (aromatic) properties and delicate salts contained in the majority of foodstuffs, and it is particularly important not to subject them to excessive heat in cooking. Seasonings which are dissimilar and opposed to each other should not be mixed together because they will either cancel each other out or will impart an offensive flavour. This crucial rule is totally disregarded every day, both in theory and in practice.

We should handle those foodstuffs which are both nourishing and toothsome with twice as much care. This is because the volatile salts and aromas which they contain do sometimes yield to the heat which has to be used to fully develop the nourishing properties.

There is, however, a fourth category of foodstuffs where washing, soaking, lengthy cooking or reduction are necessary in order to eliminate some unpleasant, or even harmful, constituent. Some types of potato, for example, contain a poisonous juice, and all potatoes contain harmful juice.[28] In the first instance it is necessary to separate the juice by squeezing it out; in the latter case, which applies only to ourselves in Europe, it is sufficient to partially remove the potato juice by frequent washing and lengthy soaking in fresh water, the remainder being vapourised by moderate heat. The artichoke likewise requires lengthy soaking to remove its bitter juice; as everyone knows, salted and air-dried foodstuffs are soaked to free them of the saltpetre, salt and brine in which they were steeped.

It is very important to be able to assess the general and individual good qualities of raw foodstuffs. There is often a considerable difference between similar items. Hippocrates[29] was already lamenting that this fact hindered anyone trying to give out general, accurate information about the effects of foodstuffs. The senses of smell, taste and sight, when properly trained, can be put to good use when shopping for and selecting foodstuffs. In this connection it would be superfluous for me to attempt to explain the anatomy of the larger game and domestic animals. This is vital information for every cook, and the English methods of cookery are outstanding in their interpretation of this branch of our science.

III   The Origins and Prerequisites of Cookery

The human dentition, which in rare instances[30] resembles the eating equipment of the carnivorous animals, and the traditions resulting from mankind's original hunting existence have lead us to regard animal foodstuffs, or meat, together with the fleshy fruits, as our earliest foods. We should consider them first. The flesh of animals does in fact contain the greatest proportion of nourishing elements, from both the chemical and dietetic point of view. Therefore we need only concern ourselves with using our skills to best advantage to develop the nutritional quality of meat.

Primitive peoples, such as the Patagonians in Anson's travels, living like animals, unceremoniously consume their animal products raw. The Kalmucks and Kirghiz, who have advanced one step on the road to civilisation, already attempt to heat up their horseflesh by placing it under their saddles when they go out riding. Cultivated peoples, however, would find raw meat, and indeed semi-raw meat, quite loathsome and revolting; it would in fact appear that the cultivated lifestyle itself weakens the digestion and creates the need for artificial assistance. We use our skills to give this assistance to the refined or weakened digestion, and achieve it by the judicious employment of heat, water and cooking salt.

For many thousands of years the above-mentioned three elements have been used by countless peoples as their external digestion aids, so to speak; we are accustomed from childhood to regard the heated stove or fireplace as immutable. In some places families are even counted and valued according to their fireplaces. Nevertheless, a long time must have elapsed before it occurred to some good soul to attach his portion of the hunted meat to the end of a stick and then to expose it to the fire. Once this discovery was made, the consequences certainly mounted up rapidly.

Another epoch had to pass before a watertight, fireproof appliance was discovered, made of clay or metal, without which boiling and stewing would have been quite impossible. It is possible that man learnt by chance to heat meat over a flame, and even to use natural cooking salt. However, whoever hit logically upon the value of boiling and the use of the cooking pot without any previous experience was undoubtedly a person of unusual capabilities. It is indeed possible that the pot was originally conceived only as a drinking vessel, and that then chance or pure curiosity gradually gave rise to the notion of heating liquids in it and finally to using it as a means of heating edible items.

Nowadays it is no longer a question of whether we should use heat, water and salt in our kitchens: we are much more concerned with the best possible quality and most appropriate use of these elements.

The first and most important step is to install the fireplace so that it can be used with comfort; it is in this very area, however, that our building skills, which are otherwise quite effective, are dragging their feet; for a chimney which does not smoke has become almost as rare as a theatre in which one can hear properly. Anyone who happens to own a hearth which does not smoke should be extremely wary of sacrificing it to any wanton desire for new improvements; the first stone displaced would be bound to be the very last stone in need of moving.

A good cooking stove – and a good stove is one at which it is possible to cook without crying – should have space for a lively, blazing fire for roasting, over which a number of spits should be set at appropriate height. There should be space beyond this central heat source for kettles and all kinds of containers and pots so that the rising heat is not entirely wasted. Spaces for casseroles, or small secondary hearths in which only coals are burnt, can be positioned around the edge of the stove and in the accessible corners. Some people use ordinary charcoal in these secondary hearths. This sometimes smokes and always emits an evil smoke which has a detrimental effect on the health of the cook. I therefore advise that the burning of all fuel should be commenced in the main fire and that coals should be transferred to the side hearths only when they are well burnt through.

Various types of economy stoves and ovens have been invented recently and it is possible to read about these in highly reliable books, which give physical and mechanical details, such as Count Rumford's small volume. These valuable discoveries have only rarely been utilised, either because people simply do not readily give up their old habits, or because the traditional methods were actually better. The cooking stoves which are found in every farmhouse and servants' hall in South Germany are becoming more widespread. When the iron plates separating the upper part of the stove from the fire located below are not too thin, and therefore do not heat up too rapidly, these stoves are ideal for boiling, stewing, baking and keeping food warm. They have, however, also given rise to that dried-up roast meat which is found all over South Germany and which intelligent housewifes should banish from their cooking repertoire.

Only in the matter of the fire is the stove not the controlling factor. The quality of the fuel is much more important. One variety of wood may be better than another; beechwood is best. We should also take care to ensure that seasoned wood is always available because sappy, damp wood will not burn readily and will smoke, thereby spoiling some foods. I myself would advise that a stock of really dry twigs or brushwood is always maintained because there are often occasions when the results desired can be achieved only with a lively, blazing fire.

True bituminous coal[42] is to be preferred among the remaining types of fuel; bituminous coal is in fact best when a very intense, powerful heat is required, as it is for the roast ox joints of the English. The more clay a coal contains, the less suited it is for cooking, partly because it gives off proportionally less heat, and partly because, in burning more slowly, it emits more unpleasant odours which can very easily be absorbed by the food. Peat, or plant material impregnated with asphalt, is normally preferable to lignite or brown coal because it burns faster, with minimal odour and, once carbonised, tends to loose its smell completely. It is therefore a good idea to get turf burning steadily with twigs before setting the food over it.

Charcoal is an excellent fuel; it gives almost as much heat as a good bituminous coal fire and also emits less odour. I must, however, point out to would-be chefs that not all charcoal is the real thing, not having been processed in accordance with the true principles of the art. It may have been prepared from wood which was too damp, or was burnt in too strong a draught, or avaricious charcoal burners may have smothered the flames before all the inert substances were burnt away. Then we find that the coals become possessed by a restless hobgoblin who spits out sparks and makes noises and explosions when we apply the bellows to the fire, filling the pots with dust and specks of coal.

Enough of the fire. Water however, nature's most precious gift and mankind's best refreshment, is not regarded with as much love and solicitude by people nowadays as it was in classical times, and even in medieval times. The ruins of the great aqueducts which are still found throughout the former Roman empire offer proof that the Romans were concerned not only with the volume, but rather with the optimum quality of the water; the high receptivity of this element means that there can be considerable variations in its constituents, or rather in its chemical composition, even from springs which occur close together. Although it is indeed very important to have good drinking water, the water we use for cooking is of equal significance: not every good drinking water is fit for cooking in the same way as not every cooking water is suitable for drinking. Soft water, with a low mineral content, is best for cooking, and mildly stagnant water is even better than a mineral water because the decomposing plant matter in the former can be partially removed by skimming during boiling, while the rest, in the course of more gentle simmering, will form a deposit or sediment in the bottom of the vessel. The salts and acids in mineral water will only become more dissolved during cooking and will be absorbed by the foods.

There are of course low-lying areas, such as Holland, where people are obliged to do without decent drinking water, and there are mountainous areas which are quite incapable of producing any pure, serviceable cooking water. In these instances, man must use his skills to help himself. Stagnant water can be much improved by rapid movement through the pipes and by filtration through coal, gravel or layers of porous stone. It can indeed be brought very close to perfection. It is also possible to filter mineral waters before they are used for cooking, using chemical methods which are relatively simple and inexpensive and which render them reasonably useful. In some mountain areas, such as Carinthia and Savoy, which are noted for medical problems with goitres, it would doubtless be very valuable to treat the drinking water in this way also.

It is, however, not my place to advise home owners and local officials about the chemical analyses and improvements which could be made to their water supply. I would rather refer them to the experts in this science, and particularly to the practical advice contained in the many excellent books on this subject.

Finally cooking salt, although its principal elements remain the same, does show great variation in its chemical composition. Rock salt, which occurs in large quantities, is without question the finest, and Spanish rock salt is the best of all. Its quality shows in salt fish preparations such as Dutch herrings. Sea salt also penetrates very well, however, and is perfectly suitable for salting small fish such as the sardines of Italy and France. Lister, referring to Book nine, Chapter thirteen in Apicius, commends the use of French sea salt in the most delicious and long-lasting salted dishes of England. The best salt available should always be used for salted dishes, even if it is a little more expensive than that used every day. The spring salts show the greatest variation. They often retain excessive quantities of clay and lime, according to the relative abundance of the spring and to the skill with which their salts have been processed. A good spring salt can be recognised at first glance by the purity and transparence of its crystals. Sea salt is always dark coloured, however, because it tends to retain a little potassium nitrate. It is for this reason that it is not necessary to add saltpetre when using sea salt to prepare salted dishes.

As it is desirable to add a certain quantity of salt to most foods in order to develop the flavour and wholesomeness, I shall hence-forward take its use for granted, with only occasional reminders. The only exception to this rule will be the foods which are definitely sweet.

IV   The Organisation of the Kitchen in Accordance with the Needs of Civilised People

I have just been dealing with the pre-requisites of the art of cookery. It is now appropriate for me to break the chronological sequence of this work in order to mention the equipment required in an up-to-date kitchen. Firstly, the modern kitchen requires a certain number of spits of various sizes which are all suitable for use with the roasting jack. This can be installed in a number of different ways.

The gridiron is related to the spit. I advise the provision of several, of varying dimensions and with bars of varying width. Some should be finely worked, while others should be silver plated or even burnished on the upper surface as untreated iron cannot be kept clean.

A suspended water kettle, made of copper or iron, or else a pot of sufficient proportions, is the next absolute requirement. Boiling water should always be available for washing cooking pots, cleaning poultry and for numerous other functions.

I shall not give details of the numerous types and uses of earthenware crockery such as pots, water vessels, saucepans and bowls as they are such basic items of household equipment. Because earthenware crockery is so inexpensive, cooks and kitchenmaids tend to handle it very carelessly so that, in a trice, everything can be broken. It is therefore necessary to ensure that they put these items away carefully so that they do not acquire any little cracks which will turn into large cracks over the fire. When buying these pots, notice whether they have a lead-based glaze because this type of glaze is detrimental to the health. This fact has been proven in an excellent book, 'Der Tod in den Töpfen' (Death in our Cooking Pots) which does, however, exaggerate a little. We in Germany would undoubtedly benefit from a thorough improvement of our pottery production methods along the lines of the English stoneware goods. These pots are coated with copper to protect them from shattering and are used for cooking in a few regions, with excellent results. They heat up very slowly and are therefore not suitable for all dishes. However, meat broths, stews, potatoes, in short, anything which requires slow, gentle cooking, do exceptionally well in them.

Tinned copper, lead free vessels have been used in our kitchens for so long, but in the middle of the last century an outcry was raised against them. Occasional cases of verdigris poisoning caused by careless, unhygienic cooks led to loud and insistent demands that they should not be used any more. There were some comical incidents when hypochondriac experts disputed in vain the advantages put forward by their wives, cooks and stewards, and these have been described in various books.

A metal vessel is, however, essential where, as so often happens, a rapid transfer of heat is required. Attempts have thus been made to replace copper vessels with cast iron. This is then subject to furring and is bad for the teeth and the digestion. It should also not be forgotten that iron vessels very readily affect the flavour and colour of foods. I therefore believe that we should keep the copper vessels, but should keep them scrupulously clean.

One or two tinned copper cake-baking pans are useful but if these are not available, they can be replaced by a Dutch oven.

A few iron tripods, especially if the stove has no side hearths. A few mortars made of metal, stone and wood.

One, or perhaps two casseroles made of the purest silver possible are necessary for a variety of foods. Details of these will be given below. These must also be kept very clean because the inevitable addition of copper readily develops verdigris.

A number of tinplate bowls can be used for various purposes, for example as containers for all kinds of baked goods. It is better to flatten out the concave bases of these bowls because it will not then be necessary to solder them with lead.

A number of tinplate pudding moulds, which must be soldered with tin rather than lead. It is, however, possible to do without these and boil puddings wrapped in clean cloths. Pudding and jelly moulds made of fireproof English stoneware are available nowadays and are very good. Puddings can be baked in them.

A number of tinned copper tins and moulds for the preparation or moulding of all kinds of flour-based dishes, jellies and so on. I cannot understand why people have not started to make jelly moulds out of glass. After all, they do not have to be exposed to heat and it would be much easier to judge the colour, clarity and consistency of a jelly in a glass mould than in a copper or clay one.

Iron vessels and containers should be used only for the most lowly purposes because they very readily affect the flavour and colour of foods.

A colander made of brass or copper and various hair sieves. It is essential that these be kept scrupulously clean.

A number of graters of varying gauges so that not everything is grated on the same surface.

A slab of smooth stone with a wooden rolling pin for the working of all types of dough, to be baked or boiled. If marble is not available, a good, smooth wooden board should be used.

A special board for cutting truffles into slivers. Further, everyday boards for cutting up cabbage, apples and so on.

A chopping board of hard, well brined wood with slightly raised edges to prevent the chopped food from falling off. With this there should be a double- or multiple-bladed mincing knife, a chopping knife and a pointed knife with a serrated blade. Wooden spoons, kitchen knives and cleavers; a large, Italian butcher's knife for cutting ham, salamis, steaks, etc into fine slices; small paring knives for coring fruit and for cutting all kinds of small items into special shapes; metal tongs and moulds for shaping baked goods and so on. Finally, a Roman style soup tureen and an English steamer would not go amiss.

All of these implements must be kept very clean. Judging from the warnings of the excellent Neubauer,[32] this is not always the case in the kitchens of Germany. 'It is a matter for such pride,' he exclaims, 'when the master and mistress, or other people, come into the kitchen and see that everything is glistening like gold.' But not only the pride of the kitchen, but also the flavour of the food and the health of its consumer are at stake if all cooking equipment is not cleaned and scrubbed immediately after use. When holding up the French kitchens as an example to the Germans in this respect, Neubauer should not have omitted to mention the almost universal cleanliness of the town and country kitchens of Bavaria. A fine example of this is provided by the kitchen of the Hirschgarten inn, not far from Munich.

V   Roasting in General

I have already pointed out that the roast is very probably man's original cooked food and I therefore give it preference above all other methods of preparing food.

Strictly speaking, a roast is a piece of meat or fat from a warm blooded animal or fish which is cooked by the direct heat from a fire. In order to prevent the outer surface of a roast from drying out, it is customary to baste it with its own dripping juice and fat, or other left-over animal fat, or even butter or oil. This treatment, together with a vigorous application of salt during the cooking, gives the roast meat a particularly assertive flavour, and it is for this reason that it is served towards the end of a meal as it then revives the flagging appetite and is also more easily digested. Different peoples use different roasting techniques, not all of which are of equal value.

The English, or rather the Homeric method of roasting is based upon the principle of initially sealing the meat with a strong application of penetrating heat, which then prevents the evaporation of its valuable juices and minerals during the subsequent[33] gentler cooking period. It is therefore essential that this type of roasting be undertaken over an open fire. Excessive measures of economy have, however, banished open fires from many German kitchens. The effects of a good, blazing fire cannot be replaced by the so-called roasting machine, nor by any kind of oven, and least of all by a cooking pot or saucepan.

{I have since learnt from experience that all basting and pre-salting has a bad effect on the roast. In order to obtain a perfect result it should be placed, quite dry, over the blazing, established fire, over which it should be turned, still dry, until the outer surface is thoroughly heated. Even then it should not be basted, although any areas in danger of drying out too quickly can be spread, or rather just dabbed, with a tiny piece of butter. The butter will immediately melt and bubble on the overheated areas; very little should be used so that there are no drips. During roasting, a properly treated joint will exude that fine, tasty and wholesome substance which has been named osmazome in modern chemistry. Towards the end of the cooking period, this substance will absorb the salt which must be abundantly and repeatedly sprinkled all over the surface of the joint. If the salt were applied too early, the joint would immediately begin to drip juices, losing its best part, the osmazome. If the joint were basted from the start, or indeed if quantities of fat and liquid were poured over it later on, its outer surface would never become firm, so that the juice would evaporate and the fibres would lose texture and become limp. A good joint should swell, its fibres stretched and taut, its outer surface firm, its interior easy to carve and tender to eat. Even when cooked to the bone, it should fill the dish with its juice at the first cut. Such a roast joint scorns that greasy, smutty filth which goes by the name of Bratenbutter (roasting butter) and which is considered by those with corrupt taste as an essential accompaniment to such food. Anyone who eschews meat stewed to leather, the duplicitous mock roast, will also be capable of showing enough heroism and true determination as is necessary to stop the old routine of buying greasy, browned butter. Incidentally, a roast joint should be removed from the spit as soon as it is done; do not wait until it begins to shrink or dry out. It is not possible to give a general rule for this because everything depends upon the size and type of the meat, and the distance from the fire. A young hen, for example, requires ten to twenty minutes. Also no one should be under the impression that it is cheaper to roast in an oven; even in the towns, an armfull of wood is not as expensive as the half pound of butter which is saved by following my method.}

In places where fuel is very expensive, grilled meat can act as a subsitute for real roast meat in poorer households. The thinner cuts of meat, such as the well known beefsteaks of the English, can be grilled most successfully over a lively coal fire. All of the more robust meats, and most fish too, are very tasty when cooked in this way. It is important that the fire should be red hot and the cook must not leave the grill, so that he can turn the slices quickly when it is necessary and remove them from the heat at the very moment when they are done. A delay of only a few seconds will result in tough meat which is completely dried out. It is not necessary to baste slices of beef, veal, mutton, or of any other fatty, succulent meats with any alien fats during grilling. This would only deprive them of their own pure, individual flavour without making them any more succulent. In contrast, if fish fillets are to be cooked on the grill, they should, with rare exceptions, be moistened a little with fresh butter or a good quality oil. Fish should be salted towards the end of cooking. At this point they can also be sprinkled with breadcrumbs which will soak up the fat which may have accumulated on the upper surface of the fillet.

The thrifty housewife would be wise to abandon all the other imitations of the true roast, particularly the 'smothered joint'. The stew, however, (*stufato* in Italian) is much more to be regarded as an important dish in its own right. Further details of steaming and stewing will be given below.

VI   Certain Particular Roasts

A large piece of meat cut from around the hip bone is required for the true roast ox. The larger the piece of meat, the more the glutin within it will be concentrated and cooked away and the more the meat's own juices and minerals will be preserved. The meat should be hung in a cold place for eight to fourteen days, less when the weather is warm, in order to tenderise it. Only after this preparation should it be placed on the spit over a lively fire, its outer surface being treated according to the general instructions given above, until it is done. When such a piece of beef has been roasted correctly it should remain very succulent, but the first cut with the knife, immediately causing the reddish juices to flow from the fibres, should reveal a pale, delicate meat, almost like well-fattened veal. Following the custom of the English, a joint of roast beef should be carved in very thin slices.

This national dish has given the English the reputation for liking raw meat. This is because many Europeans are under the impression that a roast that gives out juice is quite undercooked. They do not consider it to be thoroughly cooked until it has become as dessicated as a wasps' nest. It is they who are mistaken; a good joint of roast beef is only as moist as it is because the outer coating formed during the initial application of intense heat has prevented the evaporation of the juices.

Being obliged to cater for a small number of people I have often spit roasted smaller pieces of beef, cut from the backbone of the animal; the coating of fat which these joints tend to have, together with the presence of the bone, helped to prevent drying out and we had an agreeable substitute for the more massive beef joint.

In countries where the people like a greater variety in their food than the English, one can in any case only entertain the idea of serving these vast pieces of meat in public houses or for large gatherings. It is for this reason that we have gained another excellent substitute for the English roast beef which, if I am not deceived, is an invention of the French. It is the filet de boeuf. The tenderness of this choice piece of meat can be enhanced by a dash of vinegar, seasoning and assorted fine herbs but anyone who does not find this contrived flavour pleasing would do better to hang the meat for a few days, tenderise it by beating and then roll it up as tightly as possible for cooking. This piece of meat should then be properly larded and turned on the spit, initially over a lively fire, which should then be allowed to die down. The meat should be turned until it is sufficiently cooked. {Incidentally, I think that it is preferable to spit roast a fillet quite plainly, following the above instructions. It should not be larded, nor should it be beaten or flavoured in any way.} Starchy vegetables such as potatoes and grey or Prussian peas, also fresh, young white beans dressed with oil and lemon juice make a welcome accompaniment; other potential individual accompaniments are carrots, turnips, steamed cucumbers and salad vegetables such as lettuce, endives, etc. Appropriate details of these are given in Book Two.

It is always best to roast young lambs, sucking pigs, fattened poultry and other animals which possess a thick layer of fat over a fierce flame. After this they will require only as much heat as will keep them warm until they are served. This will prevent the excessive loss of juices by evaporation.

It is necessary to protect pheasants, woodcock and other such leaner birds with a layer of thin slices of either fresh or salted bacon. This should either be sewn together like a jacket, or should be secured in some other way. The French are in the habit of also placing a sheet of paper soaked in olive oil over the bacon jacket, and this gives much more protection against drying out. In this way the delicious meat remains remarkably succulent and fresh. The jacket can be opened up just before the bird is done. This will allow the heat to penetrate to the skin and create a more pronounced roasted flavour. I do not need to remind anyone that the savoury drippings from the bird should be allowed to fall onto slices of toast during the roasting. In Italy the giblets are removed from the body of the woodcock when half cooked. They are chopped with a few anchovies and fine herbs and the mixture is then spread on slices of bread. The cooking is completed in a roasting dish.

It is better to lard meats such as veal, hare, partridge and calves' liver, or to cover their entire outer surface with a web of little pieces of bacon. Salted bacon is preferable in this instance as it provides a pleasant contrast to these sweeter types of meat. However, such matters are always governed by the master of the house and any self-respecting cook would be wise not to forget this.

It can sometimes happen that a piece of meat contains more fat than is desirable or wholesome. The eel is a case in point. Staying by Lake Trasimeno I became familiar with an excellent way of dealing with this fish, and the method can be applied more or less successfully to all fatty types of meat. The skin is removed from the eel and it is cut into pieces. These are placed on a spit over a moderate coal fire. As soon as the pieces, which should not be too close together, begin to exude their fat, they should be sprinkled with a mixture of fine salt and fine breadcrumbs and this should be continued until no more fat appears. If this is done carefully and not heedlessly, as happens in most kitchens, each individual piece becomes evenly coated with a crust which can be made more crunchy by an increase in heat just before serving. If desired, it can be seasoned (given more bite) with a little ground pepper. This crust, which I have just described, provides a very pleasant contrast to the sweetness and mildness of the eel, and its indigestible fat is partially absorbed by the dry, crusty element in the breadcrumbs, while the rest is simply sweated away. The advantages of this method of preparation must be evident and I wish with all my heart that it were in general use in Germany, to the total exclusion of the barbarous habit of roasting or stewing eel in butter. German cookery books do in fact recommend the spit roasting of eel, but they advise all sorts of artificial preparations which conflict with the good flavour of the eel and deprive it of the freshness so important to it.

Small chunks of lamb, mutton and pork can be treated in the same way, rather like the delicious kebabs of Turkey, especially if slices of Spanish or Levantine onions are interspersed with the meat. Tiny branches of bay, sage, rosemary or other bitter, aromatic herbs can also be placed between the pieces of meat as long as they do not create too strong a flavour. The pieces should not be too close together. A little more salt should be applied under the breadcrumbs than is necessary for the eel and, if desired, a little of the favourite household seasoning can also be used.

I must now take the opportunity of mentioning the Italian method of spit roasting fresh pigs' liver. The meat is cut into chunks which are salted, seasoned and also sprinkled with a little caraway. They are then wrapped in the pig's caul fat and placed on a fine spit, with fresh, wild bay leaves between them. They are then turned vigorously over a blazing fire and are served as soon as they are done. This dish is ideal in the autumn hunting season in the country; I would not recommend it to town dwellers. They would find it indigestible.

The breast meat of larger creatures, such as turkeys (Calcutta hens, coneys or young turkeys) can be cooked very successfully on the spit or on the grill. The meat should be torn from the carcases, the shoulder joint having been broken and the skin around the pectoral muscle pulled away. This type of roast, with some delicate vegetables, makes an appropriate and delicious dish. Well run households will find many uses for the remaining parts of the bird.

VII   The Basting of Roasts and Fats in General

If absolutely necessary to prevent the outer surface of meat drying out too much, it is generally best to baste roasts with their own dripping fatty juices if possible. The pure, characteristic flavour of any type of meat will be tainted by the use of an alien fat, even if it is used with caution. There are of course many foods which can be roasted but which are more prone to drying out because of their inherent leanness or small volume, and these will require some sort of lubrication or saucing while the fire is at its hottest. In such cases it is important to use a fat with as little flavour and odour as possible. Best quality butter can be used. Fine olive oil, which is of course not always available in Germany, or, failing this, fresh poppyseed oil or a nut oil, make an excellent lubricant for small birds. Olive oil, even when very sparingly used, affords the smaller birds adequate protection against drying out, which can otherwise spell disaster for them. It also absorbs salt well and helps to seal the outer skin of the bird while the interior remains very succulent. It is also necessary to reduce the fire correctly during the cooking period. I do not otherwise advocate the use of oil. This is partly because it becomes viscous and resinous, and therefore very indigestible, when heated and partly because it often develops a peculiar flavour during cooking. These are not major problems when basting small game birds because one table spoon of oil will be sufficient to keep the entire spit well moistened, and most of this will in fact be lost either in drips or by evaporation if the fire is hot.

I shall now take the opportunity to make a few general remarks about the fats which have just been mentioned.

The excessive use of fats in cooking, over-indulgence in butter, bacon, fatty meat and the like is harmful to most people. Every doctor knows, however, that a moderate intake of fat is vital to the smooth functioning of the bowels, the joints and other bodily organs. The peasant classes in all agricultural countries demonstrate this by their instinctive use of grease, oil or butter to lubricate their dry vegetable diet. In order to maintain the balance, wealthier people, who tend to consume a much larger proportion of animal products than vegetable products, should endeavour to limit the use of fat in their kitchens to the same extent that the poor people would like to increase it.

As the use of fats cannot be completely avoided, even in the finest kitchen, it is important that the best and most suitable type of fat possible should be available.

Fresh bacon should be produced from healthy, mature pigs which have been slaughtered in cool weather. Its density, colour and smell will indicate whether a salted and smoked bacon is of good quality.

The quality of butter is affected both by the suitability of the pasture and by the production method. The butters of Holstein, Holland and Switzerland deserve our preference because they combine the merits of a natural suitability and reasonably clean production methods. Their fine quality is largely due to the fact that the cream is skimmed off while the milk is still sweet and fresh. In places where milk is less plentiful and contains a lower level of fat, the custom is to allow the milk to curdle beneath the layer of cream in order to achieve a greater separation of the fat content. This procedure results in the cream unavoidably acquiring a rancid, cheesy flavour which will be preserved in the butter.

Ordinary butter can be slightly improved by working it repeatedly in fresh water or by skimming it thoroughly over a gentle heat. Butter such as that from Holstein, and especially that produced in the autumn, can be preserved through the winter if salted. Butter can also be preserved by skimming to remove all caseins, as above, and it is then known as clarified butter. Only this latter is suitable for baking.

Goose fat, which is never very plentiful, is popular in some places and is preferred for certain dishes. In Italy, where there is less butter and more use is made of bacon and pork fat, Jewish people use goose grease. I do not know how successful they are with this.

In the temperate lands, olive oil is used in the same way as the northern, and far southern, peoples use butter. We Northerners use olive oil only for uncooked sauces. It cannot, however, be denied that it is better than butter and clarified butter for baking and that there are occasions when it should be preferred above all other fats in the kitchen.

The quality of olive oil is dependent upon local conditions and situation and on the treatment of the olive tree. It can be both improved and spoilt during processing. An example of this is provided by the oil of Calabria, which would be of excellent quality if the Neapolitan government had not imposed an excise, payable in advance, upon the oil pressing mills. This has meant that those farmers who are not well off have to allow the olives to rot until they have enough money to press them. Once the olive has begun to ferment, however, its oil becomes tainted by the rancid flavour of its rotting flesh, and this flavour is never lost. In the past, people used to employ various artificial methods to purify the oil; The people of Provence have other methods. Rapid processing of the olives is therefore necessary to produce a good oil, even from a top quality growth. The first oil which runs from the olives without pressing (the virgin oil or 'eruption') is the best and finest. It can be used fresh while the pressed oil needs to stand for a good period of time so that its sediment can separate and settle before it is used.

There is more than one form of the finest oil. That produced by the Island of Capri and by Olevano and Civitella in the Papal Territories is pale, limpid and liquid, not fatty, while the oil of Lucca, Calci, Genoa and Corfu is bright yellow, transparent and odourless, but more fatty on the tongue. Greek and Spanish oils were sought after in ancient times but are now marketed under other names. The quality of the so-called Provençal oil is unreliable. A large proportion of the oil exported from there to the North has been bought wholesale in the Italian Levant and in Spain.

VIII   Roasting with Slow, Enclosed Heat

The accounts of the voyages of discovery of the English and other peoples often mention the South Sea Island practice of roasting on heated stones or in heated trenches. Such accounts can be found in the works of Cook, Bougainville and Neuere. I found this method of preparing food completely absorbing. It was employed by an entire nation, it was simple and represented cooking in its purest form. I realised of course that it could not be carried out in a thoroughly hygienic manner because it was not possible to keep the meat being cooked free of ash, coal and earth. After some consideration, however, I hit upon a way of combining this simple, primeval cooking method with the level of hygiene which is a primary requirement in the kitchens of civilised nations. I took a good solid baking pan, well tinned, placed a tinplate bowl inside it and on this I placed a piece of fatty beef, mutton or pork. I chose a piece of meat which filled the container but did not touch its sides or top at any point. I then closed the container and carefully sealed all cracks and openings with bread dough. I completely buried the container under a heap of glowing embers and let it stand for four to six hours depending on the size of the piece of meat. Towards the end of this period I added fresh glowing coals on top of the ash heap. Before the container was opened, which had of course to be achieved before the food could be served, I made sure that it was cleaned of every trace of ash, and every time a very succulent, clean-flavoured Tahitian-style roast was produced.

I advise that a fairly deep dish, either of tin or of fire-proof English stoneware, is placed under the meat. This will then hold the juice running from the meat.

I also advise that beef, and pork in particular, should be salted before roasting. The meat should be salted for eight days in winter but only for four days in summer. Mutton readily acquires a rancid flavour and it is therefore a good idea to salt it and then to wrap it in a cloth which has been soaked in vinegar.

If there is enough space, freshly peeled potatoes can be placed around the meat. These are sprinkled with salt and cooked in the same heat. They will absorb the juice from the meat and will be delicious.

The so-called roasting machine also seems to have resulted from attempts to copy the inhabitants of the South Sea Islands. It dries the meat out, however, and taints it with the smell and acidity of the coal, which is ignited inside the machine. This is totally counter-productive. This ruinous device has gained much popularity in Germany because of the stinginess and laziness of our cooks.

IX   Boiling in General

I have already pointed out the importance of the invention of the cooking pot in Chapter Three. Unfortunately we do not know the name of the inventor, nor his country; the tale of Prometheus is partly an allegory on the cooking pot. In its earthenware form it encompasses movement and fire with great secrecy and even today it stands, an empty container, as a symbol of the lack of moral values.

At any rate we must acknowledge that the cooking pot is very ancient. It appears as early as the legend of Moses, in which the Egyptian meat pot is frequently mentioned. This has become almost proverbial. Furthermore, the cooking pot is unknown to only a tiny proportion of the uncivilised peoples discovered by our recent sea voyages.

Innumerable natural products were rendered edible by the invention of the cooking pot. It added a new dimension to others. Man had finally learnt the arts of boiling and stewing and was now able to combine animal products with the nutritious and aromatic products of the plant kingdom, creating a new end product. For the first time it was possible for the art of cookery to be developed in all directions.

Cooking pot in hand, we shall now enter the realm of boiling and stewing. The definition of boiling is: rendering an item edible, or at least more edible, by the use of water maintained at boiling point.

X   Boiling Meat and Fish

When food is roasted, the end result is simply the roast itself; when food is boiled, however, we gain the cooking liquid as well as the meat itself, and this liquid can be utilised in many different ways.

People like the English who have established a praiseworthy, but rather one-sided preference for roasting, tend to maintain a prejudice against boiled meat. I must say that I agree with the view of famous doctors that a piece of meat which has been so overcooked that it is almost reduced to shreds cannot retain any nutritional value and cannot possibly constitute a tasty meal. Fortunately, however, gentle, carefully managed boiling results in a double bonus – good broth and succulent, cooked meat.

If you wish to do without the broth, it is a good idea to wrap or, even better, to sew the piece of meat up in a cloth which has been washed out repeatedly without soap. The meat is then boiled for an appropriate time, according to volume and type. The English prepare their boil'd mutton in this way, and it makes a dish which is both succulent and nutritious. When using this method of preparation, I recommend that the meat is pre-salted for twelve, or twenty-four hours, according to the volume of the piece, as it is not possible to salt it further during the actual cooking. The foodstuff is also favourably affected by the medium of the liquid in which it is boiled. During the boiling process it will absorb as much as it gives off. For this reason anything boiled in a strongly flavoured meat broth will be delicious to eat. Examples are the pot-boiled chickens which the Parisians always have on the simmer, and Donkin's Patent Meat, which is in the truest sense prepared in strongly flavoured meat broth. Apicius was already aware that salted food was rendered more palatable by boiling it in milk. Hams can also be boiled in wine, or in water with aromatic herbs and spices.

The boiling of fish involves disproportionately greater difficulties than the boiling of meat. In most areas where there is a plentiful supply of fish, and particularly in Holland, the tradition of boiling fish correctly has imperceptibly spread throughout the population, while in other places it often happens that even the most renowned cooks are incapable of it.

I have tried in vain to get to the root of the theory of boiling fish. At every attempt there are new developments according to the type and size of fish, the water in which it lived, the length of time it has been dead, the weather conditions and, finally, the water to be used for boiling. The art of cooking fish well, that is thoroughly, but not to the extent that the fish is falling apart, is thus dependent upon a delicacy of timing which must become second nature to the cook, as demonstrated by the Dutch and Neapolitan fishermen who appear on the Tuscan coast in the winter time.

The cook may have two different aims when boiling fish: the first will be that of cooking the fish itself and the second will be that of obtaining a good fish stock. In the first case, the stock not being important, the main aim will be to preserve the glutin within the flesh of the fish. This can be achieved by not placing the fish in the water until the liquid is at a full rolling boil. The fierce heat will then quickly seal the outer surface of the whole fish, or piece of fish, thus preventing the leaching out which would occur if the fish were placed in cold or lukewarm water and then heated. I have already warned that, for the same reason, fish should not be left lying in cold water after they have been cleaned and gutted. There are, however, a small number of sea fish which are appreciably improved by a light salting before cooking and which do therefore require another dip in the water before boiling. This applies to cod, which the Dutch always cut into slices and salt for a few hours at least.

Sea fish are best cooked in sea water, if this can be obtained.

In some parts of Germany all fish are boiled with onions, vinegar and pepper. Although this is not in itself a bad method, it does tend to mask the differences of flavour between individual fish. However, no fresh water fish will suffer from a few whole peppercorns and a liberal dose of salt. I use vinegar when boiling trout and salmon only when I wish to keep them for several days set in their own jelly. In some places people like to boil trout in good wine. This is not a bad idea but does deprive a fresh water trout of much of the subtle finesse of its flavour. I would always prefer to serve trout simply in their own broth, accompanied only by good bread and fresh butter.

Fresh water crayfish can be placed in cold water for cooking because they are protected by their shells. I am not, however, convinced by the notion that they taste better when cooked in this way. Some people boil crayfish with pepper, salt and caraway. These seasonings seem appropriate to me but other people may like to cook crayfish in accordance with the specific wishes of their masters.

The larger sea crustaceans, such as the lobster, spiny lobster and common crab should have their mouth parts and anus stopped with pieces of cork in order to prevent the water penetrating and spoiling the flesh. Bartolommeo Scappi, whom I have mentioned several times, recommends this. Small sand crabs can just be boiled in sea water and then sprinkled with plently of salt when they are done.

XI   Meat Stock in General

If the cook's principal aim is to make a good stock, whether it be destined for use in a tasty, well flavoured soup or for the preparation of vegetables, sauces and the like, he must take great care in the preparation of his stock pot. The meat should be lightly salted and placed in the pot, which should then be filled to the brim with cold water. It should be skimmed carefully throughout the slow simmering process. After about two hours the full quantity of salt should be added and this will force any remaining impurities and inert matter to rise to the top. All kinds of aromatic roots and herbs can then be added gradually – celery, carrots, parsley, leeks and so on, according to preference. Onions should not, however, be added because they impart a stale flavour when boiled. The stock will have been reduced by evaporation and, if possible, the cooking pot should now again be filled so that the liquid is almost at the highest level possible. The pot should then be allowed to simmer gently for another hour or so. If the herbs and roots are added too early, their aromatic flavour is often destroyed by the prolonged cooking. It is principally for their flavour that they are being added, after all. The cook must, however, beware of two dangers when boiling and stewing: the danger of burning and of the effect of the smoke.

{Deep, pottery containers are better for stock production than shallow, metal containers. As the level of liquid is reduced in a shallow container, the meat will quickly be exposed so that its upper surface will dry out and its sides may well start to burn, or go crusty. In a deep container, however, the meat is able to sink as the liquid level drops and will therefore remain covered by it. The tall, cylindrical steamers, in which soup, vegetables and meat can be prepared together, are ideal for this purpose. A bed of cabbage, carrots and turnips is placed on the grid and then a piece of beef or mutton is placed on this. A little salt is added. There should be enough water in the lower vessel for steam production and also for soup. The steamer is placed on the fire and should remain there for a few hours. The cook should keep an eye on it, adding pot herbs when appropriate and removing them later, and also adding rice, barley, cracked wheat or pasta. When these are sufficiently cooked, the pot should be removed from the fire and opened. The soup is served first, followed by the meat with its vegetables, which will have absorbed all the fat during the cooking period. It will thus not be necessary to remove the fat from the stock, as with normal boiling. I would most warmly recommend the frequent use of this device, as described above, to all households where economy is important and the money supply restricted. It is usually made of German cast iron but can also be made of tinplate.}

The depth of flavour of any meat stock is enhanced by mixing the types of meat used. It is a good idea to chop up or pound any butchers' scraps and any little bits of raw meat or bones left over in the kitchen and to add these at the outset with the main piece of meat. After this has been removed, together with the best of the stock, the deposit formed by these added scraps can be cooked right away if more water is added. The initial stock, intended for soup, should never be extended by the addition of more water. This happens all too often in German households and the resulting brew is of no value, being flat and tasteless. The addition of water which I recommend, however, can be left to cook down gradually and the result will do for the servants' table or can be left until the next day, for use with vegetables and in sauces. I do in fact advise that some stock is always held over from the preceding day. The fresh stock can then be put to much better use. The German habit of refilling the stock pot, a habit which is even more prevalent in Italy, usually results from the fact that the good meat stock has already been used up elsewhere. This habit would be rendered quite superfluous by the use of a secondary, reserve stock, as I recommend.

Some people like to remove the soup stock alone from the pot and then add fresh water to the piece of meat. I consider this a bad practice which is detrimental to the flavour of the meat, as can easily be demonstrated by experiment. It is customary in the kitchens of the rich and of busy inns to make supplies of strong white and brown stocks in advance. These are then used to extend sauces and all kinds of tasty dishes. Much time is certainly saved in this way and it explains why these coulis (one of the names given to these brews) are ideal for use in inns. They lead to too much uniformity of flavour, however, and may even spoil dishes, especially in summer, if they have been left to go stale.

The French like to cook a small piece of calf's liver or ox liver with the meat. This enriches the soup with much glutin, or gelatine, which becomes evident as the stock cools down, as it congeals rapidly. The liver does, of course, also impart a slightly bitter flavour to the stock and people may not relish this if they are not accustomed to it. The French, however, are most particular about not topping up their stock with water. They also add quantities of aromatic and savoury herbs and roots to the soup pot and leave it on the fire for the minimum time necessary. All this has the effect of masking any bitterness in the liver flavour, making it quite attractive.

When I was younger I travelled through Italy with my master and we spent some time in Rome. In our lodgings there I was allowed to use only one outer corner of the stove and there was room for only one tall, narrow soup pot. On the instructions of my lord and master, whose delicate disposition was unable to tolerate the heavy Roman style of cooking, I used to place in this pot each day: a small piece of bacon, two pounds of beef, one pound of veal, a young chicken and a young pigeon. The pigeons in Rome are particularly tender and full of flavour. When the meat had been skimmed and cooked sufficiently, I added whatever roots, herbs and fine vegetables were available in the market and let these cook. I then set the vegetable soup in the middle of the table, surrounded by the four types of meat, accompanied by anchovies, fresh butter, radishes, cucumber salad and similar dishes. As the vegetable mixture varied, and my master used to eat different meats on different days, this simplified, perhaps even refined form of 'Ollapotrida' never became tedious to him and for six weeks he did not feel the remotest desire for different food, or for food prepared in a different way. The quantities served would have been enough for several people.

Fortified stocks, or brown soups, are made by browning pieces of meat and bacon in a pan, then pouring over a well flavoured meat stock. The fat is removed and the browned meat is cooked thoroughly in the liquid. This type of stock has a stronger flavour than the usual type, which does tend to be more nutritious and has a more delicate flavour. People often add things, such as sugar caramelised in butter, to brown stocks. This gives an unpleasantly sweet flavour. I am fundamentally opposed to all such contrivances and pretences, at least in cookery.

{The broth which the French call 'bouillon de prime' is much stronger, being used to build up convalescents, particularly new and nursing mothers. The English 'fleshtea' is a basic example of this type. – Chop beef, veal and also a chicken into small pieces; take as much water as is required for the stock and let the meat soak in this for one to two hours. During this time the cold water will release the osmazome, the most nutritious and valuable constituent of the meat. The entire pot-full is then placed over a lively fire, herbs and roots are added according to taste, the pot is skimmed and the correct amount of salt added. After half an hour's simmering, the stock is ready. It is then poured off the pieces of meat. The stock is pale and thin but has a good flavour and great strength.}

Beef is the meat best suited to pot boiling in all cases. I would always advise the addition of a little beef to any other meats destined for soup. Meats such as mutton, lamb and kid, pork, goose, duck and the like, which are fatty and inclined to be rancid, are not at all suitable for the production of a good stock and should be used only in desperation.

Mutton stock can be good if rice and thinly sliced turnips are cooked in it, Italian style. The mild flavour of the rice and the piquance of the turnips help to break down the rather rancid flavour of the mutton stock. This should be compared with the steaming methods mentioned above.

A good fish stock is made by putting fish to cook with a small quantity of water, which should be cold or lukewarm. Strongly flavoured roots are added immediately and the brew allowed to simmer very slowly; fine herbs can be added, according to taste, but not until just before the stock is ready.

XII   Soups[34]

Broths are used as first courses in much of Europe. They are thickened as appropriate with bread, cereals, dough products, vegetables, minced or chopped meat and by all kinds of other additives so that they do not cause the stomach to become distended with liquid right at the start of the meal. There is, however, no artificial additive that can remedy the mistakes of a bad meat stock. A meat stock which has not been correctly simmered, which has not been carefully skimmed and salted, or into which the smoke has penetrated, or in which the fine flavour of the herbs and roots has been lost through over-cooking will always have an insipid, bad taste, no matter what is added to it.

Bread soup is probably the simplest, if not the oldest of soups. It would appear to have originated in Renaissance Italy, as the word soup is derived from the Italian *zuppo, zuppa*, which refers to spongy substances which have absorbed some sort of moisture. In contemporary Italian only bread soup is known as zuppa; all other soups are known as minestre, which implies mash or puree to us. All this justifies my intention of regarding bread soup as the original soup, placing it before all the others. A good household soup can be made by pouring boiling, well flavoured meat stock over slices of toasted bread. This is quite suitable even for breakfast and for feeding the sick.

An Italian household soup is made from sliced bread, not sourdough, made from medium quality wheat flour, and cooked in stock until it is completely dissolved. This makes a nourishing, easily digestible supper. As everyone knows, this type of mash is also suitable for infants being weaned. If the soup is for adults, some fine herbs, or any other appropriate vegetables, can be added as desired. If they do not have any stock, the Italians make this soup with plain water, cooking the chopped herbs in a little oil before adding them to the soup pot. I found this dish quite acceptable.

The soured rye breads of the Northerners do not combine as well with meat stocks. They require the addition of something sweet or else decidedly sour. Onions can be used in the first instance. They should either be sliced and baked in very fresh butter, or they can be baked whole in hot ashes. They should never be allowed to burn. If whole onions have been baked in their skins in hot ashes, they should then be peeled with great care before being sliced as finely as possible and again boiled up in strong meat stock. Meanwhile, as much dry rye bread as is needed should be sliced very finely and placed in the pre-heated soup tureen. The onions, cooked as described in good stock, should be poured boiling over the bread. If there are some very fresh eggs available, as many eggs as there are guests should be poached and placed carefully in the soup tureen. The sweetness of a fresh egg yolk does greatly help to reduce the bitterness of the rye bread. The second instance can be amply demonstrated by the example of the toasted flour soup, or burnt soup, which is made particularly skillfully in Switzerland and Alsace. This soup is so well known, however, that it is not necessary to describe it here.

After bread soup, and closely related to it, come the soups made simply from pulses or from processed, starchy grains such as rice, barley, cracked spelt, groats, oats, buckwheat, Turkish wheat and so on. None of these items should be overcooked unless the intention is to sieve them and completely separate the filaments or fibres of the grains from the starch. Sieved soups made from cereals can be thickened with eggyolk. Lemon juice improves them and croutons toasted in butter will give them more flavour. The best soup is made from porridge oats, cooked in meat stock and sieved.

Plain flour dissolves too much in boiling stock to make a decent soup. Some of the coarser starchy products, derived from various roots, are suitable, however. Travellers report that manioc, or mandiocca flour, which the English often import from the West Indies, is a good soup ingredient. In place of this, I used coarse potato starch, which I obtained in the usual way by grating the raw potatoes and then repeatedly soaking the grated shreds. To this I added more aromatic root vegetables, also grated, but not, of course, soaked thereafter. I placed this grated mixture over a gentle fire and added as much good meat stock as seemed necessary to thin the mixture. A few fine herbs, especially sorrel, go well in this soup. A little bread, toasted in butter, is also appropriate and this, when dried, can be handed round the table separately, or can be dunked in the soup when it is served. The flavour of the soup is much improved by the addition of finely chopped chicken or pigeon liver, if available.

{Not wishing to concentrate on flours, I am now going to give instructions for one gruel which has always found favour with my guests. Take one or more spoonfuls of fine wheat flour. The quantity is governed by the quantity of soup required but should never be more or less than is needed to bind the soup without making it heavy. Add a small piece of fresh butter, neither too much nor too little; stir together in a pottery vessel over the heat until it becomes really white. When it is white and cooked, gradually add meat stock, stirring all the time so that the mixture amalgamates. When the mixture appears to have reached the correct temperature, being neither too liquid nor too thick, take one or more egg yolks and tip these into the soup tureen with a little lukewarm meat stock. Then return to the stove and, just before you remove the cooking pot full of soup from the heat, add a handfull of coarsely chopped tarragon. Pour the soup into the tureen, stirring well, so that everything is properly mixed together. You should already have cut some dry wheaten bread into thin, mussel-shaped slices and toasted these in a walnut-sized knob of butter, keeping them warm and dry afterwards. These are then thrown into the hot soup, but only just before it is served, so that they do not disappear completely.}

There are good recipes in the better German cookery books for the various methods of combining flour, eggs and butter to make a dough which, when boiled in meat stock, will make a healthy and delicious soup. These soups really are a national dish in South Germany and recipes are passed from house to house, so that I think it would be superfluous to talk of them here. German people favour a soft dough for their soup, made with a high proportion of eggs and butter. In contrast, the Italians like a firmer dough, made from flour and water. This is rolled and worked a great deal to toughen it and is usually prepared in factories, air dried and thus kept for a long time. The finished dough is named according to its shape: macaroni, vermicelli and so on. The nature of the grain used and the milling of the flour affect the quality of the dough. However, it is always very soft and mildly flavoured and it is wise to combine it only with a strong, highly flavoured stock, a concentrated brown stock for example, made according to the instructions above. The Italian method of boiling macaroni should be used: the water or meat stock should be boiling vigorously before the pasta is added. These dough products disintegrate if added to lukewarm water, becoming glutinous and porridge-like.

There are two principal points to remember regarding any vegetables which might be used to make a meat soup more tasty or more nutritious. The first is that pulses such as mature peas of any kind should be cooked very thoroughly so that they can be rubbed through a sieve in order to rid them of their pods or skins, which are indigestible and without flavour. The second point is that young peas, tender asparagus tips and all the varieties of aromatic roots and herbs should not be cooked for too long so that their flavour and aroma does not evaporate away.

Soups can be given a pleasing degree of substance by using the meat of warm or cold blooded animals. Everyone knows the varieties of sieved soups (purées) made from game or the meat of domestic animals, and I shall not speak of them here. I should just like to point out that in households where money is short, any meat leftovers which are still fresh and have been kept in a hygienic manner can very well be used for soup. The meat should be separated and finely chopped while the bones and sinews should be pounded, cooked thoroughly in meat stock and then sieved. The chopped meat is then brought up to the boil again in the sieved stock. If circumstances permit, a soup like this can be thickened with an egg yolk mixed with a little stock, or its flavour can be improved by some herbs. It is better, however, to cook any fresh root vegetables from the start with the pounded bones. They can then be passed through a hair sieve or metal colander with the pulped bones. The additives mentioned should of course always be suited to the meat which forms the basis of the sieved soup.

Meats such as calf's head, which contain a high proportion of glutin, should be lightly boiled and then cooled before being chopped into very small pieces or slices; they can then be cooked, initially in a little concentrated brown stock, the level of which can very gradually be increased. This is the only way of ensuring that the mucous tissue is slowly broken down and distributed throughout the added meat stock. Madeira wine or some sort of acidic, powerful seasoning, or even a little toasted flour can be added to soups of this kind. They are indeed very nutritious but are not very palatable without some added flavouring. Hard boiled eggs, or preferably the ovaries of newly slaughtered laying hens, or little aromatic dumplings can also be added if desired, and our dish will end up with a close resemblance to turtle soup.

In Germany, turtle soup is found only in the sea ports. It is made well but tends to be over seasoned. Crayfish soups are common throughout Germany. The crayfish butter which is used to give this soup its flavour and colour is also used for various sweetish sauces. The excellent habit of stuffing the empty carapace of the larger crayfish is less widespread. The stuffing is made of crayfish meat, anchovies and a little good quality fish or veal scraps, chopped together and bound with an egg yolk and some slices of softened bread. Seasoning, fine herbs and onions can be added according to taste and inclination. Having been stuffed in this way, the crayfish shells are then painted with egg yolk, sprinkled with breadcrumbs and baked in hot fat. They are not added to the soup until it is served to prevent them disintegrating too much. It is, however, essential that they are kept hot in the interim.

The flavour and nutritional value of crayfish soups made without meat stock as fasting dishes can be greatly increased by the addition of sieved yellow peas. If the crayfish soup is being made with meat stock, it is a good idea not to cook the crushed shells and the crayfish innards in butter, but to boil them down in the meat stock and then sieve them.

It is interesting from an historical point of view that almonds and raisins are added to this soup in some parts of Germany. This is because these same regions also show a marked inclination to sweetness in moral matters. We thus have extensive confirmation of the fact that man is no more than what he eats. A healthy palate would, however, recoil from such bad practice.

Good soups for fasting days can also be created from stocks made from most fresh water fish. As I have already pointed out, the cook should take care to commence the cooking of the fish with a small quantity of water and aromatic roots. The cooking should be slow and, at the correct time, some fine herbs should be added to the stock. When poured over some sliced wheaten bread, this gives a hearty and healthy soup which is often enjoyed in Italy. Pike, which has a high glutin content and a clean flavour, is eminently suitable for these fish soups. It is possible to make sieved soups from fish, as from meat. These can be served with a dish of baked, chopped fish, mixed with softened bread, an egg yolk and seasonings to taste.

If meat stock is to be combined with fish soups, it is best to use a stock made from lean veal, preferably from calves' feet, and with the addition of a few slices of lean bacon to be cooked in it.

In the spring time it is worthwhile making plenty of soups from chopped herbs, varying the mixtures to obtain more bitter, or more strongly flavoured results. At this time of year fine herbs have the best flavour and have valuable emollient and blood cleansing properties. In winter, however, endives are very acceptable. These should be chopped to the desired length and then simmered, not for too long, in a concentrated meat stock which can be thickened with one or more fresh egg yolks. Some slices of toasted bread should be placed in the soup tureen and a little stock poured over them. When they are sufficiently softened, the endive soup is poured over them to serve. The egg yolk softens the bitterness of the endive. This bitterness is of intrinsic importance and the endive should not on any account be overcooked because it would then lose this very savoury bitterness.

Hearty soups can be made from all kinds of root vegetables, such as turnips, celeriac and sugar-beet, thoroughly cooked in good meat stock, then sieved, diluted with meat stock and brought back to the boil. Little pieces of bread, toasted in butter, go well with such soups. I shall not continue with this subject however, because there is no end to the potential ingredients from the plant world. The skilled cook and the good housewife will be able to plan their cooking in accordance with circumstances, the seasons and the supply of local produce.

XIII The Use of Meat Broth for Sauce-Making: Sauces

Gravy[35] or sauce[36] is the name given to any liquid garnish to a solid, insoluble foodstuff. These garnishes have more than one purpose. Initially they provide a liquid accompaniment to the solid, making the food more slippery, so that it slips down the throat more easily. They also serve the purpose of refining the flavour of a solid food, or of enhancing its flavour by providing a contrast. Finally they should simultaneously promote the wholesomeness and digestibility of a given food.

It is important with all sauces that they should be used with foodstuffs, the flavours of which they will compliment. A prime example of this is the preparation of a sauce from the stock derived from whatever meat, fish or vegetable the sauce is to accompany; if the food to be sauced has no stock of its own, the sauce should be made of ingredients which are as similar as possible to the food. For example, if a dry or moist farinaceous dish is to be accompanied by a sauce, it is generally wise to make this of milk, eggs, butter and flour. The acidity of fruit does also suit most farinaceous dishes. This is partly because of the contrast which it provides, which stimulates the taste buds, but also because the mild acidity is just what is needed to soften dishes of this kind and make them more digestible.

This point only concerns us here because a sauce should never be diluted with the stock destined for the soup bowl. On each occasion, the cook should consider whether the final flavour of the sauce is to be mild or strong. For mild, white sauces, for example, a little stock should be drawn from the pot before it has acquired too strong a flavour of herbs. In contrast, any stock, even the second, or economy brew recommended above, can be used for infusions, or for diluting strongly flavoured sauces. This is true no matter how much the stock may taste of overcooked root vegetables and dissolved bone marrow. Quantities of brown and white stocks (coulis) are made in advance for this very purpose in the big households, and even in busy inns. This is not possible in the poorer households, however.

Before every sauce is prepared, it is necessary to consider very carefully which flavours can be combined with the foodstuff which is to be made more pleasing and wholesome by the addition of the sauce. Once this most essential point has been cleared up, it is time to prepare the sauce, working it carefully so that it is complete in itself. This process requires a binding agent which the ancients used to prepare in advance from fine flour. They named this amylum.[37] Nowadays we prepare fine wheat or spelt flour in two different ways. For white sauces the flour is worked into good butter over a gentle heat and is stirred until the mixture becomes quite white. This is not only for the sake of appearance but, more importantly, because it develops the inherent sweetness of the flour more completely, fostering the gentle, sweet qualities which generally characterise white sauces. This delightful balance of flavour in white sauces should never be destroyed by the use of bitter seasonings, such as nutmeg, lemon peel and the like. On the contrary, only the milder seasonings are appropriate, seasonings such as truffles, the more delicate fungi, lemon juice, fresh or salt water crayfish, oysters and other similar items. One or more egg yolks, either mixed in advance with a little stock, or worked into the butter at the same time as the flour, are often added to a white sauce. However, it is always vital to check whether any alteration to the sauce will suit the solid foodstuff it is to accompany. Among the vegetables and herbs, asparagus, all types of aromatic roots, not only carrots and beets, and also sorrel and purslane go well with white sauces. Chervil, parsley, tarragon or wormwood, basil and similar herbs go better with brown sauces.

Brown sauces are bound with flour which has been browned in butter. A concentrated, viscous brown stock is even better than browned flour, if it is available. The cook should be very careful when browning flour because, if this process is rushed, small particles will become burnt and will then impart a bitter, harsh flavour instead of the requisite full, roasted flavour. It is not true that if flour is burnt, its nutritional value is destroyed – it is customary with some of our brewers to singe malt. Moreover a well browned flour has a very beneficial effect on the stomach. This is demonstrated by the burnt soup which makes a valuable breakfast food for anyone whose digestion is weak.

Brown sauces can readily be combined with all the more bitter seasonings, acid flavours and pungent roots, fungi and herbs. They will come to no harm.

When the flour, be it browned or still pale, has been cooked in the butter, it is then thinned with meat stock, which is stirred in. The mixture should be stirred carefully and slowly in *one* direction so that the liquid will gradually penetrate all of the flour particles, dissolving them and combining with them. If, on the other hand, the liquid were added all together, the result would be much more a separation of the solid and liquid. This would be most unsatisfactory to the palate and the eye.

This is not the place to talk of every sauce imaginable. I shall mention individual examples in due course. These very arbitrary comments of mine should indeed give free rein to the judgement and imagination of my readers.

XIV Jelly, particularly with Regard to Reductions of Meat Stock

Jelly is an intimate blend of glutin with any appropriate liquid. Any jelly will liquefy if temperatures rise and, if the glutin content is low, it is often necessary to use ice to help it set. It is for this reason that the French name it *gelée* and the Italians *gelatina*, something chilled. Our German word, *Gallert*, appears to be derived from these names.

Jelly is often served with all kinds of cold meat and fish dishes and in this respect bears the same relation to cold dishes as sauces do to hot dishes. Jelly does also serve as a refreshment which is both highly nutritious and easily digestible, able to prolong extensive meals in a pleasant manner. It belongs in this guise to that class of dishes which tickle the palate (*plats de goût*) and which we shall discuss finally. In fact, a carefully prepared jelly even makes a suitable restorative for those who are ill and feeble.

When a jelly is to accompany cold meat and fish dishes, it is essential that it should have a strong, acidic flavour. A sweetish jelly would be most unpleasant and insipid served with cold meats, pies or fish. In order to achieve a stongly flavoured jelly, it is customary to gently roast and brown calves' feet or, Italian style, the feet of kids and hens, with slices of bacon and aromatic vegetables. The French, however, like to extract the gelatine from the feet or other gelatinous parts of the animal by boiling in clear water. Before flavouring it in any way, they like to test the consistency of their jelly by chilling it. I consider that this procedure is necessary only with sweet and semi-sweet jellies because the sweet, gentle seasonings contribute nothing to the setting of the jelly and would also quite unnecessarily surrender their goodness and volume if subjected to prolonged cooking and clarification. In the case of concentrated meat jellies, however, the best and most enduring flavour is achieved by roasting and cooking the meat and root vegetables at the same time as the animal feet. It is for this very reason that I would advocate the German method, although I should like to stress that any acid flavourings such as lemon juice, wine and vinegar, and any spices and fine herbs should not be added to such a jelly until it has been clarified and tested for the first time. These volatile seasonings would undoubtedly be totally wasted if they were added at the start of the cooking time.

Fish jellies should be prepared from the stock of the fish itself. Setting can be achieved by the use of hartshorn or isinglass, or with the fins and tails of related fish. Fish jellies need to be seasoned with plenty of wine and lemon juice, spices and fine herbs, to make them attractive.

Decent instructions for preparing jellies can be found in even the most ordinary cookery books and this is why I have not gone into detail here. I should just like to remind my readers that they should not believe that all of the concoctions and additives mentioned in such books are absolutely necessary for the preparation of a good jelly. The important points are as follows:

The liquid should have absorbed the gelatine to such a degree that it is capable of setting in moderately cold conditions; the gelatine content should not be too high because a jelly which is too viscous will become opaque and displeasing to the eye. It will undoubtedly also have an unpleasantly gelatinous flavour. Finally, the aromatics and acidic flavourings should be chosen with care. They should blend together well and should complement the dish with which they are to be served.

As usual, any fine herbs and other volatile flavourings should be added only a short time before cooking is completed.

XV   Steaming, Stewing and Slow Simmering of Meat

This method of food preparation is one of the most important benefits which mankind has derived from the invention of the cooking pot. It is suitable for all kinds of meat but is particularly good for coarse-grained meats which can be cut into large chunks.

When stewing or simmering slowly, the aim is not simply to cook the meat itself; the simultaneous creation of a well flavoured stock is also a matter of great concern. This stock, which has collected under the stewed meat, will serve as a sauce for it. Indeed, this simple stock, with no additives, often makes the best sauce, and even when the cook does consider it necessary or desirable to add other ingredients, the stock should always serve as the basis of the sauce so that its flavour will then be in harmony with that of the meat. It would therefore be extremely foolish to prepare a particular, and separate, sauce for a piece of stewed meat.

To stew a piece of meat quite simply, place a few slices of bacon in the bottom of the saucepan or casserole and top these with some root vegetables and, if desired, some onions or shallots also. The piece of meat is then placed on the vegetables and the container, unless it is a very deep one, is filled to the brim with fresh water or with cold, leftover stock. It should then be left over a moderate fire for two to four and a half hours, when the stock should have been reduced to approximately one third of its former volume. The cook should move the meat around during cooking and should try to prevent it burning by ensuring that the fire is not concentrated directly beneath the pot but spreads its heat around the sides also. When the stock is sufficiently reduced, it should be sieved. It can then be flavoured with fine herbs such as tarragon or basil; these herbs cook so quickly that there is no danger of the meat cooling down in its serving dish while they are being prepared. If, however, truffles, morels or any other fungi are to be added to the stock, it goes without saying that they should first be partially cooked in wine, meat stock or butter. The sieved stock can then be poured over them and the mixture reheated swiftly. If olives, capers or any similar items preserved in salt or vinegar are being used, these can simply be warmed quickly in the aforementioned fresh stock.

If the stock is to have a more assertive flavour, the slices of bacon should be allowed to fry for a few minutes before the vegetables and meat are added to the pot. The resultant sauce will then be brownish in colour and will have more character of its own. It will be much more suitable for the coarser types of meat, such as beef and mutton. Before cooking these particular meats, it is a good idea to allow them to soak for a few days, depending on the weather, in spiced vinegar. They can also be wrapped in a cloth which has been steeped in spiced vinegar. It is a good idea, although not absolutely necessary, to thicken the sauce for a brown, savoury stew of this type with a little toasted flour. I do not advise the use of the so-called coulis for stews. They are a particular feature of high class kitchens, being added willy-nilly to sauces. I consider them superfluous, because any intelligently prepared stew will create its own characteristic, concentrated stock; they also have a detrimental effect on the flavour, resulting in a tedious uniformity, and never integrate sufficiently with the various types of meat to hide the fact that a clumsy concoction has been created.

A leg of mutton can be steeped in vinegar as above. The rancid fat should first be removed from it (thrifty housewives can boil this up with any other leftover fatty pieces, store it and use it as soap) and, circumstances permitting, the meat can be soaked for longer than usual. It is then beaten, larded and prepared for cooking as swiftly as possible. It should be stewed as above. This dish, which can also be served cold, is known as a leg of mock venison. Plain beef, particularly the fillet or tenderloin, can be treated in the same way. Dry potatoes, or South German dough dumplings (known as Knetl) make an appropriate accompaniment to dishes of this type if they are being served as the main meal in ordinary households. Meat cooked in this way will keep for a prolonged period, especially if it has been steeped for a short time beforehand. It therefore makes an ideal storecupboard food in country households where guests are rare.

Any type of game can be stewed in this way in a strong, brown stock and, among the domesticated birds, goose and duck are also suitable. Even veal can be gently stewed with a few slices of bacon and aromatic roots, although no acidic flavourings or spices should be added. A good piece of quality veal can be prepared according to the method described. It should be thoroughly beaten to tenderise it and should then be trimmed and larded carefully. It is known as a Fricando in this guise. This pale, sweetish meat does, however, also belong to the group of meats, including the more tender birds, the chickens, turkeys and young pigeons, which are excellent served with a mild, white sauce. I recommend that meats such as these should be put on the fire in a good quantity of leftover stock, with some root vegetables and herbs. They should be covered tightly and then left to simmer slowly, but not for too long. A white roux is then used to convert the stock into a good sauce and any suitably mild seasonings as are available or liked, can be added. Examples of these are crayfish butter and shelled crayfish, cultivated fungi, cauliflower, asparagus, black salsify or finely chopped mixed herbs.

Young poultry and lamb, if cut into small pieces, cook very quickly. I would put these into a pot with any of the above-mentioned delicately flavoured vegetables, or with baby peas, young carrots or similar items. I would then cover them with leftover stock and leave them to cook through slowly. A fricassee of this nature requires no special sauce, nor should any flour be added. It is always most delicious served in its own, natural stock.

Tender pieces of loin of veal, the sinews removed, can be cut into small, uniform pieces, beaten, trimmed, larded and then cooked very slowly in a little leftover stock. The sauce is thickened with a little, very lightly toasted flour and is seasoned either with finely chopped sorrel, or tarragon, with a touch of basil and a more generous amount of chervil and parsley.

Salmis [ragouts, esp. of game] also fall into the category of stews. They can be made with any wild game birds, especially woodcock, fieldfare and partridge.

The most delicious way of preparing a salmi is as follows: cut the breast meat with the underlying bones away from the carcase of the uncooked bird. Lard the meat and place it, meat uppermost, in a metal dish lined with thin slices of bacon. When you are ready, place the dish in a baking pan and heat it more from above than from below so that it is cooked without drying out.

The remaining carcase of the bird (the internal organs of woodcock and fieldfare can be left in place, but the stomach and intestines of partridge, wild duck and others should be removed) can then be pounded with some salted anchovies. A few shallots may also be added. Meanwhile, the cook's assistant will have lightly browned a few slices of streaky bacon, over which the pounded mixture can then be spread. A little leftover stock is added to dilute it and the mixture is cooked gently for one to two hours. When it appears to be cooked sufficiently, it should be passed through a clean hair sieve with one or two spoonfuls of tarragon or shallot vinegar. If it will not go through the sieve, it can be further diluted with a little concentrated stock. The sieved mixture is then returned to the fire in a fresh pot and is allowed to cook until it is again of a porridge-like consistency, or is at least thickened. The juice of a lemon can then be added, the mixture stirred and spread in a dish. The pieces of larded breast meat, cooked in the pan, are placed around the edge of the dish. Slices of toast can be arranged around the edge of the dish and, in this case, the pieces of meat should be placed in the middle.

When larger birds, such as wild duck or pheasants, have been used to make a salmi, the roasted breast meat should be chopped into pieces of a good, even size before serving. A salmi is always served as a side dish and it will not then be necessary to carve it at the table.

Some people roast the bird before chopping it up. This reduces the strength of flavour of the essential salmi purée. The method may be put to good effect when using up the leftovers from previous dinners but is otherwise quite reprehensible. I should also like to stress that no seasonings should be added when a salmi is being made from woodcock as this bird's fine flavour would be impaired, if not completely obliterated. Before the salmi is prepared, this bird should be partially roasted on a spit.

A few juniper berries may be crushed in a salmi made from field-fare. For wild ducks, tarragon and basil may be added towards the end of cooking, and for pheasant, finely chopped truffles may be added to the salmi purée.

The method of preparing a julienne, a common dish which stems from the old French style of cookery, puts it into the category of steamed dishes. I have found it more tasty when placed in a pudding mould made of metal or silver and cooked either in boiling water or in a baking pan. I lined the mould with slices of bacon and then added fine slices of assorted root vegetables, interspersed with fine herbs and a few florets of cauliflower or broccoli. A piece of veal, its sinews removed, beaten and larded with bacon, was placed in the middle. I added salt with the layers of ingredients. The pudding mould should have a hook so that it can be suspended in the boiling water. It should not touch the base of the water container because this would burn the food. If the mould has no hook, it is better to place it in a baking pan and cook the food slowly over a low fire.

When this creation is removed from the mould after being cooked, care should be taken to maintain the initial arrangement of the slices of vegetable. The slices of bacon should be peeled off gently and any little areas of damage repaired.

If, as often happens, the individual ingredients of this dish are cooked separately in advance, it is much easier to achieve an elegant appearance in the end. The flavour and nutritional value are, however, much reduced by this method.

For the sake of variety I have also prepared juliennes with pieces of the meatier fish, such as sturgeon, salmon, beluga sturgeon, Danube salmon or tuna. I removed the bones and fins and larded the fish with boned anchovies instead of the bacon and, in place of any other seasoning, I used a mixture of peppers and a tiny pinch of ginger.

Fish, particularly the smaller, freshwater varieties, can be simmered slowly in a little stock with plenty of savoury root vegetables of all kinds and a few herbs and whole peppercorns. A few slices of toast, spread with fresh butter, are then arranged in a warmed dish and the fish and root vegetables are set carefully on top. The small quantity of stock in which they were cooked is then trickled over. This dish is more akin to the excellent *watersootje* of the Dutch than the *matelotte* of the French.

The following is one of the very best steamed dishes that can be made with fish: Take any succulent and delicate fish, such as trout or cod, cut it into moderately large pieces and layer it in a silver casserole with knobs of fresh butter, breadcrumbs, lemon juice, fine herbs, salt and a little spice. The casserole is then placed in a Dutch oven or baking pan over the heat and is left until it is obvious that the fish is cooked through.

If a fish is to be served whole under jelly, it should simply be boiled. If, however, you wish to remove the fins and bones, as is normal with the more meaty fish, so as to create some sort of fish shape, round or otherwise, it is better to steam the fish.

Eel, salmon, Danube salmon, sheathfish and other meaty fish should each be cut across into even-sized pieces. The spine and subsidiary bones and fins should be removed carefully so that several pieces can then be formed into one larger lump. A mixture of anchovies, shallots and fine herbs can be chopped together with plenty of seasoning and can be spread sparingly between the individual pieces. A casserole or saucepan is then lined with thin slices of fresh bacon and the boned fish placed on this. Water is poured over, but not enough to make the fish swim. Place a lid on the cooking pot and leave it to stew over a very gentle fire for one and a half to two hours. Then add a few spoonfuls of strong vinegar and a little lemon juice, with salt if necessary, and leave it to stand for a few minutes longer. The lump of fish should then be lifted out carefully and can be reshaped within a metal collar until it is cold enough to hold itself together. If it is round, it can be garnished with a lavish garland of young tarragon twigs and the fish jelly then trickled over it. The fresh tarragon will not only add a pleasant flavour to the dish but will also, as long as the jelly is properly transparent, make it look pretty.

{Should you happen to have a pottery pudding mould, the boned fish with its chopped seasoning mixture can be arranged in it in whatever order you like. The mould should then be placed in the oven or baking pan in an inverted position and allowed to cook at a moderate temperature until it is done. During the cooking time it should be kept moist with a little white wine and the juice of half a lemon. The fish should be allowed to cool down in the mould and should not be turned out before serving time. When it is turned out, the natural jelly will retain the shape of the pudding mould, or jelly mould. If the mixture will not come out of the mould, dip it momentarily into a container of warm water.}

XVI Deep Frying in Boiling Fat

A successful deep fried dish, no matter what type it is, has two requirements: a good quality fat with a clean flavour should be used, and it should be heated to a very high degree. In Italy, deep fried food, *fritto*, is a national dish, and every farmer's wife knows how to prepare it properly. In the North, however, there are hardly any cooks who are sufficiently expert to make a good *fritto*.

Unsalted, clarified butter, pork fat and good olive oil can be used for deep frying. Olive oil will seal the outer surface of any fried food particularly well and is also much better for frying fish than butter or pork fat.

As I have already pointed out, the foodstuff should not be lowered into the boiling fat until the fat has been heated over a glowing fire to the highest degree possible. When the fried food begins to rise to the surface of the fat, or when it begins to crackle, it is then time to hurry and remove it with a skimming spoon before it becomes too brown; it will be sufficiently cooked and sealed on the outside when it is golden brown in colour, and will also look best at this point.

When the food has been removed from the fat, it should be placed in a heated metal colander to allow the excess fat to drip away. It can also be placed on clean blotting paper in a warm dish. As each piece comes out of the fat, it should be seasoned with fine salt but this should obviously be added in moderation.

Items such as calf's heads should be parboiled in advance, or at least cut into fine slices, as they do not cook through as quickly. Fish do not present a problem; use only tiny fish, or cut the fish up into suitably small pieces, and they will soon be done to a turn.

A coating of egg yolk, fine flour and breadcrumbs is ideal for some foodstuffs, such as cauliflower, artichokes and calf's head. Other foodstuffs, such as calves' or lambs' liver, the skins of watermelons or overgrown pumpkins and the larger fungi are better cut into long, narrow slices with no coating.

Some chopped mixtures can be worked into a spherical shape, dipped into egg yolk and coated in breadcrumbs before frying. This applies to ox muzzle, which should be cut into very fine strips and bound together with a little egg yolk or lemon juice. Rice is also suitable, after it has been soaked to make it swell, then pounded in a mortar and sieved, and bound with egg or lemon. The variety of such mixtures is infinite.

Fine herbs such as parsley and sage can be deep fried until really crisp and will make a decorative and wholesome accompaniment to other fried foods. The knack of deep frying these herbs correctly is so elusive that the task is often given to trainee cooks to test their ability.

Deep fried fruit such as plums, peaches, apples and quinces, and also all delicate flour, milk and egg mixtures require the addition of sugar. They are therefore really desserts.

All other deep fried foods are served without garnish, or simply with lemon juice. Their assertive flavour makes them ideal starters to a meal.

XVII   The Baking of Meat Wrapped in Dough

The art of enclosing meats with their juices and the aroma of delicate seasonings inside a thick dough, which is then baked, so that its contents cook in their own exuded liquids is a widespread refinement of cooking practice. I am unable to say where this custom originated.

The baking of ham and other smoked products which have been soaked in water, milk or wine before being encased in fresh yeast dough has been widespread for many generations. It is a very successful method if the oven temperature is right and the dough sufficiently neutral in flavour. If, however, the dough is too wet, falling apart when suddenly subjected to heat, even the best ham will dry out and be ruined. It is for this reason that I would advise inexperienced cooks to stick to boiling.

This method of cooking may well have encouraged people to fashion artistic shapes out of ordinary or enriched doughs. These were then filled with raw meat with all kinds of seasonings, fat and other tasty morsels and then carefully topped with a lid made of the same dough before being baked slowly at a sustained temperature. This type of dish is known as a pie (in German, *Pastete*, which comes from the Italian, *pasta*, dough). I have in fact found the earliest mention of a true pie in medieval Italy and this, together with the etymology of the word itself, leads me to conclude that the pie was probably invented in renaissance Italy.

Pies are objects of the most irritating luxury in our cities. They should be economical, everyday items, like sausages and other foods designed to be kept for a long period. In any household where there is frequent entertaining, the cook should know how to prepare tasty, long-lasting pies from the many suitable ingredients available.

Better ingredients give better results. Good truffles will impart a very fine flavour to this type of dish. In much of Europe where truffles are not readily available, however, all kinds of other seasonings can be used to make pies which can be kept cold in readiness for unexpected guests. These include fine herbs, morels and fragrant fungi, also some of the onion family; even the mild garlic known as rocambole can be used with care. Any of these ingredients will season pies with more or less pleasing results. The lack of truffles can be made less obvious by skillful selection and combination of the types of meat used in a pie.

Veal, ham and domestic poultry are meats which are usually readily available. They will make a good household pie if layered with
chopped and seasoned liver or fresh or salted bacon. Poultry can be
put into a pie in its raw state, or it can be boned to give better results.
Breast of pheasant makes an excellent ingredient in these mixed meat
pies. If the pie is to contain any sort of game, the additional chopped
meat layers can be more heavily seasoned with herbs and spices, and
a little lemon juice or strong vinegar can even be used. The breast
meat from any game birds may be prepared as for a salmi while the
remaining carcases are pounded up raw, forced through a sieve with
strong herbal vinegar and then mixed with a generous quantity of
bacon together with a smaller proportion of calves' liver. If it is
prepared in this way, the chopped mixture will be more in harmony
with the meat used in the pie.

The French believe that the meat should be cooked before being
put into a pie. Regardless of their opinions, it is important that both
the whole and chopped meat should be used raw, otherwise the
juices would be lost. Using cooked meat would nullify the essential
value of a pie, the enclosed cooking medium which it creates. There
are, however, exceptions to this rule and these are the pies made of
the livers of any domestic poultry such as ducks, pigeons, young
cockerels, capons, poulards [fattened hens], turkeys and geese.

The livers of pike or of the sea fish, particularly cod, can also be
put into pies. These pies will not travel or keep very well, however,
and the flavour of truffles and the other fungi will not be appropriate.

A cook can really use anything he can think of to fill a pie and
can use his creations to demonstrate his imagination and good
judgement.

Hot pies are actually salmis or stews cooked in a pastry case. They
are better when the filling is put into the case raw, then being cooked
inside the dough. This does not often happen, however, because the
dough will often split if its contents are too liquid. Such a disaster can
easily be prevented by adding very little liquid to the pie filling and
by keeping it moist during the cooking period by occasionally
adding a little liquid jelly through the air hole in the top crust. It is
also customary to serve a highly flavoured sauce with a hot pie.

It would be out of place to discuss the actual pastry here. We shall
deal with flour and its uses in Book Two.

A good, sharp jelly will make a pleasant accompaniment to any
cold pie. It is most important that the flavour of the jelly should suit
that of the pie.

XVIII Boiled Stuffings

Preparations of this kind really belong in the chapter on boiling meat. I have, however, preferred to make them follow the pies as they are related to them.

The bones of any of the larger birds, such as turkey cocks, capons, poulards and even pheasants which have not been shot to pieces and are still fresh, should be removed as cleanly as possible so that the skin remains intact. A mixture of chopped poultry livers and bacon is then prepared and seasoned as desired. The boned carcase is filled with this mixture, together with one or more long, coarsely cut slices of smoked ham, which should run the length of the bird. If truffles or any delicate fungi are available, these can be evenly distributed throughout the stuffing mixture. The bird should not be over-stuffed or it will burst and the stuffing will appear too uniform when the bird is carved.

If you are stuffing a really large bird, such as an old turkey cock, it is a good idea to add some tender meat from a capon or pheasant, or a few partridge breasts, or even a really tender, well beaten piece of veal. This dish is not as good when the meat for the stuffing is diced, as does occur in some places. The human tongue enjoys contrasts and likes to distinguish between them but a flavour which is too muddled will confuse the judgement. All mixtures should therefore either be so thoroughly amalgamated that they present a uniform flavour to the tongue, or so disparate that each flavour can be appreciated individually.

When the boned bird has been stuffed, the openings in the skin should be sewn together neatly. It should next be tied or sewn up in a cloth which has been washed out without soap. It is then simmered in salted water for two to four hours. Let the bird cool down in the cloth and then untie it and carefully remove the threads from the skin. A sharply flavoured jelly should have been prepared in the meantime and this should be allowed to coalesce over the stuffed bird. The strength and body of the jelly will be much improved if the bones which were removed from the bird are used in its preparation.

XIX The Various Ways of Keeping Meat and Fish in an Edible Condition for Long Periods

I did my kitchen boy's apprenticeship in the household of a wealthy nobleman. Things were different in those days; the garden and greenhouse were carefully managed, the yard was full of hens and there were all kinds of fattened cattle in great profusion. Vegetable stores were laid down throughout the summer and so many well-fattened animals were killed for the winter that I could only compare it with Camatsio's wedding in Don Quixote, or with the special killing days of Homer's times. Hospitality was always offered to rich and poor and the Lord and his servants wanted for nothing. It was not an everyday necessity to open up the household purse even though, as everyone knows, money is more easily spent than acquired.

The following stores were laid down in the autumn: countless sausages of all shapes and sizes; salted and smoked products; meat in acidulated jellies, and more. In the end everything was stowed in its rightful place, some foodstuffs being for immediate use that winter while other goods, such as hams and bacon, might be kept for years. For a whole week the noble lady herself spearheaded the general activity, dispensing instruction and demonstrations, and this despite the fact that she was skilled in many other arts and, to my mind, was no less noble in her conduct than any of the finest ladies of the day.

Years ago it was customary in Italy too, even in the largest towns, to slaughter one or more pigs for the winter stores, and this inspired men like Boccaccio and Sacchetti to write many of their best short stories. In time, however, this practice was sacrificed to the refine-ment of the female sex, a quality which was not so sought after in the wives of ancient Greece as in that ethereal being so regrettably described to us by our Wieland [Christoph Martin Wieland, 1733-1813, poet & writer]. It appears that their advancing state of refine-ment[38] is also daily rendering German women less capable of attending to the ordinary necessities of life, to the longterm provi-sion, maintenance and distribution of stores. The custom of home slaughtering livestock has indeed become much less prevalent in recent years and meat traders are profiting more from this trend than are ordinary households.

Despite this, the established traditions of the art of salting have not been interrupted and so I shall refrain from exploring them in detail.

In Northern and Western Germany in particular, people are still expert at salting and smoking. The South Germans have never had a standard procedure for this, partly because more fresh supplies were available in the more populated areas, and partly also because the distance from the sea made the correct salting down of stores appear less vital. The quality of any foodstuffs salted down is always determined to a great extent by local factors. No artificial fattening programme can better cattle which have been allowed to roam free and have then been fattened quickly in lush pastures, such as the beef cattle[39] from Scotland and the North of England in the markets of London, or those from Jutland in the Hamburg markets; or pigs which have gorged themselves in chestnut or oak woods. It is for this reason that products such as smoked, air-dried beef from Hamburg, ham from Westphalia, Bayonne or Italy, tongues from Salzburg, goose breasts from Pomerania, Dutch herrings, smoked salmon from the Rhine and sometimes from the Elbe too, and smoked eels from Lake Plöner remain unique, incomparable and unrivalled. Nature is not at all evenhanded in her treatment of the products we might cook.

It is always true that the most compact, healthiest meat, marbled with fat, is the most suitable for salting down. The fat keeps the fibres flexible and itself helps to maintain them in good condition. Lean meat absorbs too much salt, readily dries up in smoking and goes rotten more quickly than fat meat, or meat marbled with fat. The people of Saxony have the bad habit of smoking the legs of unfattened calves, while the people of Brandenburg salt down the carcases of old ewes. It is hard to imagine anything more loathsome.

The Bavarian cookbook, which has good intentions but is not sufficiently thorough, gives useful intructions for salting down and smoking. Anyone intending to use these instructions will, however, be well advised to separate general items, such as the preparation of the meat, or the properties of salt and saltpetre, from a plethora of fantasy items which, by their very nature, could only please someone accustomed to them from youth. This applies to the instructions regarding the use of spices, fragrant herbs and seeds which readily mask the true flavour of the meat and which, when applied extraneously, rapidly evaporate, leaving only the bitterness which underlies all flavourings.

The meat for any type of sausage should be scraped with a sharp knife in order to separate the fibres from any trace of skin and from all sinews and veins. Bratwürste (frying sausages) should not be too tightly compressed and it is a good idea to give them a granular texture. The meat should be minced, salted and seasoned with particular care before the cut-up or coarsely chopped fat is roughly mixed in. By contrast, smoked sausages should be packed very firmly into the skins; the more compacted they become in smoking, the longer they will keep and the easier it will be to slice them finely. For these sausages I would prefer to mix meat and fat together fairly coarsely, as in the Italian salamis, than to mince both together and thoroughly amalgamate them, in the German fashion. Incidentally, I find the garlic flavour of the Bolognese sausages unnecessary and even rather offensive.

It is essential that the skins be thoroughly cleaned and soaked for a few days in salt water before they are filled with sausage mixtures.

A loin or tenderloin joint of pork, with one third of its attached fat but all skin and veins removed, can be freshly salted and well seasoned with spices as well as dried herbs; it is then wrapped in rectal membrane or bladder and again, if these skins are strong enough, left in brine for about one day. The joint is then hung up for smoking, like the sausages, and is kept and used in the same way. The meat on the loin joint can, however, be cut away from the bone and, mixed with coarsely chopped fat, can be prepared like a sausage. I ate this excellent dish, in both variations, in the hills around Rome. The people there call it polpette and habitually add garlic and coriander to the recipe. I advise that they should be omitted.

The *zampone* from Modena is another first-rate salted product peculiar to a specific region of Italy. The skin is removed from the hock or front trotter of a pig without tearing or damaging it in any way; the meat and cartilage are then removed from the bone; chop them coarsely and mix with some tender, finely minced meat and some kidney fat; this should be adequately seasoned and salted, according to taste. The mixture is stuffed, not too tightly, into the fat-lined skin of the front trotter; both ends of this skin should be tied together as firmly as possible; place in salt for as long as is necessary to cure the skin so that it will keep, hang it in smoke and then in a dry place until it is required for use. This product must be softened and soaked before boiling but requires only about half as long as a ham. It can be enjoyed either warm or chilled, as a starter or as an accompaniment to vegetables. Obviously the characteristic high quality of the pigs of Modena is of great importance. The flesh of these pigs is particularly well suited to other methods of salting also.

The making of sausages, like pies, allows plenty of scope for invention. It is not necessary to adhere to the current sausage recipe. On the contrary, the types of meat, spices or herbs used in the mixture is a purely arbitrary matter. Each region in Germany, and throughout Europe, has its own combinations, most of which are very good. The cook should follow this or that example or, if he possesses sufficient freedom of thought, he can rely upon his own fertile imagination.

In homes in the Lower Rhine area, I have often eaten a hard smoked, very tasty liver sausage, for which I was given the following recipe. I have not yet been able to try it out myself:

Take equal quantities of fresh calves' liver, pigs' liver and white breadcrumbs which have been softened in meat stock. Clean the livers and chop them finely and then mix everything thoroughly together, adding plenty of salt and seasonings, both spices and fine herbs; then add bacon cut into small dice – about half as much as the liver and bread mixture – and amalgamate thoroughly. The mixture should be stuffed into scrupulously clean skins which are firmly tied at each end and then placed in hot water to start cooking; the last step is to remove them, allow them to cool and then smoke them until they are really hard.

Wheaten breadcrumbs may also be used in the mixture for pig's brain sausages which are made in some areas. Throughout North Germany delicious Bratwürste are made from oatmeal – also rice flour – boiled up in an appropriate meat stock and mixed with fat, blood and spices. These mixtures of blood, fat, meat stock and farinaceous materials, which recur in the Italians' migliaccio, have a slight tendency to sweetness. The common antecedents of these sausages are the goats' stomachs stuffed with blood and fat mentioned by Homer[40] and it appears that these are comparable to the North American Indians' stuffed deers' stomachs, which have been praised in the writings of various travellers. Products of this nature are characteristic of domestic cookery because they make good use of the leftovers from a slaughtered carcase, including stock and fat. Skillful blending can give such sausages an excellent standard of flavour. They are usually grilled before use.

Blood sausages containing chopped tongue and kidney are initially boiled, then smoked until really hard. They are eaten cold.

In larger households, particularly in the country, it is occasionally a good idea to slaughter young, half-fattened pigs when the weather is cool. There will then always be a supply of lightly salted meat, petit salé. All kinds of sausages not suitable for long-term storage can be made from the intestines and other offal. The loin will make a joint of fresh roast pork; the legs are better salted and can be served either straight from the brine, or boiled after a short interval of smoking.

Geese, ducks and lean pork can each be cut up into appropriate, moderate sized pieces and boiled up in an acidulated liquid with seasonings and gelatine derived from hartshorn or the like. They can then be cooled and covered with melted fat and will keep for a long time, set in their sharp jelly. Parts of the wild boar, such as the head, boned and stuffed with chopped and minced meat and fat, can similarly be boiled and preserved in jelly. Firm-fleshed fish, such as the sturgeon, salmon and beluga sturgeon, can be preserved in the same way. The fish jelly is prepared, as already noted, from hartshorn or isinglass.

In ancient times,[41] people kept meat from putrefaction by painting it with honey in order to isolate it from the surrounding air. In time a new discovery, the Donkin Patent Meat merited some consideration and Lieutenant von Kotzebue[42] made use of it on his voyage around the world. In the introduction to this voyage, Krusenstern[43] maintains that the meat is actually improved because it gradually absorbs the thickened stock in which it is stored. It appears that the keeping quality of this type of preserve is largely dependent upon the impermeability of the vessels in which it is sealed up in portions. Apicius even manages to keep oysters. He removes them from their shells, places them in a vessel which has been washed out with vinegar, seals this firmly and keeps it airtight.

Book Two :
Foodstuffs and Seasonings from the Plant World

I Farinaceous Grains, Seeds and Roots in General

All human social structures and civilisation are founded upon the cultivation and consumption of cereal crops. People who are dependent upon animals for their nutrition, whether they be hunters, fishermen or herdsmen, will always follow a nomadic way of life and will never be able to develop their faculties to the extent possible in a sedentary lifestyle. A nomadic race does not have the opportunity of preserving the experience of many generations in the shape of buildings, works of art and written works, or of developing abstract ideas through many points of contact with the established past. The pastoral tribes, however, have the reputation for frequently preserving the purest and most elevated concepts in their original clarity and for maintaining a passionate stand against the flights of fancy of supposedly superior cultures.

Cultivation of the land does, however, affect the development of man's mental faculties. This is because it establishes the tradition of fixed settlements and also causes these settlements to multiply. Compared with animal herding, let alone hunting and fishing, diligent cultivation of cereal grains results in disproportionately more secure and more plentiful levels of food production from the earth. At this point we are reminded of the fact that, whatever our sentimental contemporaries might say about it, food does exert an incalculable influence upon mankind's moral development.

Most of the cereal grains are derived from grasses, which are believed by some to have originated in the plains of Asia.[44] The most ancient civilisations in India and China were not founded upon the cultivation of these grasses, however. They were much more dependent on rice. Furthermore, judging from the descriptions of

121

Herodotus,[45] the many varieties of profitable grains which he encountered on the valley floors of the Tigris and Euphrates appear to have been maize or Indian corn. The early cultivation of these grains must have led to the genesis of the ancient civilisations of the Near East. European culture is, however, founded upon the cultivation of the straw-producing cereals, and these would appear to have reached Europe via Persia and the Pontus Mtns. It is not possible for us to trace the wanderings of wheat, barley and the leguminous crops back into the dim and distant past because the majority of the cereal grains and pulses had already spread as far as the coasts of the Mediterranean before the dawn of history. Even the most cultured race of all time revered the memory of the benevolence of Ceres and Triptolemos in its myths and religious practices, honouring thus the conditions which allowed its unsurpassed mental development.

The number of cereal types gradually increased, partly by the creation of endless variants of the existing species, and, more significantly, by the arrival of the starchy tubers and roots of the new world. Trade eventually brought the pith of the sago palm into European kitchens. I do not intend to give details of all the different species of cereals, pulses and potatoes. Many of these are not cultivated in Europe and are prepared in very similar ways.

Many things are edible in their natural state. In the case of all the cereal varieties, however, artificial measures must come to the aid of the digestion. We should consider initially those grains which cannot be boiled, baked or rendered edible to humans in any other way without first being crushed. The straw-producing cereals all belong in this category – wheat and its variants, rye, barley, oats and maize or Indian corn. In ancient times these grains were crushed in individual mortars; this was slave work of the hardest and most feared kind. For this reason alone, mankind owes a great debt of gratitude for the invention of water and windmills. This also applies to mechanisation generally, to the machines which are so often unjustly reviled today. It is not the fault of ingeniously developed machines that so many people are unable to find proper jobs nowadays. Much more to blame is the indolence and lack of understanding of those who possess enough power and influence to deploy the potential which is no longer required by the exigencies of daily living. This potential could be motivated towards greater and better goals.

That's as may be; it suffices for us to note that simply crushing the grains results in a coarse flour (groats or semolina) which is little suited to bread making and can only be softened and made digestible by boiling. To reduce these hard grains to true flour they must be crushed much more thoroughly and sieved through cloths to remove the fibrous skin layer, or bran. Repeated sieving or bolting will produce a finer flour of varying degrees of coarseness. It is curious that flour is sifted through hand sieves throughout Italy, where there has so far been a rejection even of the simple machinery required in Northern Europe to set the flour bolters in motion.

To prepare other grains, such as rice and buckwheat, for cooking, it is necessary only to remove their woody husk. These grains can also be ground into flour. Barley can be treated like rice in that once its husk is removed, producing pot barley [or pearl barley if all husk removed], it can readily be softened by boiling. Millet can be softened in its whole form or in crushed form while maize is processed to a coarse flour which does not require bolting or sieving because the outer coating of this grain is not excessively fibrous. Pulses are softened by boiling and do not need to be crushed first. This is also true for the softer starchy tubers and roots, which are on a par with chestnuts, and also for the vegetables such as pumpkins and artichokes which have a high starch content.

II   Flour and its Use

The term flour is applied to the fine, nutritious dust which is produced when grains are crushed to remove their fibrous outer layers. The more these fibrous outer layers are removed by sieving or bolting, the more nutritious the end product will be.

In order to release and develop the nutritional element, or gluten, in the flour, it is mixed with a liquid and exposed to heat. This may be achieved by boiling up the mixture in a fire-proof container to make a porridge or purée, or by binding the flour with a small amount of liquid, kneading it into a dough and then exposing this to a dry, enclosed heat, baking it. The latter form is known to us as bread.

I believe that porridge is the older of the two preparations. The ancients were already convinced of this,[46] and they knew both leavened and unleavened bread. Furthermore, porridge, and not bread, is the normal staple for peoples who cling to the lowest rungs of the ladder of civilisation. In interior Africa a porridge is made from maize, and in Upper Egypt and Nubia it is made from lentils. The pilau, or rice porridge, is consumed throughout the Orient even in modern times. Despite this, we shall deal first with bread because, in the context of our style of eating, porridge is better classified with the vegetables.

III The Baking of Bread

Like the maize cakes of the North American settlers or the loaves of
the Persians, bread was originally a flat disk or cake made of solid,
unleavened dough. Bread in this form is prone to going mouldy and
is difficult to digest because the dense dough does not allow the
proper evaporation of moisture during baking. Hippocrates[47]
remarks that leavened bread is more easily consumed but is less
nutritious than unleavened bread.

Once mankind had become familiar with the details of fermentation, a very important natural process, someone had the bright idea
of utilising it to raise bread dough. The first leavened bread was
probably raised with wine or beer yeast.[48] Beer is very likely to be the
more ancient in Asia, for the simple reason that it occurs in China
where no wine occurs. In many parts of Europe today, bread is raised
by keeping a small portion of dough from one baking session to the
next. In other places, particularly where the acid flavour developed
by old bread dough, or sourdough, is not popular, the dough is
raised with a small quantity of stored wine or beer yeast. A bread
dough which is too sour is not enjoyable unless people are used to it
and will only be considered digestible if local circumstances dictate.
The leavening of bread should never be carried beyond the stage of
raising the dense mass to a moderate extent. A spongy, porous loaf,
such as those produced by town bakers trying to economise on flour,
is just as unpleasant as a soggy or doughy loaf. The capacity of a
spongy dough to cause flatulence is just as detrimental to the health
as the heaviness of a soggy one. The evil characteristics of a soggy
and doughy loaf are usually the result of adding too much liquid to
the dough mixture. They may also arise from the fact that the oven
was not hot enough for baking, or, due to faulty construction, did not
retain the heat for long enough.

The French, particularly the Parisians, use pigeons' droppings to
raise their bread rolls. They are filled with air bubbles and, after they
have expanded in the oven, this results in particular development of
the upper surface, which bakes into a hollow crust. This crust obviously becomes very dry and a little overcooked and, for this very
reason, most tasty and digestible. Doctors may also like to decide
whether continued consumption of heated pigeons' droppings might
impair the health.

I consider that one of the best breads is that made in Florentine
households from fine wheat flour, lightly salted, leavened with a

piece of the previous day's dough, or with a little yeast, then baked at the right temperature until crusty and left in a dry place to mature for twenty four hours. This is, in fact not dissimilar to the household loaves of France and England, but English bread tends to be more heavily salted and made from coarser flour.

Rye breads, which keep longer than wheaten breads, usually have a rather more acid flavour. This is because they are made with sourdough kept for long periods between baking sessions. The addition of a small quantity of wheat flour, which is not as susceptible to becoming over-acidic, will soften the flavour. If rye breads are thoroughly kneaded, neither too sour nor too salty, and, having risen properly, are baked until really crusty, they will be hearty and nourishing, worthy of comparison with the best varieties of bread.

Breads made of very coarsely ground flours can become very indigestible if the dough is too wet or too acidic, or if they are not baked properly. The so-called black bread, rough bread or ration bread, made from rye flours from which only the coarsest bran has been separated, demonstrates this. In contrast, however, if they are leavened with care and baked thoroughly, like the Pumpernickel from Westphalia, these breads can be wholesome and even quite delicious. It is, of course, quite possible that the farmhouse loaves of Westphalia derive their good flavour from the characteristics of the local grain, which would exert a decisive influence on the flavour and nutritional value of the bread, no matter how it was handled. The fame of this bread's flavour has even spread beyond the German borders.

My knowledge of the Scottish oatmeal breads and the Scandinavian crusty breads (Stampebrö) is limited to the descriptions of other people. I have tried breads made with an equal mixture of potato and rye flour in Germany and have found them soggy,[49] heavy and insipid. During a period of scarcity in Italy, I sampled a loaf which included crushed Egyptian beans in its mixture. I did not like the flavour; this mixture must be bad for the health. I am convinced that, in times of shortage, it would be much better for people to consume these moister starchy products in the form of stiff porridge. I am reminded of the fact that when the grain crops failed in England during the civil wars, people used to eat potatoes baked in hot ashes and then scrubbed, instead of bread. This happened even in the rich households and I consider it a better substitute than the normal potato bread.

In the cities of Europe the craft bakeries produce all kinds of bread rolls, biscuits and pretzels (Kringel) and the quality of these varies with the quality of flour used. Their characteristic flavours may be developed by careful handling, or ruined by superfluous additives. It is customary in some places to mix seasonings such as caraway or coriander into bread dough, or to sprinkle them on top of loaves. The taste for these doubtful flavours must be acquired young. They are not acceptable otherwise. It often happens that these ingredients are added to breads which have been badly handled or baked. They may be too acidic, soggy or spongy. Wherever artifice is used, there is something essentially lacking. Anyone who is capable of developing the food value of a decent flour by kneading it into a dough with the correct amount of water and then baking it in the appropriate manner would not dream of ruining the simple goodness of the bread by adding an evil, chemical flavouring.[50]

IV   Baking in General

Bread in its simplest, unseasoned form may act as an accompaniment to any type of food. The universality of its flavour forms a foundation, and at the same time a connecting thread, or leitmotiv for even the most complex meal. On the other hand other baked goods, unless making an appearance as an individual course, often act only as trimmings or additions to particular foods, in which case their composition will reflect the flavour of the food they are to accompany.

The French are the undisputed experts when it comes to making firm pastry for cold pies, pastry which can be moulded into any shape or form. The making of this pastry, and of many other baked goods, has become second nature to them. Their recipe books have the last word in this matter and I have borrowed the following instructions from them:

Quantities: six pounds of flour, three pounds of butter, two ounces of salt and ten egg yolks. This quantity may be halved, quartered or doubled, according to requirements.

Method: Take the flour, heap it on a table and make a hollow in it; put the butter, salt, egg yolks and a glass of water into the hollow; the quantity of water will depend upon the other ingredients. Work the butter with the water, yolks and salt and be sure that the butter is well softened; work the flour in gradually and draw the mixture together into a lump. When the dough is holding together well, knead it with the fingers until it is thoroughly amalgamated. If it is too dry, add a little more moisture. It is dangerous to knead this dough more than twice because it could become too grainy and would not then stick together properly. This is especially likely in summer.

It is extraordinary that the fine strength and attractive golden appearance of French pie pastry promotes the practice of partially casseroling the meat before it is used for a pie. This method is recommended in the best cookery books and is doubtless good for the outward appearance of the pie. On the other hand, however, the basic purpose of the pie, that of providing an enclosed cooking medium, is largely lost. This can be clearly demonstrated by preparing two pies with the same ingredients. The meat for one of the pies should be pre-cooked in the French style while the meat for the other pie, with its seasonings, should be placed in the crust raw. The pies should then be marked and baked. The flavour of the meat which was not pre-cooked will be much cleaner and stronger, with more juice.

Some of the puff paste, or rich pastry recipes in the cookery books are useful whilst others are not. The making of a good rich puff pastry demands sparing use of choice butter, high quality fine flour and slow, careful preparation in a cool place. I have found the following method very successful over the years:

Quantities: one pound of the finest wheat or spelt flour; three quarters of a pound of butter, which should either be unsalted, or have the salt removed by repeated washing; two fresh, whole eggs; one tablespoon of good French brandy; one tablespoon of fresh cream.

Method: Heap one half of the flour on a marble slab, or, failing this, on a smooth, clean table. Make a hollow in it and place the eggs, brandy and cream in the hollow. Work the mixture into a firm dough which can be rolled out. Take half of the butter and position this on the rolled-out dough, then fold the dough up and around the butter. Use some of the remaining flour to dust the work surface again and then invert the lump of dough onto the newly floured area. Roll the dough out again and follow the same procedure with the remaining butter, until the flour is used up.

The dough should then be rolled out quite thinly and cut into the shape desired. It is arranged in layers to achieve the required thickness and each layer should be painted with a little egg yolk. The outer surface of the pastry should also be painted with egg yolk to give it an attractive golden colour.

Some people use a slightly different method; the French, for example, use a very large quantity of butter for this type of pastry and this makes it fatty and heavy. Other people add salt to the dough, which does not harm it.

Rich pastry makes an ideal accompaniment to nutritious meals and is also an excellent medium in which to serve stewed fruit and other sweet mixtures.

Small pies made of rich pastry may be filled with a variety of delicate meats in thickened, slightly acidic sauces; veal sweetbreads for example can be lightly boiled and the most tender pieces diced before being warmed through in a white sauce, either alone or with truffles, morels or other delicate fungi. The hot pastry cases are then filled with the mixture and served. Cleaned crayfish claws and tails may also be used with morels in a less acidic sauce, thickened with a little crab butter. The livers of all sorts of small birds are suitable too.

Items such as ox cheek, the udders from female calves and cocks' combs are prepared in the same way as the sweetbreads. Oysters may also be served in this way but should not be boiled, only gently warmed in the sauce off the heat. As the famous Scappi notes, they would otherwise become hard and indigestible.

The procedure for making little pies from salt-water crabs and lobsters is as follows: cook the animals by boiling them, remove the contents of the heads and chop this meat with a shallot, fine herbs and the flesh of one sardine. Stir with a few spoonfuls of strong vinegar and a little oil or butter over a gentle heat until almost boiling. Dilute with a little lemon juice and white meat stock and then pass through a clean sieve. The tail and claw meat from the crabs should meanwhile be diced and then added to the sieved sauce. Add salt and a little seasoning and heat the mixture. Fill the pie cases.

To make little shrimp pies: cook them, remove the fleshy tail parts and put aside; pound the rest and heat with butter or a little veal stock. Sieve this and then thicken it with a little white roux, an egg yolk and a little lemon juice. Add a pinch of salt, warm the tail meat in this sauce and use to fill the pie cases.

Any tender, tasty pieces of fish or meat are suitable for these pies. The cook can give free rein to his imagination here.

When lunch is being served for numbers of people together, the cook may present any number of side dishes in an ornamental fashion by enclosing them in a good puff pastry on a serving platter. Salmis and the various lightweight steamed dishes are suitable for this. It is not, however, a good idea to put too many different creations within the same pastry enclosure as one flavour would spoil another.

A good Swiss cream cake, or ramequin, made of cream, butter, egg yolks, potato flour and parmesan cheese will be very successful on a puff pastry base.

Puff pastry may also conclude a meal, providing a medium in which to serve cooked and preserved fruit, or any other sweet mixtures. In this guise it may well be known as a fancy cake, or tart. The term is also applied to other baked goods made from different dough mixtures and, of these, the sand cake, or crumble cake, is the most easy to digest, and by far the best. It is customary in many places to make tart pastry with ground almonds but I would not advise any self-respecting cook to do this. Not everyone likes almond pastry and it is always very indigestible. People who eat quantities of marzipan and almond confections find that their teeth are ruined. Whole communities have been known to inflict the most serious damage to their entire digestive systems by the consumption of almond pastries and cakes. I have even heard of one woman who killed herself by eating marzipan.

Pâte à brioche is one of the French baked goods which can be thoroughly recommended on account of its simplicity and digestibility. Every French cookery book has a recipe for it. It is much better than the related German *Butterleibel* and *Süsterkuchen*.

Doughs of varying degrees of dryness, fattiness, firmness or slackness can be made into cakes and tarts of many shapes and forms. These trivialities can be seen in the cookery books which are so full of them but it is much better to follow local traditions of mixing and processing the doughs. Female cooks are always more expert in the matter of local baked goods as they tend to travel less than male cooks. These details are really not of any great importance. The cook should insist upon fine flour milled from ripe grain harvested dry and on top quality butter and very fresh eggs. The best way to ensure the quality of the flour is to purchase the wheat or spelt oneself and then send it to the most skilled miller in the neighbourhood, without counting the cost. It is also important to beware of adding too much fat or moisture, put the dough into the oven at the correct time, before it sinks, bake it thoroughly, but without burning, and do not, as so often happens, add a whole chemist's shop full of additives which would only alarm and confuse the senses.

In many German towns, pastry and cake 'factories' have risen from the ruins of the art of true housekeeping. I have seen cakes emerging from these places with layers of tart fruit, chocolate, vanilla, almond paste, sour preserves and insipid sweetness. Hypochondriac consumers took eager bites out of these confections, their mounting stomach aches temporarily forgotten. Their enjoyment was obviously painful, nothing like the relaxing pleasure of satisfying a healthy appetite.

V   All Kinds of Boiled and Baked Cereal Dishes

I have no intention of making an exhaustive study of this category of foodstuffs but I consider that the soup ingredients are the most important in the group on account of their general usefulness.

Soup noodles like the Italian macaroni and vermicelli are usually made in specialised factories. Housekeepers and cooks therefore need only to be able to distinguish between good and bad products. They will soon learn to do this. Good Neapolitan macaroni should swell by two thirds of its volume when boiled and should become very pale. The macaronis of Lombardy and Genoa are usually rolled out flat and contain a little saffron. They are rightly considered to be inferior to the Neapolitan product.

The water or stock to be used for cooking macaroni or vermicelli should be brought to a good rolling boil before the pasta is added. It would dissolve into a floury porridge if added to cold or lukewarm water. I do not, however, think that macaroni makes as good a soup ingredient as cut noodles. These should be made of fine spelt flour, kneaded into a firm dough with a little water and approximately the same volume of egg yolks. The dough is worked thoroughly, rolled out as thinly as possible and then cut into fine shreds. These noodles are improved if made a few days in advance and allowed to dry in the sun. They will not, however, keep as long as macaroni because of their egg yolk content.

Like macaroni, cut noodles can be boiled in meat stock as well as in salted water. They can then be served as a side dish with toasted breadcrumbs, or with butter and parmesan cheese.

It is a tradition in Austria and Bavaria to press the noodle dough together into a disk shape and then to grate it. The coarse shavings are then air-dried and will constitute an excellent soup ingredient.

If a little butter and some eggs, beaten to a foam, are added to the dough, it will become so slack that it can be cooked in the boiling stock in larger lumps, as dumplings (*Klösschen, Nockerlen*) and thick-cut noodles (*Spatzelen*). Any kind of coarsely crushed grain may be used as a change from flour and will produce the substantial semolina dumplings so rightly beloved in South Germany.

There is no end to the variety of these pastas, and the boiled types are preferable to those fried in fat, which are used for soup in some places. The latter variety tend to make the soup greasy and this spoils not only its flavour but also the essential wholesomeness of the dish.

As its name suggests, pudding is a dish of English origins. Before potatoes became widespread in England, people used to eat a pudding made of a flour and water batter with their roast beef. This was wrapped in a cloth and then boiled, and it is still cooked in this way in the country. In Tom Jones, Fielding measured the tutor's prosperity in the frequency with which he consumed roast beef with this pudding.

This dish has now been developed to such an extent that it may be regarded as one of the best foods for toothless gourmets. Whether it be boiled or baked in a mould, the pudding should be very light and spongy and this is achieved by beating foaming eggs into the mixture, filling it with air bubbles which will expand on heating. As the basic pudding ingredients are flour, eggs and butter, it can easily be made sweet or savoury by the addition of further ingredients. Recently the English plum pudding has become the most popular variant. This has a robust flavour, not normally characteristic of these dishes, derived from the addition of a moderate amount of good beef marrow and fresh calves' fat.

Ground almonds are often added to sweet pudding mixtures, but make them heavy and indigestible. Cooked almonds of any kind are unhealthy and this explains why they taste unpleasant to those people who remain more in touch with their own instincts and who otherwise enjoy eating fresh or airdried almonds as dessert. The transformation which occurs when the oilrich almond is boiled or roasted is the same as that which makes any cooked oil indigestible. Despite this, burnt almonds are a harmless confection; the burning has the effect, not of turning the almond oil to resin, but rather of completely destroying it.

Before we leave the subject of the pudding, which is known as a *Knopf*, (or *knob*,) in South Germany, probably because it is usually boiled in a table napkin, we must mention those smaller knobs known as dumplings (*Klösse* or *Knetel*), which are fairly well known. Bavarian Knetel are made of bread croutons mixed with eggs, flour and milk, or preferably with meat stock. Half of the croutons used should be toasted in butter. These ingredients are mixed to form a firm dough which is then shaped into marbles. The marbles are turned several times in dry flour to coat them before they are dropped into the boiling water, or rather, stock. These simple dumplings make an ideal accompaniment to all kinds of dishes. In Bavaria, an excellent variation is the addition of a little chopped bacon or minced calves' liver. The dish is then known as bacon or liver dumplings and is robust, popular country food.

Bavaria is also the home of the famous stewed dumplings [*Dampfnudel*], raised noodles and similar light, cereal-based foods. The high quality of these products is largely due to the excellence of the Bavarian beer yeast.

The soufflé is more of a delicacy. Stir fine spelt flour and milk together over a fierce flame to make a firm porridge; let this porridge cool down and let it stand until half an hour before serving time. Then stir some good butter, a few egg yolks and a little sugar into the milky porridge, without heating. When everything is well mixed, add egg whites, beaten to a foam and flavour the mixture as desired. The most suitable individual flavourings for this light and gentle dish are cinnamon, vanilla and the volatile oils of lemon or orange peels. The chosen flavouring should be used sparingly. {A soufflé should rise well. Its crust should be firm and cracked and it should lean gracefully to one side. The cook may achieve this, partly by making sure that the batter does not become too thin during the mixing process, and partly by maintaining a greater heat from above than from below during baking. This dish does have a tendency to become unpleasantly sloppy and, for this reason, coarser grains, especially corn grits, are more suitable for it than fine flour. It is important to cook such coarse grains in butter before adding the milk.

This dish is known as omelette soufflé in French.}

VI   Porridge in General and in Detail

As I have already mentioned, porridge, or purée, is the most ancient of the common cereal dishes. This is due both to its intrinsic qualities and to historical circumstance.

A porridge, in the widest sense of the word, is a solution of the starch inherent in the floury grains, seeds or roots. The solution should be as complete as possible and is created using the medium of a liquid kept at boiling point for a certain length of time. It is for this very reason that a good porridge is one of the most nutritious foods derived from the products of the plant kingdom. It is used for weaning babies and, in agricultural areas, it is the refuge of the poorer people. It is, therefore, no surprise that Cato makes repeated references to porridge in his work on agriculture and that even Hippocrates[51] gives porridge preference to bread in certain instances.

There are considerable differences in the degree of solubility of the various plant products suited to porridge making. Some have constituents which must be removed at all costs, and some have properties which are always worth preserving. Thus there are various points to remember when preparing a porridge.

Rice, for example, dissolves readily and contains much sugar. It should be cooked in the oriental fashion, only for long enough to ensure that the individual grains are saturated with moisture. This is swiftly achieved and the hot water is then poured away. The grains are cooled by pouring cold water over them, or simply by taking the pot off the fire. The dish is finished by adding the ingredients desired.

Pater Angeli[52] informs us that oriental peoples find overcooked rice quite repulsive, a fact which is confirmed by other travellers. The Orientals maintain that the dissolved gluten/starch distends the stomach. Indeed any Europeans who settle in the Levant are soon converted to this opinion.

The following recipes are examples of daily variations in cooking methods which are widespread among Eastern peoples.

'The rice is parboiled in water and the water is then drained off completely. The lightly cooked rice is spread on a bed of small pieces of meat with a little butter, also onions, almonds, raisins, peppercorns, cloves, cinnamon and cardamom and the mixture is cooked over a gentle flame. At the end of the cooking time, the heat is increased sharply and the dish is drenched in butter. It is popular throughout the Orient and is known as pilau.'

I would advise anyone following the above-mentioned pilau recipe to omit the almonds and raisins.

Another recipe: 'Boil rice in a small quantity of stock. The liquid should be sufficient to just swell the individual grains without making them stick together. When the grains have absorbed all of the stock, pour melted butter over them.'

All kinds of robust and savoury sauces, eggs, vegetables and fruit juices may be added to or poured over pilaus in place of the butter, meat stock or meat. The inventive cook can really let his imagination run wild!

The Italians also parboil their rice, let it absorb butter, sprinkle it thickly with parmesan cheese and then sit boiled capons, poulards, or any other less dainty poultry on it. If the rice has been cooked in the poultry stock rather than in water, the flavour of the grain will blend beautifully with the flavour of its accompanying meat. Milanese rice is cooked as follows:

Pick over the rice and rinse it several times, then let it dry. Melt a little fresh butter over the fire and toast the rice in this until some of the grains appear to be turning yellowish. Pour over small quantities of poultry stock, waiting until each amount has been absorbed before adding more. When the rice has absorbed enough liquid and is sufficiently soft, serve it with the boiled poultry. Beef marrow may also be added and, in Milan itself, a type of fatty sausages, cervellati, are served with the rice.

Millet and buckwheat groats may be treated in almost the same way as rice. Millet is often consumed in porridge form in the Bavarian Forest, a region in which grain supplies are scarce. The millet is lightly salted and allowed to swell in milk, after which it is removed from the fire. An earthenware pan is buttered and the millet mixture spread over it. This is put into the oven and left to cook slowly. Some knobs of butter can be placed on top of the millet so that it will develop a crust.

Buckwheat groats are prepared in the same manner. In Holstein and Denmark buckwheat groats are commonly served swollen in milk and then dressed with butter or cream. The dish is nutritious but rather heavy. The flavour of ripe buckwheat which has been dried by the sun is intrinsically sweet and pleasant and therefore any wise cook should be prepared to use it to enrich his special dishes. An excellent polenta can be made from buckwheat flour. It may be flavoured in a number of ways or may accompany meat dishes and is always very tasty.

If cornmeal, or maize, is tipped into rapidly boiling water, it will make a stiff porridge, polenta, which is the favourite food of the people of Lombardy. This grain has a mild, rather sweet flavour and can therefore be combined with strong, contrasting flavours. Polenta is dry and indigestible if served without plenty of fat. The detrimental effects of this foodstuff are painfully obvious in some parts of France where people consume maize without any sort of milk, fat or meat. In Lombardy on the other hand, and especially in the prosperous Papal provinces, polenta is usually served with assorted rich meat dishes and here it does its job properly.

Polenta is excellent when cut into slices using a wire in the proper fashion and then layered with fresh butter, salt and slivers of truffles to form a cake which is painted with butter and then baked gently until crusty, either in the oven, or in a baking pan.

A similar dish can be made using parmesan cheese in place of the truffles.

{In his account of his difficult journey through the northernmost parts of America, Mackenzie gives the following recipe for preparing the smallest practicable amounts of maize for the use of the fur trappers and traders.

'Boil the uncrushed grain in water containing a strong solution of potash until the outer husk is removed. Then wash it thoroughly and allow to dry on special racks. When it is dry, or rather dehydrated, it can be packed and is ready for immediate consumption, if prepared in the following way:

Boil it in water for two hours over a moderate fire; when it has been boiling for some time, a few small lumps of animal fat or butter are added. When cooking is complete, a little salt can be added (if the corn were salted earlier, the salt would arrest the softening process, or might stop it completely) and this will make a healthy, appetizing and nutritious dish. One pound of thus dehydrated maize will be sufficient to satisfy and nourish a fur trapper for 24 hours.'

This recipe is always better than the groats which are prepared in a similar way in Northern Scandinavia. The groats are boiled, chopped and dried and then given to the men of Sweden to keep them going when they have to travel far afield to work.}

The Italians eat polenta made from chestnut flour as a fasting dish but this rarely appeals to northern people because of its sticky texture and sweetish flavour.

The result of attempting to make porridge by stirring fine flour into a liquid would be an indigestible gluey substance which would stick to the teeth. I would therefore advise that flour should first be worked together with good butter over a gentle heat until it is quite pale. Only then should water, meat stock or milk be poured on to dilute it. If milk is used, it will be appropriate to add sweet flavourings to the porridge. In the case of water, it would be wise to choose strong, assertive flavourings such as diced, fried bacon, onions or fine herbs.

The people of the Lower Rhine like to make a thick porridge by boiling rye flour in water. They then take spoonfuls of the mixture and arrange these in a hot dish lined with slivers of butter. This is a tasty dish but its tough, sticky texture makes it extremely difficult to eat.

As I have already pointed out, rice, the various coarse grains and also polenta need to be prepared quickly. Being readily soluble, they should not be reduced to glue by overcooking. Legumes, on the other hand, should be cooked for a long time because their outer skins are most indigestible, so that the softening process is much more protracted. The skins of properly cooked legumes can be removed by sieving. It is, however, possible to reduce lentils to a rough purée simply by cooking them slowly and stirring frequently. To serve them Egyptian fashion, allow their cooking water to evaporate completely and then add a generous amount of butter, salt and some seasoning; fried onions are also appropriate. This is a dish much praised by travellers, but its wholesome flavour must be largely due to the natural quality of the Egyptian lentils.

A purée made of mature peas has a natural tendency to bitterness but this is avoided in Bavaria by the customary addition of wheat flour mixed with butter. Pea purée is a national dish in Denmark, and here celery hearts are cooked in with the peas.

The people of Tuscany are in the habit of eating a purée made of cooked white beans served over boiled purple sprouting broccoli[53] and slices of bread. This is lubricated with a little clarified butter or oil and is not unpleasant.

A purée made of chick peas (*cicer, ceci, garavanços*) dressed with a little oil, lemon juice and pepper is a tasty fasting dish in Italy and Spain.

The processes of soaking and cooking thoroughly, and then finishing in steam, are especially important in respect of potato purée, which is the favourite staple dish in North Germany. The potatoes should be peeled and cut up and then soaked in water for several hours, the water being changed more than once so that the maximum possible amount of poisonous juice is removed from them. They should then be boiled in water with plenty of salt until they collapse, whereupon any remaining water should be drained off. The potatoes should be left near the fire for another half hour to allow the evaporation of further moisture. They should be stirred occasionally during this time. Finally they should be thinned a little with milk or stock, some butter should be added and the mixture seasoned and finished as desired.

A variation on this method is to add a little more butter and some egg yolks mixed with stock, stirring them into the puree until it is really smooth. Shaped like an omelette or French pancake, it is painted with butter, coated thickly with parmesan cheese and allowed to brown a little on top, either in the oven, or in the baking pan. Thick cream may be substituted for the stock and a little cinnamon added with a generous quantity of salt. A very thorough stirring and beating before baking will make this dish even lighter and it is even possible to add beaten egg whites.

Potato purée can be sieved together with a mixture of fine herbs. One half of the quantity used should be spinach, and the other half sorrel, chervil, parsley, purslane and tarragon. These herbs should be heated in a little concentrated stock so that they retain their fine green colour. Then chop them, taking care not to loose their juice. Take a quantity of dry potato purée which is twice that of the herbs with their juice and pass both potatoes and herbs through a coarse sieve, or through a metal colander. Return the sieved mixture to the fire with a little butter, add salt and allow it to just heat through. Then take it off the fire, cover it and keep it warm until serving time.

In the sixteenth century, a purée made of the flesh of overgrown pumpkins, mixed with milk and seasoning, was served even on Papal tables. This purée is most insipid and rather sweet when made with milk but is much better if strong stock is used and the mixture is then served buttered, with fine herbs and spices.

As a final point, we have proof in Count Rumford's soup which, by virtue of its origins and characteristics, is a scholarly purée, composed from experience of chemistry, that, even in modern times, this type of food has been considered worthy of the attention of philanthropists.

VII   Vegetables in General

People tend nowadays to use the term *Gemüse* [vegetable] for all dishes made from plant materials. I believe that this is because most of them are served in some sort of puréed form.

With the exception of the dried pulses and starchy tubers, the majority of vegetables are of little nutritional value. However, when combined with other, more nutritious foods, individual vegetables may have a very beneficial effect upon the body. Some act as purgatives while some refresh and cleanse the body fluids; in short, if consumed in sensible quantities, vegetables are veritable household medicines. Every good housewife should be aware of their different effects and be able to utilise them in accordance with the seasons. We are afforded the clearest conception of the importance of vegetable consumption in the accounts of travellers who, reaching land after long sea voyages, soon restored the health of their sick simply by feeding them fresh vegetables.

In connection with cookery, vegetables may be divided into three categories. The first group comprises those plants which do contain nutritional elements, although they do not quite compare with the aforementioned dried pulses. The second comprises those vegetables which have a high fibre content, rendering them difficult to digest. Their nutritional value is almost negligible but they do contain various fine salts and useful acids. The third group comprises all of those plants which have a fine cell structure and powerful aroma. Their essential value is therefore not as vegetables, but as flavour enhancers for other foods.

VIII   Nutritious Vegetables

The potato,[54]   that most excellent tuber, rightly takes pride of place in this category. I must repeat that the potato's juice, which tastes unpleasant and is mildly toxic, should always be extracted.

The wonderful flavour of potatoes baked in glowing embers is a direct result of the fact that this cooking method causes all of the juice to evaporate, leaving only the starchy substance. The English style steamed potatoes are successful for the same reason, particularly if the cook has taken the precaution of soaking them for a few hours beforehand.

It is customary in Holland and in the adjacent parts of France to steam potatoes in butter without boiling them first. The longer and more thoroughly these potatoes have been soaked beforehand, the better they will taste.

I have already dealt with potato purée. Potatoes may be served as a vegetable with butter and meat stock, with cream, with herbs and with powerful sauces made of chopped herrings (or preferably sardines), shallots and fine herbs. In the Rheinland, potatoes are often prepared as above, boiled and then dried off at a moderate temperature and finally coated with breadcrumbs toasted in butter. It is also necessary to know how to treat the different varieties of potato, as some are floury and some are waxy in texture. The floury varieties are better served as purée, or, in dry form, as an accompaniment to roast beef, boiled fish, boiled bacon and so on. The waxy varieties are best served as vegetables with some sort of sauce, or in salads. Watery potatoes which collapse readily are suitable only for animal fodder. In Italy and South Germany, people have been careless enough to allow this variety of potato to infiltrate the stocks of good seed potatoes, leading to a general degeneration of the good stocks.

The Artichoke[55]   For three months of the year, the artichoke occupies approximately the same position in the diet of Southern Europeans as the potato has occupied for a generation in the diet of the Northerners. The heart of the artichoke is rich in starch and even the outer leaves are fleshy and nutritious before the flower begins to develop. In common with the potato, the artichoke contains a bitter juice which should be diluted or removed. This is achieved by soaking in fresh water, by boiling in salted water and by the gradual evaporation of this same water. It is also achieved by baking in hot embers or on the grill.

This method of preparation is best for old artichokes, or those which have finished flowering. The pollen filaments and half-developed seeds should be completely removed, the artichoke heart placed on the grill and melted butter or good oil poured into it. Add plenty of salt and pepper too. After a while, more butter or oil can be added if needed. This dish is traditionally the frugal food of the cobblers of Rome and Naples. These people make the braziers on which they warm their awls do dual service as cooking stoves, a very economical practice. It is also possible to arrange the hollowed-out artichoke hearts in an enclosed baking pan. They are lubricated and salted as described above and cooked over a gentle fire.

The Italians tend to consume artichokes very young, before the filaments have begun to form. It is then necessary simply to break off the outer leaves and trim the tops of the inner leaves and these small artichokes will be very tender and good to eat, whether boiled or baked.

In France, tender artichokes are eaten in a white sauce flavoured with lemon juice and thickened with egg yolks. In Italy they are served with oil, salt and lemon juice. After being soaked, they can also be steamed in a strong meat stock and then combined with fine herbs or baby peas which will sweeten them in a very pleasant manner.

I have also used artichokes in a fricassee made of poultry, veal or lamb with a medley of other vegetables such as small pumpkins and delicate root vegetables. The mixture was finished with fine herbs and a little lemon juice.

As long as they are finely sliced and are soaked in salted water for a few hours beforehand, young artichokes are most successful baked in clarified butter. They should be painted with egg yolk and coated with breadcrumbs before baking. This will give them the characteristic gilded appearance.

Artichokes may be kept throughout the year if they are picked very young. The outer leaves and inner leaf tips are removed and the artichokes are quartered, boiled gently and then hung on threads to dry in the air or over a gentle fire. It is, of course, necessary to soak them overnight before they can be used.

Small, quartered artichokes can be steeped for an hour in a mild ash lye. They are then rinsed in several changes of water and dried with cloths before being placed in a brine in glass containers, like salted olives. Ten percent saltpetre should be added to the salt to improve the colour of the artichokes. When this preserve is served,

142

the artichoke pieces should be rinsed in clear water, dried with a cloth and then dressed with a little oil and lemon juice.

Cardoons[56] are a variety of artichoke of which the stalks are eaten. The fleshy stalks are boiled in salted water, after which the outer layers can be peeled off by hand. They are then cut into pieces and can be steamed over an acidulated liquid or coated with egg and breadcrumbs and baked with other vegetables.

Cardoons can also be peeled raw and then steamed. As with artichokes, their characteristic bitter flavour is not, however, to everyone's taste and this has led to the practice of boiling them initially. The artichokes and cardoons of Northern Europe do tend to be less bitter than those of Italy and Spain.

Pumpkin   Both our common pumpkin[57] and the more elongated variety, the bottle gourd,[58] are frequently consumed as vegetables in Southern Europe and in Southern Asia. The bottle gourd is allowed to grow to the length of a normal cucumber whilst the melon-shaped pumpkin is restricted to the size of an apple. This fruit is easily digested and has some nutritional value. The Southern peoples find it refreshing.

The pumpkin can be enjoyed in a salad if it is boiled in salted water, allowed to cool and dressed with oil and vinegar with a few delicate, aromatic salad herbs. Another easy method is to boil it in strong meat stock and then season it with chopped fine herbs and a touch of pepper. It can also be baked with a coating of egg and bread-crumbs but should be parboiled first. The larger varieties can also be stuffed and then steamed in concentrated meat stock.

Pumpkins can be preserved by boiling them in salted water until they are just done. They should then be dried and packed into glazed containers with red Spanish peppers, tarragon, basil and other fine herbs. The containers are topped up with strong, boiling vinegar. If they are compressed or tied very tightly together, the pumpkins will keep in this way for weeks and can be used to extend small starters, or to accompany boiled dishes.

The flesh of ripe pumpkins is sweetish and rich in starch. They can be prepared in the same way as swedes, i.e. sliced or diced, boiled in strong meat stock and then sweetened with a pinch of sugar caramelised in butter, or made more savoury by the addition of fine herbs, pepper and lemon juice.

Such pumpkins can also be used as a soup ingredient, often mixed with rice.

The flesh of ripe pumpkins has some value as a binding agent for other foodstuffs. The basic ingredient of the excellent and renowned pan forte of Siena is none other than the cooked flesh of certain local pumpkins, which have an excellent flavour.

Green, unripened legumes Young peas, broad beans and semi mature white beans are difficult to digest because of their skins but do have some nutritional value.

Young peas[59] contain a great deal of sugar. This is very probably their most valuable component. In order to preserve this sugar, the green peas should be steamed in meat stock or in a little water with some butter. They should not be boiled in water first. In many parts of England and Germany, however, people have got into the habit of boiling green peas in quantities of water. They then throw away the liquid, together with all the goodness from the peas which it contains, and serve the impoverished vegetables dry, or with butter. The original flavour of the peas is even restored artificially, with sugar and seasonings. I am sure that the intelligent reader will be able to decide which of the two cooking methods is better.

Young peas can be combined with other vegetables such as asparagus, turmeric roots, artichokes and young pumpkins; ,they are also compatible with pieces of meat such as poultry and lamb. Furthermore, they make excellent soups; see Chapter Twelve in Book One.

When young, broad beans[60] can be prepared and served in the same way as peas. When fully grown but still immature, the larger broad beans are filled with a starchy substance which is most attractive. These fully grown beans should be boiled in water with plenty of salt until they burst. They should then be dried with a cloth and served in a napkin with melted butter as an accompaniment. The beans are eaten individually, dipped in the butter, their starchy heart being sucked from their hard, indigestible skins. It will be obvious that a dish like this is only suitable for family consumption. If fully grown broad beans are to be served at a larger, more special meal, they should be skinned in the kitchen and then mixed with meat stock with a little butter and fine herbs. They can also be served stewed in English fashion with pieces of streaky bacon. The skinned beans are boiled in the bacon stock and are then served arranged on a dish in ornamental concentric rings.

The Italians make a commendable dish with semi mature kidney beans[61] which they boil in salted water, cool and then serve with oil, lemon juice and pepper.

The pods of peas and beans can be eaten as vegetables and in salads if they are picked young. We shall return to these in the next chapter.

Green chick peas[62] make an excellent and delicious thickening agent for sieved soups, or purées. Their skins are very indigestible, rendering them less suitable for consumption as vegetables. They are rarely cultivated in the North, although they will grow.

Fleshy roots   The roots of celery[63] are aromatic and nutritious. Its leaves are simply aromatic and are mainly used to flavour stocks. The Italian variety does not develop tubers and concentrates its growth more in its leaves. It has a milder flavour and the entire plant can be eaten, the roots and leaves being served either boiled or steamed as a vegetable side dish.

Celery roots can be used in soups and in any mixtures of chopped, sweet vegetables such as juliennes. They may also be served as a vegetable in their own right.

Celery root can be hollowed out and stuffed with a mixture of finely chopped tender meat and fine herbs. It should then be placed in a dish with some butter to be baked in the Dutch oven or baking pan and served with a white sauce. It is even better simmered in a strong meat stock and served with a brown sauce.

Celery can be cut into matchsticks, painted with egg and bread-crumbs and then baked with other tiny items in clarified butter or oil.

It can be blanched and served in mixed salads.

Parsnips[64]   This rather sweet, but nutritious and wholesome root makes a welcome addition to a mixture of other, more robust root vegetables. It can be combined with roots such as carrots, celery and Hamburg parsley to make sieved soups and is also suitable for juli-ennes. Parsnips can be diced up with a little celery and plenty of black salsify and placed in a casserole with a generous joint of veal, tied in a rectangular shape. The casserole should first be lined with a few slices of fresh bacon. Add a little salt and a small quantity of water and cover the casserole. It should be allowed to steam over a low fire for approximately an hour and a half until everything is cooked without burning at all. The veal is served as the centrepiece, surrounded by the root vegetables. If it has cooked correctly, so that it is really tender and pale in colour, it will make a most appetising dish. The bacon should, of course, be put aside when serving. The flavour of the dish can be sharpened with a few drops of lemon juice or a touch of seasoning, if desired.

Carrots[65]   This is a delicious and most wholesome vegetable which can also be used to season stocks. Young carrots are particularly tender and possess a welcome sweetness which makes an excellent flavouring. It is a good idea to serve them steamed in good meat stock, perhaps with a little chopped parsley. If there is no decent stock available, they should be put into a pot with just enough water to cover. This should then be allowed to steam off, after which the carrots can be dressed with a little fresh butter. A few slices of smoked bacon will not go amiss; these should be used to line the saucepan or casserole, with the carrots placed on top.

Carrots may be combined with all sorts of other vegetables such as asparagus tips and green peas; they may accompany other roots in dishes such as juliennes and matelotes. In some parts of Germany, a good robust piece of bacon steamed with carrots and well soaked potatoes is a regional dish. It is traditional in England to cook carrots with a joint of beef. The carrots gradually absorb the meat juices and are finally served as a vegetable with the meat.

When carrots have been kept through the winter, their sugar content is not as high as in young carrots. This can be rectified somewhat by adding a pinch of ordinary sugar when cooking them.

The flavour of concentrated jellies and brown stocks can be greatly improved by the addition of some lightly browned carrots.

Black Salsify[66]   This is a delicate and attractive winter vegetable. It can be served boiled in meat stock which can be thickened with a little white roux, perhaps with a touch of lemon juice. See above to combine salsify with parsnips. It can also be served mixed with winter asparagus in a sharp white sauce.

Some people like to boil salsify in salted water, clean it and then serve it in a sauce made specially for it. I would recommend this practice only when the vegetable smells unpleasantly of manure or rotting straw, which can happen with winter vegetables.

Turnips   The turnip[67] family is most extensive and its individual members differ widely from one another.

The round, white turnip[68] is used mainly as a spring vegetable and has a pleasantly sweet flavour, being rich in sugar at this time of year. It does also have a trace of bitterness, but this is easily ignored. The turnip can be combined with rice in strong meat stocks and it makes an excellent vegetable, particularly if steamed in fatty mutton stock. A healthy and tasty dish, a sort of olla or julienne, can be made by combining white turnips and other root vegetables with the more robust types of meat. Those who have weak digestive systems will not, however, find this dish beneficial.

Some people like to boil turnips in salted water and serve them with butter and chopped parsley but this method results in the loss of a great deal of their natural sweetness.

Swedes[69] and the other hearty winter turnips are best cut into large matchsticks and steamed in household stock. When they are sufficiently cooked and have become tender, a pinch of ordinary sugar should be browned in butter in another pan. The swedes are then tossed in this until they are coloured a little.

In some parts of Germany and the Slavonic countries, people use these larger turnip varieties to make a sort of turnip sauerkraut. The turnips are mashed up, salted and left to ferment like cabbage for sauerkraut. This turnip kraut provides a useful and beneficial winter preserve when there are no other soured vegetable products available. The flavour resembles that of radishes and I personally have never been able to get used to it.

There is one variety of turnip which is carrot shaped and has dense, white, very sweet flesh. It is a native of Brandenburg and is marketed under the name of March or Teltower turnip. The seed of this turnip tends to degenerate in different soil and this leads me to believe that a similar, but more fleshy variety which occurs in Bavaria has the same origins. The two varieties are prepared in the same way. They should be steamed and then attractively coloured with a little toasted flour.

Hamburg Parsley[70]   These roots are used mainly to season soups and sauces, or they may be combined with medleys of other vegetables. Used alone, their flavour would become rather tedious in the long run.

Hamburg parsley can be combined with freshwater fish, poultry and the tender breast and rib cuts of veal, lamb and kid. The roots should be cut up as desired and added to the liquid in the common cooking pot at the start of cooking, during cooking, or even at the end, depending on the length of time needed by the type of meat chosen.

The Mangold or Beet[71]   Due to their excessive sweetness, the common red beetroots are rarely served as a hot vegetable side dish. They are either pickled in vinegar or served in salads, mixed with bitter herbs and potatoes. The Italians bake them in the oven after the bread, or in hot embers on top of the stove, producing undeniably tastier results than boiling them in water.

The yellow beet[72] has a much better flavour than the red variety. It is steamed in stock with a spoonful of strong vinegar and some pepper, and served as a vegetable.

Cucumbers[73] I hardly dare include these strange vegetable fruits in the nutritious category because they are coarse textured and indigestible and held by Southerners to be fever-inducing. Despite this, their insipid sweetness makes them equally unsuitable for inclusion in either of the next two categories. Therefore, in view of their excellent juice, which clears the blood and strengthens the lungs and liver, we shall place cucumbers in this first group of nourishing vegetable plants.

Unripe cucumbers are normally peeled and sliced raw, and eaten in salads. Their juice, the only useful part of these indifferent fruit, is usually pressed out on these occasions.

A pleasant vegetable side dish can be made by peeling and chopping unripe cucumbers and then steaming them in a strong stock which has been well seasoned and acidulated. They can also be hollowed out and filled with a meat stuffing. {Prepared in the following manner, cucumbers can stand on their own as a vegetable: Peel the cucumber, remove the seeds and cut it into pieces. Place in a pot lined with a few slices of bacon or some butter and cook on the fire. As soon as the cucumber begins to brown, moisten it with a spoonful of good meat stock. Let it simmer until it is really tender and has absorbed the stock sufficiently. Season as desired, using a drop of lemon juice or vinegar, chopped fine herbs and pepper.}

Cucumbers are, however, most suited to the creation of assorted pickles. Their glasslike, spongiform cell structure renders them exceptionally receptive to the introduction of outside flavours, and to the development of flavours inherent in them. Small cucumbers are pickled in vinegar, flavoured as desired with dill, horseradish, garlic, whole Spanish peppers and Nepal pepper. The important point is to pick the cucumbers on a dry day and select good, unblemished specimens; furthermore, a strong wine vinegar should be used; lastly, the containers should be sealed thoroughly and stored in a cool, dry place.

Larger cucumbers which are still not ripe can be placed in a brine with dill and vine and cherry leaves; they should be allowed to ferment gently so that their flavour is mid-way between that of a salt pickle and a vinegar pickle, just like a tasty sauerkraut. Quantities of excellent preserves are made with these fermented cucumbers in Bohemia, Lausitz [ie around Dresden] and all over the Slavonic North. In Northern areas, fermented vegetables act as substitutes for decaying fruit. However, I believe that Dutch soured cucumbers are the best. This is partly due to the essential superiority of the long, white, bristly cucumber which the Dutch prefer to cultivate and also to the fact that they like to add a few Spanish peppers and other seasonings which improve the flavour and help to preserve the cucumbers.

Cucumbers which are almost mature and are beginning to turn whitish yellow should be peeled and sliced lengthways. Their seeds should be removed, together with the fibres, and the hollowed cucumbers then placed in a dry container with salt, whole mustard seeds, horseradish, peppercorns and a little garlic, if there are no strong objections to it. A bay leaf and a split Spanish pepper will make welcome additions. Bring some strong vinegar to the boil and pour it, still bubbling, over the cucumbers. Over the next few days, repeat the process by pouring away the vinegar, boiling up fresh and pouring it hot over the cucumbers and seasonings. The container should finally be firmly sealed and placed in a cool, dry place until needed.

IX   Vegetables which season more than nourish due to their rigid cell structure and indigestibility

In this category, **asparagus**[74] is undoubtedly the most popular.

Asparagus is often to be found growing in its original wild state in the marshes of Southern Europe and even in England. Some species of wild asparagus are hardly edible while others are sought after, regardless of their diminutive size, on account of their attractive flavour.

In sandy areas, garden asparagus is set deep in the earth and is cut as soon as it appears at the surface. It should not be set so deep on heavier soils, however, and should be allowed to grow to a height of one inch above the surface before being cut. Asparagus is more tender when cut at surface level but its flavour is stronger when it is cut according to the second method. The Italians cook their garden asparagus too little, the Germans cook it too much; I suggest the happy medium in this matter. Asparagus should certainly be tender to eat but its valuable salts should not be dissolved and boiled away by overcooking.

Asparagus should be cleaned only shortly before it is cooked. Wash it quickly, without leaving it lying in cold water; tie it in bundles and do not place it in the cooking pot until the water is at a rolling boil. Add plenty of salt to the water and when you wish to check whether your asparagus is cooked, test the tips and not the bases of the stems, as inexperienced cooks tend to do.

Having been boiled in this manner, asparagus can be served in the Italian fashion, cooled and dressed with oil, lemon juice, salt, pepper and mustard, or it may be served in the German fashion, in a white sauce made of butter, flour and egg yolks.

Asparagus may be combined with other vegetables in chopped mixtures and in soups. Tender asparagus tips may be pickled in vinegar with pepper, salt and other seasonings and, like other tender vegetables, they can then be kept for use in garnishing boiled dishes.

Cabbage Varieties Cauliflower.[75] As a rule there is only one variety of cauliflower available in Germany: that with white florets. The Italians, however, have lemon yellow and sea green varieties and, in addition, they have a most delicious brownish-red cauliflower which is known as broccoli.[76] This is particularly prevalent in Rome but often stinks and tastes of all kinds of manure. This is so often the case with winter vegetables, due to the slack attitudes of the growers. Anyone whose experience of Roman cabbage is limited to such foul examples will be amazed at its high reputation.

Cauliflower may be blanched in salted water and then served with oil and lemon juice, or in a white sauce. Cooked cauliflower has more flavour if it is cooked in a steamer. Excellent results can always be obtained by boiling it wrapped up in a clean cloth.

The natural sweetness of cauliflower is actually preserved much better when it is slowly steamed in meat stock or in butter with a little water. It is preferable in this case to use those heads which are rather less well formed. They can be cut or broken into pieces without offending the sense of beauty. The flavour of steamed cauliflower may be sharpened by the addition of a little lemon juice or very finely chopped sorrel. It may also be sweetened with a sauce made of fresh cream based on a white roux with an egg yolk. Crayfish butter and cleaned crayfish tails may be used to season this sauce.

Small cauliflower florets can be steamed and mixed with chopped lobster meat and then dressed with a cold sauce made of finely chopped and pounded herbs together with the minced head meat of the lobster. A few spoonfuls of good vinegar are added so that the mixture can be forced through a clean hair sieve and the resultant purée is then brought to the boil and seasoned with plenty of salt, black pepper, white pepper and a pinch of cayenne. The sauce is cooled and finally moistened with the juice of a lemon and several spoonfuls of decent oil. A shallot may be chopped and pounded with the basic herb mixture, and this may be lubricated with oil without any heating at all. However the sauce is prepared, it is important that the finished dish should be pleasing to the eye. A good arrangement is to place the lobster meat in the centre, encircle it with the cauliflower sprigs and then make an outer moat of the thick, creamy sauce, which should have an attractive green colour.

Cauliflower florets can be used in vegetable soups and in chopped dishes. They may be parboiled, painted with egg and breadcrumbs and then baked with lemon juice.

Broccoli is sometimes eaten cold as a salad vegetable and in this case it is best when spiked with bitter oranges. It may also be served steamed in stock or pigs' fat with a generous amount of pepper. The Italians acknowledge the Romans as born experts in the art of broccoli steaming – the end product is known as broccoli strascinati.

Hearted Cabbage[77]   The common hearted cabbage[78] contains a great deal of natural sweetness and it is important to try to preserve this when preparing the cabbage for consumption. This is because the dense cell structure of the cabbage affords it little else to recommend it, condemning it rather to the group of indigestible, flatulence-inducing foodstuffs.

Chopped cabbage leaves, thoroughly cooked, will impart a pleasant flavour and a certain amount of body to soups. The tough midribs should be removed when cutting up the cabbage leaves as these will not soften readily in cooking and have very little flavour. Cabbage should, of course, be cooked in meat stock; it may be combined with carrots and fine herbs.

A delicious way of preparing early, spiky white cabbage is to halve it, remove the coarser stems and place it on a bed of sliced ham and beef scraps. Add a little stock and let it cook very gently. It can then be served around a joint of boiled beef. The stock which will have collected under the cabbage should be poured off and sieved to remove the little pieces of meat and it can then be poured around the cabbage on the serving dish.

White cabbage can be preserved by shredding or slicing it finely and then simmering it slowly in stock or in a little animal fat, adding a drop of vinegar to sharpen it. Red cabbage[79] is more often used for this purpose. A little caraway is a welcome addition to either type of cabbage. White cabbage is also one of the ingredients in the famous *olla podrida*, the delicious blend of vegetables and meats which is a favourite dish in Spain.

The fleshy main stem of a hearted cabbage is normally cut out and thrown away or given to the animals, but in thrifty households it may be chopped finely and steamed in stock with vinegar and caraway. It may also be sweetened slightly with butter and a little milk. I do believe that this less aromatic part of the hearted cabbage is actually the most nutritious.

The well known sauerkraut is made from shredded white cabbage, the flat autumn variety in particular, which is salted and allowed to ferment. A barrel which has been used for white wine will initiate a gentle fermentation in the cabbage and will give it a pleasant, sharp wine flavour. If the process is to be started in a new barrel, crushed grapes should be placed in the bottom of it. Good sauerkraut should smell fresh and should be a beautiful bright yellow. Sauerkraut should not be stirred when it is being cooked, otherwise it will lose its fine colour. If it is steamed very slowly, it will not burn and will not need to be poked about too much.

Sauerkraut is often combined with fish, oysters and other fasting foods but I think that it is best served in true German fashion, with a dish of salt pork, accompanied by a potato purée with white beans or yellow peas.

A few Borsdorf apples are sometimes cooked with sauerkraut to sweeten it. Refined cooks also like to create a dainty and charming dish by layering the cabbage alternately with meats such as sliced beef and fresh or salted pigs' trotters. After a long, slow period of cooking, the cabbage will have absorbed the juices and goodness of the meat.

Juniper berries, caraway seeds and peppercorns are often added to sauerkraut at the time it is packed into the barrels. A long sojourn in brine has a bad effect upon the flavour of such spices, however, so that I think it is best not to add these aromatic seeds until it is time to actually cook the cabbage. They should be added only if their flavour is liked.

'Wirsing' [Crisped] and Savoy Cabbage[80]   This is the most tender and tasty variety of hearted cabbage and it quite rightly bears the name of Savoy because it is the favourite vegetable in the entire Piedmont area. The local people cook the chopped leaves with rice to make a soup which is also frequently consumed next door in Lombardy.

If Savoy cabbage has not spent the winter cloaked in rotting straw or manure but has been exposed to all weathers, it will not need to be doused with water, nor will it require pre-cooking of any kind. It should be cleaned dry and then rinsed off quickly before being steamed in meat stock, or with butter or a piece of fresh meat. It should be cooked until it is just tender so that its flavour is not lost. If, on the other hand, it has been grown in a trench or has been heaped with manure, it will be necessary to spend an hour or so washing it in several changes of water and then to parboil it in salted water before preparing it for serving.

Wirsing [crisped] cabbage is related to the variety known as Brussels sprouts, which are very tasty. The two types are prepared in the same way. Brussels sprouts can be steamed in a light meat stock or with a little butter and then garnished with tiny omelettes.

I believe that when Cato waxes so enthusiastic about cabbage that it is to Wirsing that he is referring. He pickles the cabbage leaves in strong vinegar, serving them raw as a salad to fortify the stomach, and the green variety of the Savoy cabbage would be most suited to this procedure. Fifty years ago, people were still in the habit of serving the new shoots of some of the turnip/kohlrabi varieties as winter salad.

Kohlrabi[81] Kohlrabi derives its name from the Italian cauli rape and is an excellent vegetable when eaten young. The turnip-like main root should not be allowed to grow any bigger than a medium sized apple and, together with the more tender stems, should be cut into small pieces. The green leaves may also be chopped or cut up very finely but should not be added to the cooking pot until the fleshier parts of the kohlrabi are beginning to soften. As long as they are neither overcooked nor still raw, and retain their pleasant green colour, these leaves will flavour the dish and enhance its appearance.

The kohlrabi is not well regarded in North Germany. This is because people have the incomprehensible habit of bringing the vegetable to market only when it has become quite overgrown, hard and tasteless. The kohlrabi is very much inferior to the swede and the other winter turnips when consumed in this overblown state. It should be used as animal fodder, rather than for our tables.

The **musk cabbage**[82] is a delicious variety but is difficult to grow and hardly ever used.

The Italians' **purple sprouting broccoli**[83] is similar to our red and green winter cabbages. Grown in the dry hills of the Chianti area it is tender and delicious but in the well-watered gardens of Florence and Rome it is a very indifferent vegetable. It is normally boiled in salted water, dried, cooled and served in oil and vinegar but may also be prepared like our German red cabbage.

We very often forfeit the strong, characteristic flavour of our native red and green cabbages by boiling them and pouring away the cooking liquid before serving them. They should be picked with great care and scrupulously cleaned; a pinch of sugar should then be browned in butter, the cabbage placed on this and allowed to cook very gently in its own juices. If it threatens to dry out, a little butter, water or meat stock should occasionally be added, but never so much as to cause an accumulation of liquid in the bottom of the saucepan.

Green beans, French beans We have mentioned the dried beans of the phaseolus plant in the sections on cereals and purées. We shall now concern ourselves with the bean pod which is a popular vegetable when eaten in the immature state, before the beans are formed.

The Italians eat the pods of their dwarf beans very young and therefore simply top and tail them before cooking, without cutting them up at all. They are blanched, cooled and eaten with a dressing of vinegar and oil. They may also be steamed in meat stock, butter, pigs' fat or even oil, and are then always served with a good dose of pepper.

Sword beans are popular in Germany because they remain tender for a long time and give a lot of nourishment for their size. In this country they are normally parboiled in salted water before preparation. This may be just a matter of habit, or it may be because people are not very fond of the strong natural flavour of these beans. I cannot deny that green beans, especially slightly overgrown sword beans, do have a hint of unpleasant bitterness about them. This could, however, be removed simply by dousing them once with boiling water.

French beans, finely sliced in the German fashion, can be prepared in numerous different ways. They may be cooked through by steaming in stock and finished with butter, flour and chopped parsley. They may also be steamed in butter, garnished with a little vinegar, tarragon, basil and other pungent herbs. Finally, they may be served in a sweeter medium, with fresh cream and a little butter and flour.

Pearl beans are also known as salad beans. They are prepared in the same way as the other beans. In the Lower Rhine area, pearl beans are boiled in salted water and served with a sauce made of sour cream with a little egg, butter and flour. This is quite a tasty dish.

Green beans are also preserved for the winter store cupboard. They are dried in the air or over a gentle heat and are soaked before use. They may be sliced or left whole and are salted down in barrels or pottery vessels, being soaked as mentioned. Small, tender French beans are excellent pickled in boiled vinegar with an assortment of spices. Cloves should be used very sparingly, however, the emphasis being on the more bitter spices such as the various peppers.

Most of the more tender and fleshy vegetables, such as asparagus, cauliflower and young pumpkins can be pickled in vinegar and preserved in this way. The Italians are quite happy to make use of certain fleshy sea plants[84] which do indeed make a wholesome accompaniment to boiled dishes.

X   Vegetables which nourish a little but
      distinctly affect flavour, having a fine cell
      structure

The garlic family,[85] including onions, clearly takes pride of place
here. This is partly because mankind's oldest historical documents
describe it as a favourite of the Jews whilst, according to Pliny, the
Egyptians honoured it as a deity. The principal reason, however, is
that its use remains so very widespread today.

Consumed in quantity, common garlic[86] is bad for the breath. Its
fibres are indigestible and cause belching. In the Mediterranean coastal
area, however, people regard garlic juice as a prophylactic against
fevers. Garlic can certainly be used as a flavouring, if sparingly and
in conjunction with various other aromatics, in the majority of
robust, solid and fatty dishes. It is always a good idea to separate the
juice from the fibre and to keep this fibre well away from the dish
because there is no doubt that it is the cause of the evil smelling
belching which makes garlic so unpopular with fastidious peoples.

This separation can be achieved in a variety of ways. If a sauce is
to be flavoured with garlic, it will be sufficient to rub a small piece of
garlic around the inner surfaces of the casserole, saucepan or cooking
pot to be used for the sauce-making. If an Italian fasting soup made
of pulses is to be flavoured with garlic, a few slices of bread are
toasted and rubbed with a piece, so that the bread absorbs the juices.
The bread is then placed in the soup bowl and the hot soup poured
over it. Finally, garlic can be pounded in a wooden mortar to extract
its juice. This is then mixed with strong vinegar, whole cloves, pepper and ginger and is firmly sealed up in bottles, to be kept in a
sunny spot so that the occasional spoonful can be added to a mixed
dish or sauce.

A few cloves of garlic can readily be added to any type of pickled
preserve because only the volatile, aromatic element of the garlic is
transferred to the vinegar or brine.

When I am making a cold pie, I put my garlic in the bottom of the
pie and put a little pastry lid over it to separate it from the filling.
This method causes the garlic smell to retreat humbly, subtly
flavouring the dish from its covered position.

A slice of hot, fresh toast, lightly rubbed with fresh garlic, moistened with good oil and generously salted is a country breakfast dish
in Italy. It certainly tastes much better than it smells.

In many countries, people love a leg of mutton steamed with quantities of garlic. This dish requires a very strong digestion.

Rocambole[87] is a small variety of garlic. It is more delicate, with a less powerful odour, and its bulbils, and especially its seeds, can be used in any type of filling for cold pies without any offence to the olfactory nerves.

Some people choose to classify onions[88] quite separately whilst others include them in the garlic family.

The onion has a less powerful odour than garlic and is more pleasant and tender to eat. It is also a little easier on the digestion. Onions are therefore much more suitable for consumption as an individual vegetable dish than garlic.

The longish variety of onion, known in some places as the Strassburg onion, makes an excellent accompaniment to boiled dishes, especially when it is young. These onions should be cleaned and then allowed to steam very gently in meat stock over a few slices of lightly browned bacon. They should be cooked until they are as soft as butter in the centre, whilst still retaining their decorative shape. At this point they should be removed from the fire and left to soak up all of the stock before being attractively arranged around the boiled joint on the serving dish.

Fully grown Spanish onions[89] can be hollowed out and filled with a favourite stuffing. They should be placed in a shallow casserole or saucepan in such a way that they cannot move, because otherwise the stuffing would fall out. The cooking pot should then be filled with stock or water to a depth of two fingers and should be allowed to steam away very gently. Every now and then, a few more spoonfuls of stock should be added, as necessary. When the onions are thoroughly soft and saturated with liquid, some butter should be added to the pot so that they brown a little. They are then ready for serving with a sharp brown sauce.

Small white onions can be boiled and served in a brown sauce with boiled dishes. They can also be included in chopped mixtures.

Sliced and lightly browned onions are used to enhance the flavour of all kinds of dishes. Chopped onion is included in various stuffings and sauces and is even combined with other vegetables. The onion flavour is indeed most appropriate on many occasions, but sometimes it is used in the most absurd manner. In German kitchens, I have seen spinach boiled in water and then wrung out with the hands so that it could not possibly retain any flavour or juice. After this treatment it was chopped up with raw onions and returned to the fire with some butter or stock. No-one will be surprised to hear that this tasted like a green onion purée, its colour alone being reminiscent of spinach.

With regard to flavour, the shallot,[90] a superior and well known type of onion, is preferable to the larger varieties. Its flavour is, however, too strong for it to be served as a vegetable dish in its own right.

Chives[91] are a popular flavouring in some areas. They are chopped or sliced finely and added raw to foods. I do not like them in soups but they are quite good mixed with small salad herbs and dressed with oil and vinegar, although I still find their flavour a little unpleasant.

The common leek,[92] which is also known as *Porree* in Germany, is a member of the garlic and onion family. It will give a good flavour to meat stocks when combined with other pot herbs, but it should not dominate. Young leek (the stem and fleshy base) is eaten as a vegetable with boiled joints. This dish has historical significance in Germany and, in some areas, it is still connected with particular days. In the extreme North, people look forward to it with pleasure as an early vegetable which relieves the long winter.

This edible part of the leek is known as *Kopflauch* in Germany [i.e. 'head' leek] as it also has a fleshy bulb at ground level. The word *Kopflauch* is good, pure German and should always be used in preference to the foreign *Porree*.

Spinach This plant,[93] with its pretty colour and mildly aromatic flavour, is very often consumed as a vegetable. Apart from its advantages from a dietetic point of view, it manages to flourish throughout the year, baulking only in the face of the sharpest frost or most persistent drought.

In some areas, people have fallen into the bad habit of boiling spinach in water, which is then poured away while the spinach is chopped and steamed in butter or meat stock before being served as a vegetable dish. As mentioned above, the spinach may also be given a new and foreign flavour by the addition of onions, and other intruders such as beurre manié and breadcrumbs may be used to bind it. This treatment of spinach is really most unsuitable.

If you like to eat your spinach finely chopped, it should, like so many other herbs, be blanched and then chopped. It can then be steamed very gently in water or meat stock over a moderate fire, with butter and salt being added as necessary. Flour and breadcrumbs will deprive spinach of a great deal of its natural freshness and flavour, but, if people insist, the use of these two ingredients is certainly preferable to that of chopped onions.

The Italians dig up the entire spinach plant when it is still in the first bloom of its youth. They remove only the outermost leaves and fibrous roots and steam the little plants whole, without cutting and chopping them. The roots of young spinach plants are indeed very tasty, imparting a trace of aromatic bitterness to the sweeter leaves and creating a flavour which will please even the most indulged palate after a few samples.

The combination of spinach and sorrel, steamed as above, is first rate.

A quantity of spinach will have a pleasant, mitigating effect upon the strong flavour of the bitter spring herbs. These are mostly wild and possess many beneficial properties, but many people, accustomed to sweet flavours, find them unpleasant. A good proportion of dandelion and watercress should be used in this herbal spinach, chervil, parsley, lettuce and any other aromatic herbs being added in smaller quantities. The mixture is chopped and steamed as above.

It is traditional in some parts of Germany to gather all sorts of wild herbs during the Easter week. Varieties such as orache, nettles, dandelions, watercress and young caraway shoots are chopped and combined to make a most delicious vegetable dish, similar to spinach. It is known as Negenschöne in the Saxon dialect.

One particular variety of beet[94] is cultivated only for the sake of its tender and edible leaves, which are prepared like spinach. As these leaves remain green, becoming even more tender, in the worst winter weather, the plant is often known as spinach beet. Quantities of it are grown on the barren upper slopes of the Swiss Alps, particularly in Urseren, and it has in the past been known as the Swiss beet because it spread throughout Europe from Switzerland. The juice of the true spinach has a very pleasant green colour and mild flavour so that it can be used to great advantage to give a good colour to all kinds of dishes and sauces. The pressed juice of raw spinach is indeed very unlikely to spoil any dish in which it is employed as a colouring, regardless of the amount used. It is ideal for giving an attractive shade to cold herb sauces.

To make a cold herb sauce, take one half part spinach and one quarter tarragon, the last quarter being a mixture of sorrel, purslane, parsley and chervil. Add a tiny shallot, or half of a larger one, with a few basil, marjoram and thyme leaves. Pound the mixture in a mortar made of wood or stone. Use a wooden spoon to remove the pulverized herbs and put them with boiling vinegar through a fine hair sieve into a clean earthenware pot. Put this pot on the fire and bring it just to the boil, then remove it. Salt and a pinch of saltpetre should be added at the outset to improve the colour. Allow the mixture to cool slowly, stirring it frequently so that it does not lose volume. The sauce may be thickened with olive oil, egg yolks, or a little semi-solidified white stock, as appropriate.

Sorrel Sorrel[95] leaves can enhance the flavour of stocks, they can flavour a variety of sauces and can be consumed as a vegetable, either alone, or mixed with other herbs.

Sorrel is especially mild, with a pleasant bitterness, in winter and spring and it is therefore particularly important at this time of year not to deprive it of this fine acidity by blanching it before cooking. It becomes more robust in summer and the pedantic German habit of blanching it before chopping and cooking is then less damaging to it.

Some people, being unable to stand any assertive flavour, like to add sugar to their sorrel dishes. I have reason to believe that sweetened sorrel actually engenders acids whilst the unsweetened version eliminates them.

It is quite appropriate to thicken steamed sorrel with an egg yolk mixed in a little stock.

A sauce can be made by boiling freshly chopped sorrel in meat stock and a variation is made by steaming tender sorrel leaves in meat stock, diluting this a little and then thickening it with a few egg yolks.

Endives We utilise two varieties of endives in our salads and vegetable dishes, the common broad-leaved type[96] and the curly endive.[97] The first type is less tender and tasty in salads than the curly variety but is better served as a vegetable. Broad-leaved endive should be cleaned, chopped and steamed in a little meat stock without further additions. It should never be cooked for so long that it loses its verdure because the loss of colour would indicate that most of its flavour had also been boiled away.

Broad-leaved endive may be made into a soup as follows: chop the leaves finely and cook them in plenty of meat stock until they still retain a little bite; thicken the broth with a beaten egg yolk. Toast slices of bread, place these in the soup tureen and pour over the endive soup.

As a winter vegetable, endive has extensive healing properties. If regularly consumed raw, it cleanses the body fluids and is particularly soothing to those with gum problems.

As I have said, curly endive is tastier and more tender and wholesome than the broad-leaved when eaten raw in salad. Despite this fact, this excellent variety has virtually been banned from most of our market places by the unrestricted laziness and malice of numerous German kitchenmaids who cannot be bothered to clean the curly leaves properly, checking through them for dirt and insects. A general agreement between these young women has meant that the growers who bring curly endive to market find no purchasers. There is no doubt that the male chefs themselves would also have had a hand in this conspiracy if they had not been in the habit of palming off on the fairer sex the lowly tasks of picking over and cleaning.

Lettuce   The term, salad, is used to describe all the various types of lettuce[98] which are used in the kitchen, although it actually denotes a particular method of preparation rather than a plant.

There are countless varieties of lettuces, though, on the whole, only a few are cultivated in Germany. The most popular types are the green and variegated lettuces which can also be used as salad herbs when picked very young. The excellent Roman lettuce does not appear to grow properly in Germany.

Like spinach, all of the lettuce varieties can be used as a vegetable. They can be included in a herbal spinach mixture and in herb soups. It is, however, more normal to serve them raw, dressed with oil, vinegar and salt like other salad vegetables. {To prepare lettuces as a vegetable, dip them in boiling water to make them collapse and immediately press the water out. Put them [in a pot] on the fire with a little butter and allow them to brown slightly. Add a drop of stock occasionally – just enough to keep the lettuce moist. Shake; do not stir. Cook the lettuce slowly and gently.

Other leafy salad plants such as endives and purslane may be treated similarly.}

Pot Herbs   We have already mentioned celery and sorrel. These two herbs are usually accompanied by parsley,[99] chervil,[100] purslane and tarragon in the stock pot. Any imaginative cook will know how to vary quantities and proportions according to circumstances.

Parsley is an ancient aromatic herb which has always been held in the highest regard, despite the dangers of confusing it with young hemlock plants. Apicius himself includes it in all kinds of stuffings and sauces and it does indeed give an attractive colour to any meat dish whilst also being compatible with a host of vegetables.

It is important not to overcook parsley, as this destroys its aroma and flavour. The principle to remember is that parsley will be tasty as long as it retains its beautiful green colour. Experience and practice will teach the cook just when to add this particular herb to the cooking.

The same details apply to all the other aromatic herbs, although tarragon can tolerate being boiled for longer than parley.

Herbs which have a strong and characteristic flavour and are therefore suitable only for certain dishes Nowadays, marjoram[101] and thyme[102] are hardly used except in sausages, and then they are used in dried and powdered form. Employed sparingly, they can, however, give an excellent flavour to other chopped mixtures. A few leaves of fresh marjoram will take the rancid flavour away from minced lamb and kid.

Basil,[103] especially the small-leaved variety, is a very pungent herb which should be used in minute quantities. It is always mixed with other herbs which soften and tone down its flavour, so that its musky quality does not become dominant.

Strictly speaking, angelica[104] is compatible only with sweet things. A good sweetmeat can be made by boiling it in sugar. The Italians use it raw with assorted mixtures.

Nowadays wormwood, both the common variety and the Roman,[105] is utilised only in distillations intended to fortify the stomach. The ancients used it much more assiduously. I must admit that I have little idea of how wormwood might be used with other foods. A very delicate wormwood flavouring would perhaps complement venison, or perhaps wild boar.

Capers[106] are the seeds and buds of a plant which frequently grows on walls and rocky areas in Italy and Greece. They are preserved in vinegar and we add them to sharp sauces and eat them raw in salads.

Saffron[107] is an absurd seasoning which is esteemed in some countries just for the sake of its beautiful yellow colour. Its flavour is quite weak, though not unpleasant.

Lovage, or ligusticum, is rarely used as an aromatic herb. It is mentioned by Apicius.

Tomatoes[108] are used to flavour sauces and soups in Southern Europe. They impart a pleasant, sharpish flavour and a fine orange colour. They are said to thicken the blood if consumed in excessive quantities. I have no idea why people are not attempting to cultivate this savoury fruit in Germany.

Apicius includes both mint[109] and lemon balm in those endless mixtures which we modern people would find most unpleasant. These plants are now used only in distillations. Some varieties of mint[110] are occasionally grown in garden frames and the new shoots used in mixed salads. A few leaves of mint and lemon balm can also be included in the herbal spinach mixture, if desired.

Rosemary occurs in various sauces in Southern Europe and is also used in stuffing poultry. Young branches of mugwort are used in a similar way in some parts of Germany.

Sage[111] makes a much better combination with roasts of all kinds. If little branches of common sage or Roman sage are placed between small birds on a spit, they will flavour the meat in a most appropriate manner. Sage can be placed between pieces of fresh eel on a spit, to be thoroughly roasted with the fish. It can also be crisped in clarified butter and used as an accompaniment to a variety of other baked goods.

The North Germans are fond of an extraordinary soup which is known as eel soup but could equally well be called 'Four Seasons' or 'Four Elements' soup. Sage is a traditional ingredient, without which the soup would hardly be edible. The powerful and assertive flavour of the herb is needed to give the muddle of ingredients a definite theme.

The flavour of rue[112] is so strong that it is not generally popular as an ingredient in herbal spinach, herb soups or in herb sauces, either hot or cold. Those who do like rue can add its fresh shoots to these herb mixtures.

A healthy breakfast to cleanse the blood can be made by eating rue, either alone, or mixed with other herbs, on slices of bread and butter. Young shoots of rue can be added to a green herb salad.

Some people add elderflowers,[113] which are known to be sudorific, to sweet dishes. They impart a rather flat, sweet flavour which is inclined to become unpleasant.

The South Germans use the young shoots of mugwort to stuff geese and ducks which are to be steamed or roasted. This plant flourishes around human settlements.

In North Germany there is one garden herb which traditionally accompanies broad beans and is therefore known as 'bean herb' [Bohnenkraut]. This is dill,[114] which is otherwise almost exclusively used in pickling cucumbers.

Nasturtium flowers can be pickled in vinegar and used like capers. They are my last entry in this list, which misses out several other less significant aromatic plants.

Mild flavoured salad herbs　When eaten raw, dressed with oil and vinegar, endives and all the lettuce varieties are not only pleasant to eat, but also very healthy.

Among the pot herbs, tarragon and purslane can also be used in green salads in combinations with milder herbs. The aromatic buds of nasturtium flowers will also improve the flavour of a mixed salad.

An excellent spring salad can be made by combining small garden cress[115] with young dwarf lettuce.

Watercress,[116] which I have already mentioned in the spinach category, makes a most wholesome salad.

A delicious salad can be made with the leaves and roots of rampion.[117] The knotty parts of the roots and outer, tougher leaves should be removed.

Scurvy grass, or Indian cress[118] will continue to flourish under winter snow. It is an excellent, healthy salad herb with a very bitter flavour. It is combined with sliced beets in winter.

The Italians use the bulbs of one of the fennel varieties in salads and desserts.

The leaves of pimpernell[119] may be included in a mixed salad.

Chopped borage,[120] dressed with oil and vinegar, is served as a garnish to boiled dishes.

Dandelions and the young shoots of all kinds of cultivated and wild plants are best eaten in spring time.

People have their own favoured methods of making all kinds of salads from herbs and roots, either cooked, raw or pickled, combined with meat, fish or salted products. German people are quite familiar with mixtures such as the so-called Italian salad and herring and sardine salads.

Fungi　The truffle is by far the best of the edible fungi. No-one will dispute that it is the jewel in the crown of any lavishly dressed table. Not all truffles are equally fragrant and tasty, however. The best come from the Périgord area and the Etsch valley, near Trento. The truffle should also be fully mature, without being over-ripe. Truffles which are beginning to decompose should be thrown away, even if they do retain a certain amount of goodness.

Any attached soil is normally removed from truffles by immersing them in simmering wine. Some like to peel them but their rather woody skin actually has the best flavour.

Truffles can be simmered in a mixture of wine and meat stock with whole peppercorns. They are then drained thoroughly, spread out on a cloth and served with fresh butter as a starter.

An Italian method is to heat slivers of truffles on a plate with oil, salt and pepper. Lemon juice is squeezed over them before serving or they may be sprinkled with parmesan cheese. The mixture can be served on slices of toast.

The entire civilised world is familiar with the truffle's power to flavour sauces, pies and stuffings. Once people realised what an effect foods can have upon human emotions, they started to make extensive use of delectable meals on ambassadorial missions. The channels of diplomacy have thus become a fine means of disseminating knowledge of special and rare flavours. Any ambassador who represents his master in words only is hardly regarded as doing his job properly. Regrettably this has led to an increase in the price of this ambiguous natural product at its very source, with the result that the pleasure of the quiet truffle gourmets is somewhat curtailed.

I have encountered one small variety of woody fungus, the prunjoli, only in Italy. This fungus is the equal of the truffle in terms of aroma and strength of flavour but is much less substantial. It may be added to all sorts of chopped mixtures and may, for example, be served on toast, combined with some sort of animal product.

Cultivated fungi, or mushrooms [champignons], are grown in special beds or can be found wild in horse pastures. Of all the fungi found in Germany, mushrooms have the most tender flesh and the best flavour. The English make a very spicy ketchup from old mushrooms and this has been confused with the Indian soya in our German cookery books.

There are many varieties of edible fungi. It is, however, easy to make a mistake and pick a similar, poisonous variety instead of an edible specimen. This explains why many people who value their lives refrain from consuming any sort of fungus at all.

There are some excellent books on the subject of fungi in general and in detail, and householders and cooks should be able to learn from these. Nature delights, however, in cloaking deadly poison and magical flavour in identical garb. There are various suggestions for testing whether fungi are poisonous. These include using onions and dipping in silver spoons. Some believe that they can tell from the smell of a fungus whether it is edible.

XI   Seasoning seeds, barks, roots, leaves used in dried form; also essences used for seasoning.

The dried and pulverised leaves of marjoram and thyme are currently the commonest indigenous seasonings of this sort. Other leaves may be mixed with them. We also have the bitter caraway,[121] a better variety of which is cultivated mainly in Malta, coriander[122] and anise,[123] which, in Southern Europe, is consumed in its immature state, rather like a fruit. Many German people have become accustomed to using these seeds. Like juniper berries, caraway can be used in many instances where the intention is to create a strong, robust flavour. Caraway is an ideal flavouring for boiled crayfish while juniper berries are good in a salmi of small birds.

Bay leaves, both fresh and dried, have been used for centuries. The ancients also made use of myrtle berries but these have been neglected in recent times. I shall not deal with mustard[124] because it is so well known.

Many more spices come from outside Europe, mostly from the Tropics. Pepper is the most useful of these. Every housemaid knows that there are black and white peppers which have a very similar flavour.

Spanish pepper is a capsicum[125] which has a similar flavour to vine pepper but surpasses all other spices in its warming and inflammatory effects. Cayenne pepper, which has recently become so popular, is prepared from one capsicum variety.[126] This spice is the salvation of anyone whose digestive system has suffered in a hot, moist climate and was first used widely in the swamps of Guyana. The large numbers of people with consumption and liver problems sadly indicate the damage done by our seafarers in trying to transplant the lifestyles of the Indies, West and East, to Europe. Every year, these sufferers travel from England and the continental seaports to Southern Europe and contemporary English doctors have become expert at selecting the best places where their consumptive patients may end their days.

A less hot variety of Spanish pepper is grown in sheltered areas in Europe and is used, when still green, to flavour pickles of all kinds. If used with discretion, a few fresh green chilli peppers will improve the flavour of pickled cucumbers without being harmful to the blood. The Italians and the English are in the habit of pickling large jars full of chillies and their habit of using two or three to garnish meat broths can be most agreeable.

Some Italians adulterate their wine with this spice.

Ginger[127] is another very hot spice. As a result of one of mankind's inconstancies, which continually puzzle historians, it has recently fallen from favour and is now hardly used. I cannot really think where to include ginger in the framework of cookery. I have occasionally made use of the rather milder cardamom, in goose-liver pie for example. In the East Indies, fresh ginger is used to make a valued and stimulating drink.

Cloves are a little milder than pepper but do have a tendency to sweetness. The current bad habit of combining them with all sorts of foods is therefore not appropriate. The clove is a most delicate and effective flavouring if it is used with care and mixed with other ingredients.

Allspice, or Jamaica pepper, is less sweet than cloves and can therefore be more widely used.

Cinnamon[128] and vanilla are used in sweet dishes in rather the same way as orange and lemon peel. In Germany these peels are all too often used in savoury, strongly flavoured dishes also. The flavour of cinnamon is, however, used to good effect in certain savoury dishes such as pilaus, polenta and juliennes.

Pistacios, pine nuts and almonds are being used less and less in European kitchens. They make sweet dishes heavy and indigestible and the flavour and colour which they imparted to creams and jellies is now being supplied by other starchy fruit. Many people cannot bear the flavour of the oil contained in these aromatic nuts. Tamarinds are frequently used in the East but not at all in Europe.

The English have assimilated certain Indian dishes through their conquest of that continent, and their increased use of all the hot spices has engendered those powerful fish essences which are known to our epicures under the general term of soya. Chinese and Japanese soya is prepared from vegetable substances which are malted, crushed and fermented. Please refer to the learned Beckmann on this subject.

In Tonkin, people salt down crabs and small fish in stoneware jars. These are sealed and left alone until their contents have broken down into a thick liquid. This evil smelling essence does have a pleasant flavour and spiceloving Europeans use it as the basis for their soya.

According to Forster, the Moluccan Malay people in Jakarta and Capetown garnish all of their dishes with a savoury sauce made of some sort of small fish, salted down. They add spices, and probably garlic, to this sauce, which they call achar.

The famous sauce known as bakassan is prepared from tellin[129] in Indonesia, particularly on the island of Ambon. According to Rumphius,[130] who describes the method of preparation in detail, there is a white and a black variety. The black sauce is made from the dark, fatty substances, with spices, while the white is made from the flesh itself, with vinegar and plenty of spice. The English are exporting these sauces to Europe but I am not at all sure of the quantities involved. There is no doubt that many people confuse the English ketchup, made from salted mushrooms and spices, with the Indonesian soya.

It is very likely that these essences date back to the earliest times in Indonesia and we can safely assume that the Greeks and Romans used them as a model for their garum and liquamen. Why should we allow our own laziness, this crippling symptom of our apparently busy age, to prevent us from making soya ourselves. Why should we not prepare the delicious garum sociorum by the Straights of Cadiz as in Roman times? If only some enterprising Englishman could rediscover the recipe for the king of all the sauces, then the secret would be out and the course of world history made clear, Gibraltar would be occupied by the British and gloriously defended by Elliot. After all, the frugal Spanish, who have no industrial development, can never be expected to enrich the world's food repertoire in any conceivable way.

XII   Sugar, Fruit and all Kinds of Sweet Things

I ought now to write about the history and widespread use of raw sugar but it is more appropriate to refer to the Swede, Bengt Bergius,[131] who devotes half of his most informative book to observations concerning this commodity. He did not know of the more recently discovered sugar substitutes but, although these are historically important because of the Continental System [Napoleon's plan for shutting out England from all commercial connection with Europe], from a culinary point of view they are too insignificant to merit more than an occasional mention. Honey however, although its culinary applications are not as diverse as those of straightforward sweet sugar, is being neglected too much nowadays. Its complex, aromatic sweetness attains a magical quality in the fine mountain honeys produced in the South and is infinitely better than the finest sugar in certain recipes, such as the famous pan forte of Siena. It is most regrettable that people in the North have almost abandoned the making of honey wine, or mead, in their homes. This type of drink must be better than all the artificial wines which ruin the teeth and the digestion, and may even damage the central nervous system, if consumed regularly.

On the other hand, sugar does blend much better than the rather resinous honey with all kinds of cereal dishes, milk and egg dishes, creams, whipped snow puddings and so on. The Romans and Greeks were not nearly as advanced as we are in this particular aspect of cookery.

Sugar also combines much better than honey with the acidity of all the various fruit juices. Our fruit preserves must therefore be considerably better than those of the ancients.

The subject of confectionery covers fruit preserving as well as the wideranging topic of the preparation of sweet dishes. I shall therefore leave it out.

I shall simply point out that any fruit which is to be preserved should be picked in dry weather. Stone fruits which are to be dried in the oven or boiled in sugar should not be used until they are tender and ripe.

The art of making dry conserves was formerly very widespread in the South. People used to exchange whichever fruits were most luscious and ripe in their areas. Guzman[132] gives an interesting description of this. Nowadays the French are the experts in this subject. The dried fruits and fruit jellies of Havana are still excellent, however.

XIII   Teaching People to Cook

The art of cookery itself presents no problems when people are learning to cook. This is amply demonstrated by my book. The basic rule could not be easier to grasp: make the very best of every edible substance. No other sphere of man's knowledge and activity contains so many connections and logical progressions. Even if he is not very experienced, a cook can easily progress from one step to the next. The difficulty does not therefore lie with the art itself, but in our ability, or rather inability to learn it properly.

Many boys and girls who set out to learn the art of cookery are not truly dedicated to it. Their thoughts are on the respectable financial reward when they should at first be concentrating on the skill they are learning. Once mastered, the skill will soon bring its rewards, as a tree bears fruit. No-one is likely to do well in a subject if he did not have a basic feel for it in the first place.

Infected with an excessively servile veneration of his master, a young cook will often lose himself in the maze of unnecessary complications left over from outdated styles of cookery. He will not be receptive to new views and will be unable to learn from his own experience and thoughts. I have actually seen young cooks spending entire days practising the art of sprinkling salt over dishes but I very much doubt whether the food would have tasted any better.

Then we come to the real spanners in the works: the pushy upstarts and young know-it-alls. There is nothing to be done about these. At the age when I was still cheerfully washing dishes and basins, picking over spinach and undertaking other elementary duties, no kitchen boy today can be seen for dust. He wants to be at the front line, bungling the skilled jobs and pushing ahead of his master before he has even a basic grounding in hygiene and orderliness, before he has learnt the basic principles by watching and listening. This situation should not be tolerated any longer. Nature has turned on her head and history gone into reverse.

Female cooks are totally lacking in basic training. Their minds are so full of cleaning, fashions and other idle notions that there is no room for a proper understanding of principles. Their hearts are rarely in their cooking. This makes them all the more obstinate – they will not be diverted from their familiar path. I have tried in vain to improve the ways of hundreds of German cooking women. Whenever I have poked my nose into a German kitchen run by women, the early morning scene has resembled a washhouse, despite my attempts to enlighten them by my words and deeds. Here would be a basin of pot herbs, swimming in water, there would be the day's salad, similarly inundated; here the soup meat would be steeping in cold, or even lukewarm, water, there the roasting meat and fish in the same state. I am amazed at the power of German pedantry, its lack of sexual bias, even if it does stem from our old tradition of integrity. Cooking-women seem to believe themselves entitled to dispense with all such traditions, however. Unfortunately the order of the day is cheating over the shopping because housewives have grown too lazy, too ignorant and too falsely refined to keep proper storecupboards. This means that every day of the year brings its necessary expenditure, and the women will always think of themselves when spending money, resulting in chaotic penny-pinching in bourgeois households. The high drama and domestic battles are causing unprecedented restlessness among the kitchenmaids in our German towns.

I should like to contrast these tales of abrupt proceedings and garish scenes with a pleasant picture of peaceful, resigned domesticity. Excellent serving women and good housewives do exist and I hope that some of them will read these pages. The numbers of these fine serving women would be greatly increased if only they were properly paid for their work and were treated with more justice and less caprice. There are still only a few people who follow the advice of the aforementioned Rumpolt,[133] who begins:

'The master should be in command of his servants but should be able to handle them in a friendly and amicable way. His words of command should not be proud, inflated, overbearing, immodest, violent. He should not rant and rave but should behave with great gentleness, sweetness, friendliness and modesty so that his running of the household takes the form of amicable requests and demands rather than a series of harsh orders. A lot of violent ranting and raving will confuse people, making them more stubborn and unwilling, and little will be achieved.'

Anyone who wishes to devote himself to cookery should grasp the concepts of orderliness, hygiene and punctuality early in life. He should not be allowed to read novels; if he wishes to develop his intellect he should study the natural sciences, history and mathematics; these will exercise his intelligence, improve his memory and give him knowledge which he can later apply to cookery. He should also read my book and no other.

Book Three :
Eating

I   Teaching People to Eat

It is not sufficient to return to the basic principles of food preparation and to demonstrate the application of these principles by examples. The entire art of cookery would just be a useless contrivance if it did not succeed in promoting and maintaining a feeling of healthy well-being. This state can only be achieved through sensible eating, which would at first appear to be a natural instinct but is in fact a great art, requiring more education than anyone would imagine.

One only has to associate with the uncivilised people in the far corners of the world, or to sit at the table of a father who, as so often happens, is bringing up his children like wild animals, in order to realise that clean, modest and peaceful eating habits do not come naturally to mankind. Such habits are, however, necessary for social eating, and for the very health of the consumers.

Three different methods of teaching people to eat have followed each other in quick succession in those countries where people have not neglected so-called social education. The old-fashioned fatherly approach came first in all cases and although this had its advantages, the method was flawed in that it placed artificial restrictions on nature rather than encouraging natural development.

The attached copperplate,[134] by an artist who experienced and clearly remembers this period, depicts one of these traditional households. The lady of the house has the word but the father employs his bearing and sharp eye to uphold the rules and authoritative decisions made by his wife. He is the director and has banished under the table any potential naughtiness on the part of his repressed children. The servants are even more intimidated, of course. After the sound of the dinner gong in such a house, the people would be able to dish up the food, carve it and eat it without smashing the dishes, cutting their fingers or burning their mouths but this is not the natural, inborn way to behave. If the lady of the house were to allow her tongue a rest and the master were to relax his right arm, the pleasing state of order would rapidly dissolve. The children and servants would probably revert to the most uncivilised behaviour patterns if relations and neighbours did not take charge of the neglected household.

In recent decades, the spirit of the times has gradually led to the suppression of this rigid way of bringing up children. And as people always have a tendency to go from one extreme to the other, there was a great rush to emancipate children from their general oppression, restriction and constraints. It is a feature of the new humanity that children are also granted rights but people should not have forgotten that this made it all the more important to instill in them an awareness of their duties. The newly released prisoner needs to understand wrong from right more clearly than anyone else.

I have found an old book[135] which expresses the duties of young people at table in the following words:

'How a boy should prepare himself for a meal and how he should prepare the table. Before you sit down to the table, you should have everything ready and in its proper place; that is, the water, wine, beer and so on; wash and clean the drinking vessels, lay the tablecloth and put out the knives, saltcellar, plates, spoons and bread. If the bread is rather burnt and has any ash, cinders or other dirt sticking to it, you should slice it finely and distribute it among the plates.

'When the meal is finished, the table should be cleared correctly; first the plates, etc, and lastly the tablecloth, which should be shaken out over an ordinary basket. If anything edible is left over, it should be taken away so that it can be put to good use either for people or animals and will not be wasted.

'Before the guests sit down at the table, you should fold your hands and recite the grace slowly and clearly. You should say "Aller Augen, Vater unser" (Our Father, all eyes) and "Herre Gott himmlischer Vater" (Dear God, Heavenly Father) etc, as described in Luther's Catechism.'

How a boy should behave when waiting at table.

'First of all you should stand up straight, feet together, and watch carefully to make sure that nothing is missing, goes astray or is broken. This applies to bread, plates, spoons, salt and other items. And when you are serving food, passing it to people or placing things upon the table, you should conduct yourself sensibly, modestly and slowly so that nothing is spilt.

'Do not speak to anyone who is already engaged in conversation; nor should you eavesdrop whilst keeping silent yourself; you cannot

worry about what you do not know. You should give your full attention to your duties and do not allow yourself to be distracted. Try to do
as you are bidden and avoid those things which do not concern you.

'If anyone asks you a question, reply briefly. At night time you
should trim the lamp with care and be sure that you do not offend
anyone with the bad smell caused thereby. Be sure that you do not
extinguish the lamp completely. You must not nibble any food which
is being removed from the table or kept, nor must you conceal
any food about your person. Certain scroungers at court are in the
habit of doing this and it looks bad and will have evil effects in the
long run.

'When everyone has finished eating and the table has been cleared,
the final prayer and thanksgiving should not be forgotten.'

How a boy should behave when he joins others for a meal at table.

'If you are to join others for a meal at table, you should behave in
the following manner. Just before the meal, cut your nails so that
they do not look as if they are trimmed with velvet, wash your hands
and take your place quietly. Sit upright and do not be the first to grab
the dishes. Do not slurp your soup like a pig; neither should you
blow the food so that it is splashed over the table. Do not snuffle like
a hedgehog; do not be the first to drink; be moderate and avoid
drunkenness. Drink and eat as much as your body requires; once you
are satisfied, do not make yourself ill. When everyone has had a
helping from the dish, you can take your turn.

'Do not let your hands rest on your plate for any length of time. Do
not swing your legs about under the table like a linen weaver.

'If you have a drink, wipe your chops with a napkin, not with your
hand. Do not drink with your mouth full of food. Do not dip anything which you have bitten back into the serving dish. Do not lick
your fingers and do not knaw on bones – use your knife to cut the
meat you want from a bone.

'Do not poke your teeth with your knife. Use a toothpick or quill.
The knife will make your teeth go rusty, just like water with iron.
Keep one hand in front of your mouth if you must pick your teeth.
Do not cut the bread across your chest. Eat whatever is in front of
you at the time and do not reach across the table; do not turn the dish
around so that you can reach something that you particularly like.

'If you wish to carve meat or fish, do this with a knife and not with
your fingers as do the people in some countries today.

'Do not scoff your food noisily, like a pig. Do not scratch your
head or pick your nose while you are eating.

'Do not speak with your mouth full. This is a coarse habit.

'Frequent sneezing, blowing the nose and coughing will not be popular.

'If you are going to eat an egg, you should cut up the bread first. Do not make the bread soldiers too large or too long. Be sure that none of the egg drips and eat it swiftly. Do not break the egg shell – it should be replaced in the serving dish. You should eat the egg properly, not drink it.

'Do not spill food on the tablecloth or down your clothes. Do not make a spoil heap of bones, crusts and other refuse around your plate like someone digging for treasure.

'Do not throw bones under the table. This might cause a fight amongst the dogs and would displease the other people at the table. When you have finished eating, wash your hands and face, rinse your mouth and offer God your praise and gratitude for his fatherly blessings.'

These instructions to young people are certainly quite reasonable and it would have been a good idea if people had referred back to such standards of behaviour when they threw off the iron yoke of the distorted customs of a few decades ago. For, although it would have been harmful to young people to force them into dogged, rigid behaviour patterns, it would not have been necessary to renounce totally their natural sense of order. Nowadays the parents are all too often the first victims of the revolution I have described. How often do we see mothers deferring to their daughters and sinking before them into a state of unseemly servitude, when the daughters are certainly no better at running the household.

As a contrast to his first picture, my artist has attempted to depict a meal time in a liberated household which is being run according to the latest fashion. The woman of the house, who is probably a writer, appears to be reading through a proof sheet and is so absorbed in her cerebral activities that she is forgetting all about the basic reality of eating. The husband, on the other hand, seems to be concerned only with satisfying his hunger as quickly as possible. The unkempt and grubby children are knawing bones, messing about with the bowls and dishes and making themselves and others more dirty.

Today's school of thought – if something which has hitherto been no more than a trend can be referred to thus – has perhaps set its goal too high. It is attempting, so far unsuccessfully, to realise the ideal state. We shall refrain from offering a picture of something which has not yet happened. If, however, we were to attempt to put these exalted aims into words, they would run something like this:

The children shall be allowed to say 'we are hungry, we are thirsty; we would like such and such a food, or such and such a drink'. The parents, however, reserve the right to grant the necessary permission; no child is allowed to help himself without parental sanction.

The children are also expected to comb their hair, wash themselves and be properly dressed. On the other hand the parents allow them to enter the room freely and confidently and to take their places without being asked.

Finally the children are allowed to choose whether they wish to say prayers before eating. As long as it does not annoy their parents, they are allowed to talk at will during the meal.

It must be quite obvious that the new school of thought is attempting to be all things to all people. On the other hand it must be evident that this striving is going to encounter some obstacles in its path. A child might, for example, crave a dish which the father wishes to reserve for himself and this will displease the father, regardless of whether he refuses the child the dish, or whether he allows it.

I am afraid that people are likely to persist in this behaviour rather than returning to the habits of former times because their laziness predisposes them to abandon anything difficult. It is therefore vital that all parties are made fully aware of their duties, as well as their rights. It would be useful to instill in them a certain sense of what is reasonable. This would then teach them, without their realising it, not to crave things which would demand too great a sacrifice on the part of the person granting the permission. Children tend to have a good appetite and the parents should not of course deny them plenty of healthy food, whether for reasons of general stinginess, or because they themselves have a greedy desire for the food in question. On the other hand, the children should start by getting used to the fact that adults do take precedence over them.

On the subject of good behaviour during the business of eating, it is necessary to convince intelligent children that it is in their own interest to deport themselves correctly, to be clean and to eat quietly, chewing food slowly; also that nothing is achieved by noisy, idle conversation; that chatter is an affectation or an unconscious addiction to a specific form of physical exercise [i.e. of the vocal chords!]. In his natural state, man prefers silence to talking and any educated man will say only as much as is necessary. There is little to be done if the children are not very bright. It will be necessary to resort to physical punishment to make them learn.

A great deal depends upon whether children are instructed from an early age in the proper use of cutlery, forks, knives and spoons. Etiquette varies in this respect too. For example, the English place the knife on the right hand side and the fork on the left. They cut the food with the right hand and use the left to transport it to the mouth. This method simplifies matters and should therefore be recommended to Europeans who tend to put down their knife after they have cut off a morsel so that they can then take their fork in their right hand and use this to conduct the food to the mouth. When they have drunk their soup, the Bavarians tend to lick their spoons clean and then keep them on the table because they are afraid of missing out on the sauces served with subsequent dishes. The wealthy Dutch lay from six to eight silver spoons at each place for the same reason. It is true that foods should not be served swimming in sauce in the style of South German country people; a sauce of the right consistency will cling to each mouthfull and any that is left over can be mopped up with pieces of bread.

It would be so easy to win over our growing youth to the simplified English way of eating and to break them of habits such as licking their spoons, chattering and making awful noises whilst eating.

178

II   Simplicity or Complexity of Dishes

The ancients are divided in their opinions as to whether a simple diet or a mixed diet is the more beneficial to mankind. The followers of Hippocrates are for simplicity while the Aristoteleans defend complexity. Emphasis was, however, placed upon the fact that not all nutritious foods are equally digestible. Rules were applied only to individual meals, not to the annual calendar of consumption. If we had more precise knowledge of the properties of individual food-stuffs we should be able to envisage a meal structure in which a perfect balance of nutritious items was achieved each time. The suitability of a meal is affected not only by the properties of the food-stuffs but also by the digestive abilities of the individual consumers. Every person would therefore be wise to make a mental note of his food experiences, so that he eats only those things which, either alone or combined with others, really suit him.

Bearing this point in mind, a meal for a small number of people should consist of a small number of suitable dishes while a feast for many people should comprise many dishes so that each person may choose his ideal food.

For the same reason, any generous table set for a convivial meal should include dishes fit for all of the participants. These dishes can be offered to anyone while the spread should also include items likely to appeal only to certain individuals. When feasting, Nordic people, and also the Germans, often make the mistake of passing every single dish around the table, with the result that the guests overload their stomachs out of sheer boredom and weariness. I intend to suggest some ways of avoiding this evil in my chapter on the organisation of feasts and banquets. Following my examples, the emphasis will be placed only on those guests who are greedy enough to want to try everything. It will be a service to such people if each course is removed as quickly as possible, the meal being structured so that even the most industrious eater can get through a maximum of two dishes in each course. In this way the honour of the house will be maintained, leaving an impression of generosity and good order. The health of the immoderate eater will not be impaired while the sensible guest will not feel that he has been force-fed or even choked.

To return to the main point, it appears that the followers of Hippocrates had lost sight of the effects of chemical breakdown in their consideration of how foodstuffs are combined. Cooks do have a vague feeling for these effects. If ingredients are skillfully combined in a dish, or in a series of dishes, each food type can encourage and assist the breakdown of the others, for dry foods and moist foods will help each other, as will fat and lean, cold and hot.

Furthermore, we do not eat purely to nourish ourselves. Eating can also bring about the thinning or cleansing of our bodily fluids as well as either stimulating or calming us. A healthy human being will instinctively seek out or avoid these effects in foods, as will the more intelligent animals. This is why the same dish may appeal to a person at one age and not at another, or even in one particular state of health, and not in another.

The increase in variety of foodstuffs is also of importance in world history. People who have a mixed diet are able to position their settlements closer together because they are less likely to experience famine. Different grains, plants and animals require different temperatures and different soils. A seasonal pattern which is damaging to one species may encourage another. Fate affects different areas and climates in different ways and it is fortunate if, in the event of a crisis, people know how to utilise the products of other lands.

An over simple diet has concentrated the population of China in the ricegrowing areas, where water is plentiful. There are said to be vast numbers of people who do not have enough to eat. There are suggestions that the Chinese ought to be able to introduce the cultivation of rye, barley, oats and potatoes in their barren Northern provinces which, according to the accounts of travellers, are as devoid of people as the great river valleys and plains are overpopulated. Each year it would then be possible to send colonists from the overpopulated areas to the empty regions, which appear to be very extensive indeed.

When we think of the ready progress of European culture, we do not often remember how much we have to thank the ancient Greeks and Romans[136] for their developments in agriculture and the art of cookery. The ability to feed a large population, even on relatively infertile land, is a legacy of the ancient world which was faithfully preserved like an insignificant curiosity in the monasteries of the Middle Ages, to be passed on to a new, hard-working, but most ungrateful, generation.

In recent times we have gained much from the discoveries of sea voyages and science. Such a huge abyss remains, however, between the ponderings of the theorists and everyday life that only a few foodstuffs, such as the potato, have become truly widespread.

Despite this, the increase in quantity and variety of edible natural products has outstripped demand in recent decades. We need an overall increase in the population. We need improved laws and better governments in the countries bordering the Mediterranean, and in the New World, to encourage a growth in population to suit their expansion and to utilise the fruits of our industry. Alternatively, we should emulate the Romans and the other civilised peoples of the ancient World in attempting to deploy the resources of an idle population, which we are able to feed, but cannot fully occupy, in great public works. Some of these works, canals and major roads for example, will be of lasting benefit to the fabric of the country, while other constructions will improve the quality of life. If, as some people maintain, there is insufficient finance for such works, there is still no shortage of grain to feed the workers, and the imposition of a tax on the less marketable natural products would not be too burdensome at present.

If only people were willing to make the mental leap from abstract considerations of hard cash, or even imaginary sums, to the reality of everyday circumstances, it would be easy to conquer the most excessive of all the evils, the evil of excess. When a country has people whose potential is not employed in the private sector, but for whom there is sufficient food, we have a state of true affluence and an excess workforce for deployment in special projects. Public works such as the aqueducts, bridges and military roads of the Romans and the irrigation systems in Lombardy owe their existence, not to money, but to man's steadfast perseverance, because such works can only be undertaken where there is an excess of human potential.

III   Emotions and States of Mind which should not be stimulated or encouraged while eating, either in oneself or in others

There are some emotions which occasion an excessive surge of bile; others excite the nervous system and cause harmful contractions of the digestive system; some states of mind actually impair the function of these organs.

The following emotions will have the effects mentioned:

Firstly: Indignation. In this case the provocation occurs when an unexpected occurrence gives offence to our own person, to our friends or even to our opinions. Anyone with proper feelings will not inflict a personal insult on someone else without good reason but it is particularly important that intentional insults be totally avoided during mealtimes. Inexperienced people who are not accustomed to social intercourse are, however, very likely to fall into the trap of unintentionally insulting others. Any intelligent person who notices them should therefore not take them too seriously. He should control himself, so that he does not himself become the victim of pointless indignation. On the other hand, it is easy to offend people quite unintentionally if they are not very bright and do not have the capacity to interpret correctly every nuance of an expression. When speaking to stupid people, intelligent guests will therefore measure their words much more precisely, taking special care to avoid irony, which is usually completely lost on the simple-minded. If everyone at the table is stupid, it is most fortunate if they are all of a phlegmatic temperament. If the reverse is true, it will be useful to play loud music during the meal, a practice which I reject as harmful and disruptive in any other circumstances.

We tend to be much more ambivalent about insults offered to friends than about those which affect ourselves. It is, however, impossible to suggest any firm rule here because the social nuances of friendship are so very varied. Suffice it to say that we should take particular care to protect both very new friends and our long-established, well-tried friends. This is because those friends who are neither brand new, nor semi-retired, tend to be more ambivalent towards us.

Insulting a man's opinions is a most delicate matter which should be avoided if at all possible. For people have the highest opinion of their own opinions; they treasure them like children; in fact, the more they feel unable to formulate different or new opinions, the more they will value the existing ones.

There are two distinct types of opinion. One type will gradually become firmly embedded in the soul during a man's lifetime while the second type will strike the soul like a flash of lightning. The first type should never ever be approached too closely but the second type can always be assailed through jokes and other intellectual artillery, so that they explode and rumble around as they did originally.

Secondly: Anger. Anger is aroused by provocative speech which imperceptibly increases a man's indignation until it becomes a lasting mood. Therefore anger is no more than a state of prolonged indignation and is induced by the same factors. If one refrains from arousing indignation, anger will also be avoided. Once a man's indignation has been aroused, however, there is still time to divert his anger. As we may occasionally prevent a conflagration by tearing down a building, a state of indignation can likewise be soothed by calm and indulgence, together with appropriate apologies. The threat of approaching anger will then be quelled.

Thirdly: Annoyance. This is a state of suppressed anger which is again induced by the same factors as the above. The difference here is that the angry man is unable to express his feelings, either because he is overexcited or because he is nervous and afraid. As the vicious hyena is the most terrible of the hunting animals, so this particular mood will be the most detrimental to a meal.

The following states of mind will cause contractions of the stomach:

Firstly: Embarrassment. This normally arises from conversations in which no-one succeeds in expressing his opinion properly. The people most prone to this harmful state of mind are married couples and friends who are harbouring some sort of mistrust, grudge or resentment against each other but are not yet ready to give vent to their feelings. It is best in such cases if the parties concerned have a good, frank discussion some time before the meal and, if they find themselves unable to iron out the misunderstandings, they should not eat together. Embarrassment may also arise where the people around a table are not equally endowed from an intellectual point of view, or where their standards of education and cultivation are too disparate, so that no one person is willing to drop his guard before his fellows. During a meal therefore, no-one should boast and press his superior knowledge, nor should he hold forth in languages which are not adequately understood by the other guests. I should even like to advise people against vague, half-baked attempts at making their fellows aware of any class differences because this can cause a certain degree of embarrassment where their intellectual capacity is otherwise equal. Embarrassment will reach its most dangerous extreme where people get involved in conversations in which they find themselves unable either to agree wholeheartedly or to openly disagree. In such circumstances it is useful to call upon people such as diplomats who are accustomed to not speaking their minds too openly in their tinpot political discussions. In this particular case, it will be a great advantage if such a person is well schooled in the art of charming others and is graced with a lively and sociable sense of humour. He will then find it quite easy to engage others in innocent, amusing conversation which will not dry up.

Secondly: Humiliation. A table-fellow will feel humiliated if attention is drawn to any of his physical or spiritual defects or weaknesses, infirmities or even vices, which are not suitable for mention in polite company. We all encounter some unfortunate incidents during our lives and allusions to these can be most unpleasant. We tend to feel much more ashamed about specific incidents in our lives simply because we feel that others then consider us capable of, or likely to, cause such incidents. People who have an exalted opinion of themselves, or who at least consider themselves superior to others should never be made to feel their vacuousness and negativity during the course of a meal. If action becomes unavoidable, corrective sermons should be preached during the hours of the morning. Unless the offenders are totally inured, they will necessarily feel very ashamed. People who are very foolish will also feel ashamed if they are made aware of a superiority of rank or wealth.

It is merciful to spare people other forms of humiliation and, when at the table, it is wise to harden oneself against all types of shame.

Thirdly: Uneasiness. This arises when conversation is fickle and irrelevant; when everyone tries to speak at once; when no-one has any accurate knowledge of the topic of conversation and, finally, when illogical people try to debate a subject, even if they do have some knowledge of it.

The threat of uneasiness can easily be avoided during a meal if people try to control themselves and restrain their own vanity and egotism.

Fourthly: Stress. This is caused when people try to express concepts which others find irksome and difficult to understand. Conversations touching upon metaphysics and mathematics should be banned forever from our tables. Admittedly, the Greeks had quite different ideas on this subject but we poor Germans even find it difficult to express ourselves clearly and succinctly on matters of domestic and public life.

The following states of mind may impair the function of the digestive organs:

Firstly: Sleepiness. This dangerous mood may be caused by a person's own thoughtlessness but is more likely to arise when one particular guest monopolises the conversation, rolling out meaningless thoughts in a wearisome tone.

Secondly: Stupefaction. This is the result of excessive noise or meaningless, confused talk, violent laughter and other exaggerated behaviour. Playing music during meals tends to stupefy people and is therefore reprehensible. Many years ago, Shakespeare accused the Germans of being too noisy at the table. Nowadays this reproach applies only to the public rooms in German inns or to the civic banquets held in some areas, rather than to the German nation as a whole.

IV   Correct Employment of Meal Times in the Home

I make no bones about the fact that it is much more important to have an adequate, decent, hygienic and appetising meal every day of the year, than to have splendid and opulent dinner parties now and then. Although it is both amusing and expedient to give the occasional banquet, to gather one's friends around and let one's hair down a little, it is really the daily pattern of ordinary meals which nourishes and invigorates, fortifies and restores our strength.

This is why I have concentrated on describing the most straightforward methods of preparing the cheapest and most wholesome foodstuffs in my books. In places where I had a choice between a rare delicacy or an everyday domestic dish of the country, I have preferred the latter.

Anyone who has grasped my basic concept will not lack inspiration and will be able to provide an adequate, pleasing meal every day of the year, even if supplies are limited. The prudent housewife[137] will start her meal with a hearty soup which can be made very simply from meat or fish stock, or even water, with any sort of puréed cereal matter, after which she will have the choice of the entire range of salted products and pickles, fresh butter, radishes and so on. She will be able to serve dainty items such as salt herrings and pickled gherkins, radishes and fresh butter, slices of quality sausage or smoked ham in elegant small dishes, and the remains of any kind of salted joint will provide her with the wherewithal to serve three or four little appetisers, without any great trouble. A boiled joint will follow, then vegetables, accompanied by baked or grilled meat and fish, depending on whether impoverished circumstances permit the daily consumption of a roast. Finally there will be light puddings, clotted cream, or cheese and fresh or preserved fruits to close the meal.

Examples
A family meal for a fasting day

Soup made of grated potatoes with fish stock (see Chapter Twelve), or crayfish with a pea purée, or greens wilted in freshly melted butter, or other ingredients.

Appetisers: Fresh herrings or sardines, smoked salmon, caviare, or other smoked fish, such as eel and the black trout from Berchtesgaden, which need to be warmed through on the grill; also marinated fish. In coastal areas, oysters, mussels or crabs may be served. As a contrast there may be sour cucumbers or small gherkins, French beans, cucumber and other vegetables pickled in spiced vinegar. There may also be a dish of small radishes or large black radish with fresh butter or, if these are not in season, a little blanched, sliced celery with salt, pepper and vinegar.

Main Course: A boiled fish served on potatoes which have been boiled dry, then allowed to absorb some of the fish stock on the serving dish. If the fish is not an oily one, the dish may be spread with some fresh butter (see Book One, Chapter 10).

Some mild vegetables, such as spinach, sorrel or a herb mixture with baked fish or, if there is no fish, with eggs or toast.

To finish, a spit-roasted or grilled fish with salad; or some sort of pudding sweetened with fruit or sugar.

A family meal for a normal day

Meat broth with bread, vegetables or some sort of flour-based preparation.

Appetisers: A few slices of ham or smoked sausage; a small dish of cold meat, roast or otherwise, in jelly. Vegetables as above. A skilled cook will sometimes add variety by serving a few delicacies fried in clarified butter.

Main Course: Boiled meat, served on its own or garnished with vegetables.

Vegetables with baked or grilled meat. If a roast is served, it should be accompanied by salad and the vegetables can be served in two smaller dishes with the boiled meat. Fruit, cheese and cold milk puddings form the dessert.

The Italians are more accustomed to beginning their meals with appetisers than are the Germans. The practice allows economical use of delicacies which are often expensive. These delicacies impress people more at the start of a meal. They stimulate the digestive juices and take the edge off peoples' hunger, so that they do not gobble up the meal in a way which would be harmful to them. In the Hildesheim area, the cold meat leftovers are often served after the soup. This would be a commendable practice if only it were accompanied by a sense of beauty and order.

Clean table linen is very important at mealtimes. Most people object to things they find disgusting, and clean, well-ironed linen will contribute to the general feeling of wellbeing which one should always try to promote during a meal. I would certainly not dissuade anyone from decorating their table with a pretty flower arrangement, even for a family meal. My only stipulation would be that this should not entail great expense but should make use of what is available seasonally.

It is important to try to avoid the above-mentioned emotions at family mealtimes too. The husband should never bring his business problems, or even any irritation with his wife, to the table with him. It is quite bad enough when the children, if there are any, have to witness the displeasure of their parents from time to time, without the adverse consequences of anger and annoyance vented during the meal! It is much better to resolve domestic discord in the privacy of the bedroom, although this method is not without reproach either.

I should like to take this opportunity of pointing out that the best housewife or cook will sometimes produce an unsuccessful dish. There will be a reason: the cook may be out of sorts or weather conditions may prevent a dish from rising properly, or one particular ingredient may not be up to standard. Married couples and house-holders must learn to restrain themselves in such circumstances because their indignation will not improve the meal before them, nor will they gain any future benefit from an unjustified outburst.

V   Entertaining and Banqueting

People have always tended to go over the top when arranging feasts. Appetite and greed are not the only factors involved here. The throwing of a great and plentiful banquet will also gratify a man's vanity and desire to show off.

Peoples who are normally sober and unusually frugal in their lifestyles tend to be fond of gluttonous repasts. This is because opposites attract each other, so that their feeling of emptiness will incite them to stuff themselves. People who have a good, plentiful diet are rarely inclined to gluttony. However, there are instances where uncultured people, who have few aesthetic sensitivities, amass huge wealth. Gluttony will then be manifested in the daily life style. This occurred in ancient Rome towards the end of the Republic, and then again before the collapse of the Empire. When incomplete intellectual development combines with a moral structure which also remains in its infancy, man is very likely to descend to the most soul-destroying of the material vices.

I would say that the middle way, the path of moderation in fact, is the best bargain in this case, as in all material matters. It may, however, remain intolerable to the spirit.

As the sea and the starry heavens suggest infinity, so prosperous, cultured people should be capable of giving an impression of plenty when they entertain. The individual guest should, however, remain all the more aware of his own limitations so that he does not strive for the unattainable, but returns to the comfortable thought that there is room for his own individuality in the great plan of things. Like the fish in the torrent, he will be able to move freely in this space.

Just like a family meal, a festive meal should be based upon four dishes which are likely to suit everyone. These should be served in large dishes and offered to every guest. They should be: soup, if appropriate, boiled meat and roast meat, and boiled fish and roast fish. These dishes should of course be prepared in the most simple and natural way possible and, with the exception of certain meats and fishes which would be too solid or fatty, should be suitable even for those who are ill or infirm.

All other dishes, be they complex or simple, stimulating or soothing, easy or difficult to digest, should be served individually around those four basic dishes. They should be positioned so that they are visible and available to all.

I believe that my readers will thank me for giving the following example of the procedures I used to follow during my years of apprenticeship in the homes of counts and princes:

1. Soup; if the table is round, there should be just one soup which should be really substantial but made with ingredients which are easily digestible and suit everyone; if the table is long, there should be two, contrasting soups such as calf's head soup (see Book One, Chapter Twelve) and crayfish soup (*ibid.*); or strong broth, in which macaroni has been thoroughly softened, served with parmesan cheese, partnered by a soup made of herbs or puréed peas, root vegetables or cereals.

Four, eight or twelve appetisers should accompany the soup, depending upon the size of the table and the number of guests.

If they are well made, the soup bowls themselves may look quite decorative on a table. Occasionally however, they are not put on the table, but on the sideboard. The servants will then hand them round. When this happens, special table decorations will occupy the places which the soup bowls would have filled. In the days when people wore wigs, these decorations were normally foolish porcelain figures arranged on stands. People had at that time developed a wonderful capacity for tolerating ugliness. This was partly due to the influence of the Chinese. They were much admired and the factories of England and France were producing Chinese-style artefacts for the rest of Europe. Expert representations of ancient statues and temples have recently appeared as table decorations but even these display a narrowness of spirit and lack of imagination, although they are more pleasing than those dolls. The popular bronze figures produced by the French suffer from a tendency to look soppy. Nowadays the most appropriate decoration is probably afforded by alabaster vases, as long as they have been modelled on the true, classical pattern. They can be filled with fresh flowers and their natural bounty will go some way towards cloaking the inadequacy of modern art.

If the table is round, it is a good idea to place a decent sized alabaster vase in the centre of the side dishes. The vase should be filled with beautiful, but unscented, flowers. When it is time for dessert, this splendid arrangement should be replaced by another of fragrant flowers. During the main part of the meal, the mixing of the fragrance of flowers with the steam from the meat and fish dishes would cause a most unpleasant smell. Furthermore, the constant nervous irritation would disturb and upset those eating. However, the scent of flowers has a beneficial effect during dessert as it will draw out and dispel the old food smells. This is why people used to hand around scented toothpicks during dessert.

Two vases are better than one if the table is long. Four small entrée dishes or side dishes should be positioned around each vase. A low table decoration, such as an imitation stone plaque or antique-style porcelain plate, appropriately painted, should be placed in the middle, exactly midway between the two vases, and also surrounded by four side dishes. During the dessert, an antique dish like this may be filled with posies of violets or other fragrant flowers, and these can then be offered to the women at the end of the meal.

Having digressed, I shall now return to the subject of appetisers. These should be small, mainly cold dishes which will stimulate the acid juices of the stomach and take the edge off people's hunger. Excessive hunger can be harmful. All the salted products, such as tongue, ham, smoked sausage, herrings, sardines, smoked salmon, caviare, botargo [salted roe] and olives are appropriate here, as are all the marinated salt fish such as Baltic herring from Norway, lampreys and eels. All of these delicacies should be served in thin slices or small chunks or, in the case of caviare, on tiny slices of toast. They should not be consumed in large quantities and guests should never incite each other to overeat.

Four dishes of salted products may alternate with four of fresh foods such as oysters. These should always be offered on all four plates. Dressed crab may also be served on slices of bread and butter, or with oil, salt, pepper and lemon juice; smoked eel may be soaked in hot water, skinned, seasoned with pepper and then grilled in individual chunks, wrapped in paper, and then served with lemon juice. Other products, such as trout from Berchtesgaden, smoked salmon from Lake Stahremberg and many other regional specialities may be served grilled. Finally, all sorts of tender cuts of meat can be served. These could be thin slices of cold roast pork or small cutlets or chops of lamb or veal, cooked in strong stock or grilled en papillote. Italian style truffles, pickled mushrooms, radishes and other small vegetable items can be included here and there.

There should also be four dishes of little pies, baked savoury mixtures or small baked fish such as fresh sardines, loach or sliced trout.

If only four appetisers are being served, you should offer a selection from all three types so that people have variety.

If oysters are very plentiful it is better to pass large dishes of them around the table than to offer them in the dishes of appetisers.

2. A large, handsome joint of boiled beef. If the table is large, it will also be possible to carve and serve a joint of roast beef or a joint of smoked or air-dried Hamburg beef. If the table is small, it will be better to make do with the boiled or roast beef.

I advise that the popular accompaniments to meat, sauces, potatoes and the like, should be passed around rather than being set on the table. The other dishes which form part of this course should be composed of plain or garnished vegetables or of poultry and other tender meats in various guises. These side dishes should never require carving – each person should be able to help himself with his own fork or with a spoon.

3. A large fish, either boiled or roasted. If boiled meat has already been served, it will be best to serve roast fish, and vice versa.

There should be four, eight or twelve side dishes offering a selection of dishes prepared from smaller fish. Others may contain tasty sausages, salmis and fricassées, some of which may be garnished with rice. Others may have a pastry base. Finally, there will be robustly flavoured cereal dishes such as macaroni or potatoes with parmesan, polenta with truffles, and so on.

4. The roast, the principal dish. This may be a leg of veal, a turkey, three pheasants or nine partridge or woodcock.

The side dishes will be composed of salads and cold, jellied confections of dainty fish, poultry, ham or wild boar. To finish, there will be tarts or cakes and sweet, floury puddings leading into the dessert.

5. Dessert. This should consist of foods which are easy to digest and will help to thin and dissolve the food already eaten. There may be cooked and preserved fruits, jellies, creams, tasty milk puddings, iced puddings, preserved spices and other confectionery, delicate cheeses and all kinds of fresh fruit.

If plenty of fruit is available, it should be arranged so as to emphasize the impression of great profusion. Pineapples and melons can be placed in the centre of antique-style raised dishes, with high feet and wide rims. These can be surrounded by peaches and figs, with grapes draped over the edge. A shortage of fruit can be disguised by skillful distribution of whatever is available in a series of small dishes or fruit baskets, whichever one has.

The meal is now served. Dear reader, kindly be seated.

VI   Cookery for those who are ill and convalescent

{NB This entire chapter not in First Edition!}

These three books already represent a style of cooking which conforms faithfully with the principles of dietetics. I have not, however, paid particular attention to those who are ill and infirm and this is why I am now taking the liberty of adding this new chapter. It owes its conception to the multifarious requests and inquiries of kindly doctors, but I would still refer the reader to the preceding books.

To be honest, there is no food that will really serve the needs of someone who is truly ill. The unwell eat more from force of habit than because they need to. They certainly do not require the nourishment, although a degree of comfortable satisfaction may be desirable.

I am referring only to the true state of being ill. In the interim stages there will, of course, be a temporary need for food, and it is then most important that the invalid be correctly nourished.

The following soup will be the most beneficial and likely to be tolerated by even the most seriously ill person: any type of grain, either whole or appropriately crushed, softened in water, with a walnut-sized knob of butter placed in the middle, and then salt added at the end (see above for Mackenzie's accurate observation on the effect of salt on the process of solution by boiling). Buckwheat should be cooked for a short time only and should not be over-softened. Rice comes next (I advise that a little beurre manié be added to rice, also some finely chopped herbs, according to the taste of the invalid). Barley, crushed spelt and oats require long, slow cooking. Indian corn grits are only palatable when cooked in meat stock. To complete the above list, we have an almost meat-like substance which is made from stale wheaten bread, soaked in water for a long period and shaken, not stirred, to which a little butter is added. This is most receptive to aromatic seasonings such as parsley, tarragon and basil. Although these soups should not resemble porridge, they should have a tendency that way. I recommend that these soups be served alternately to restrict the diet of the true invalid, whose fancies and desires should not be aroused and excited.

The various drinks known as tisanes (for the tubercular) and gruels clearly owe their origins to the same sort of observations as those on which I have based my counsel. They are usually sweetened and made palatable by the addition of lemon juice. It is also normal to offer them to invalids all through the night, as well as all day, and as a drink rather than as food. As a result, the invalid's digestive system, which is in a weak state anyway, is constantly disturbed by these tisanes, which also provide him with substances which are not good for him, at least in his current condition. In cases of prolonged illness, patients always develop an aversion to the sort of sweet-sour drinks which are normally offered to them. This reminds us of the effect of lemonade drunk shortly after a meal. The broth made from rice in chicken stock, which is traditional invalid's food in France, and the barley gruel in thin veal stock served in the Rhine area will both hold their own for longer than the sugary drinks. Although they make excellent soups, however, they are too substantial to be served as drinks.

More extensive meals are required by those who are gradually wasting away due to some illness, and particularly by those who are convalescent. In these cases it is especially important to avoid preparations which catch the eye and tickle the palate of the patient. Foods should be beneficial to the patient's condition and should not mislead the appetite, whether it be recovering or simply stimulated by illness.

The following preparations are the most reliable in these circumstances: Of the soups, the French 'bouillon de prime' (see Book One, Chapter Eleven) may be offered as a drink or served on slices of lightly toasted bread as part of the meal. Even if they were of some little value, the very method of preparing jellied consommés from overcooked meat renders them useless. Further suitable foods are: The more digestible types of meat, either grilled or spit-roasted (Book One, Chapters 5, 6, 7); chopped mixtures of poultry, veal and certain types of game (Book One, Chapter 15), any bitter, hot or stimulating seasonings being left out, however; boiled poultry and veal, which is best served straight from the cooking broth, as boiled joints tend to harden rapidly once they are out of the liquid.

Among the vegetables, the carrot is good if boiled slowly in meat stock. Potatoes should be soaked in plenty of water and then boiled in salted water until they collapse. Meat stock and a little butter may be added to them towards the end of the cooking time. I would recommend lettuce and endive of the green leaf vegetables. Young green peas may be offered in soup or may be cooked in plenty of meat stock for serving as a vegetable. They should not be cooked dry because they harden rapidly without liquid. Dwarf beans, picked young, may be lightly boiled and then steamed in meat stock. The white roots are all good but there should be no turnips, cabbage, broad beans, artichokes or cardoons. Steamed cucumbers and boiled and steamed young pumpkins will make additional little vegetable dishes which are refreshing and easy to digest.

I have my doubts regarding spinach. It will sweeten and improve watercress and dandelions but they in turn will deprive it of its character.

Doctors and nurses should be able to use these short notes to find those sections in my first two books which are of practical value to them. I am anxious to avoid the sort of repetition which would arise from any attempt to delve more deeply into this subject.

Appendix

Extract from the travel notes of my cousin, Ernst Kruesch, former valet, now host at The Bear in Aranjuez.[138]

Anyone with a few days to spend over his preparations for a trip to the Pyrenean peninsula could not do better than to spend them in the well appointed St. Etienne Hotel in Bayonne. This establishment also bears the name Posada de Sant Esteban, depicted in gold letters. He should be sure to sample the local delicacies of this prosperous area; the succulent ortolan, which is at its best in this region; the famous cuisses d'oie, which are made into a particularly delicious jellied preserve in the town, then to be distributed in pots and consumed after a quick roasting. If it is possible, he should not forget to consume a slice of Bayonne ham with a fresh, green fig and, turning to the wonderful selection of sea fish, he should sample freshly caught, marinated tuna.

The thought of these pleasures will serve to fortify him in the face of the deprivations confronting him. The Spanish 'Venta' has absolutely no knowledge of cookery other than that which the traveller manages himself. He may shoot a partridge or acquire one from the farm lads, there may be a couple of wild pigeons, or he may purchase trout, a few eggs or goats' milk on the way. All the Posada has to offer are a few quite dreadful meals, prepared in a quasi-French style.

As in all countries, the national dishes of Spain are to be found in the homes of the prosperous farmers and the middle classes. Spanish cuisine is quite limited, not artistic, and is often distorted, overrefined and suppressed, either as a result of misinterpreted arbitrariness and invention, or as a result of an even more unfortunate emulation of foreign traditions.

Judging from hearsay, people tend to regard the so-called olla potrida as Spain's only national dish. Furthermore, they regard it as a great muddle of edible ingredients. There are several misunderstandings to be cleared up here. First of all, in Spain itself, we have never come across this dish described as anything other than simply olla. It appears that the adjective dates from long ago and has been pre-served in travellers' accounts, but has disappeared in the country itself. It is also important to understand that olla is a most intricate dish which probably developed in stages. We should consider both its origins and its simplified version. Before dealing with olla, we should therefore explain the characteristics of puchero. Although this is itself a complex dish, it possesses a particular individuality, representing a most practical combination of all the nutritious and wholesome elements required for a meal. Puchero consists of vegetables and meats cooked together in the same pot until the juices are thoroughly amalgamated while the actual lumps of food remain separate.

Mutton (*carnero*) is the meat which is used most often and is regarded as most suitable. Beef (*vaca*) is also often used and some-times a little of each will be preferred. The vegetable, which is added later, according to the length of time it needs to cook, may be white cabbage, kohlrabi, broccoli or carrots, but chick peas, the favourite vegetables of the Spanish, must never be forgotten. The puchero will be all the richer if additional chick peas are included. It is, however, important to stick to the principle of one type of meat and one type of vegetable cooked together in a tight-fitting container, without worry-ing about using the cooking liquid for soup. This will result in the perfect puchero. The poor man may season his puchero with toma-toes, leeks or onions while the prosperous man will add some of the spicy sausages which the Spanish call chorizos. The best quality chorizos are made in Estremadura and distributed throughout Spain. People maintain, quite wrongly, that they are made of mule meat. A piece of bacon (*tocino*) or ham (*jamón*) is usually added to the puchero to soften and bind it and this is good practice in view of the leanness of the original meat used. In poorer households this bacon or ham may actually replace the mutton or beef. The soup, meat and vegeta-bles are then transferred from the one cooking pot to one serving dish. The fine local wheaten bread is dunked in the broth and the dish constitutes a healthy and tasty one-pot meal.

If we now expand the basic principles of puchero and apply them to a composition of all available kinds of meats and vegetables, including game birds, then we have olla. This arrives on the table with the characteristic appearance of a stratified mountain range, with mighty boulders and eyries. It is structured so that the huge joint of beef represents the rounded summit of the central mountain, against which the less stable forms appear to lean, while the lower slopes are formed by the different vegetables, kept as separate as possible, and linked by a line of fragrant chorizos which encircle the foot of the mountain. Olla requires a great deal of preparation and some skill on the part of the cook to ensure that each component is correctly cooked when it reaches the table. It also requires a large number of consumers, and the Spanish are not in the habit of eating in large groups. Therefore it cannot be considered as common, nor is it a true national dish, whereas the comfortable, unpretentious puchero is encountered everywhere. It is found in a hundred variations because it scorns no ingredients and can profit from any opportunity, from any market leftovers. It can be all things to all people.

We shall pass over a number of dishes which are mixed, baked or stewed in various arbitrary fashions. These may be the pride of their local area, but I cannot understand why, because they are neither practical nor tasty enough to deserve special mention. We shall turn instead to another national dish, gazpacho, which also appears in two quite different forms. It is found in the homes of ordinary people and on the tables of the rich.

This dish has also developed from a basic combination which was the most simple, cheap and nourishing in the circumstances. Doubtless it dates back to the earliest days of a warlike and hardworking race. It was food for the wandering herdsmen, the soldiers and emissaries, making use of the natural products they found around them. It was something which did not take up a lot of precious time, and which could be prepared without the aid of fire, a light and digestible, but sustaining dish, ideal for steeling the nerves and digestive system against the debilitating effects of the burning sun.

Gazpacho is prepared as follows: A large lump of fine wheaten bread is placed in a mortar and moistened with a fragrant, strongly flavoured olive oil. Salt and a few cloves of garlic are added, and perhaps a few small green or red peppers. The mixture is then pounded to a stiff purée and eaten straight away,[139] with the hands. We have seen working men eating this pounded creation with evident pleasure. We have also observed them undertaking the most strenuous and prolonged physical work in the burning sun of midday, having eaten only a handfull of this mixture for breakfast. It kept them going for the greater part of the day. We have, moreover, seen further evidence of the fortifying effects of garlic. Gazpacho appears to come from Andalucia.

Gazpacho takes a different form on the tables of the prosperous. A great selection of marinated fish, crab and pickles, sour cucumbers, tomatoes, peppers, anything which will tickle the palate, is served up in a large dish, surrounded by a cold, jellied, omelette-like mixture and dressed with oil and vinegar.

The Valencian method of preparing rice deserves a special mention. It would appear to date back to Moorish times. The grains are light and quite tender, but remain separate. It seems that they retain their golden colour through the use of oil in the cooking, and the addition of tomatoes gives the whole thing a most attractive reddish tinge. Arroz a la Valenciana is highly regarded throughout Spain.

Puchero disappears at the Portugese border. From Badajoz onwards, the national dish in the towns and prosperous farmhouses is polho com arroz, boiled chicken with rice cooked in the manner of an oriental pilau. The grains of rice are separate, as in the Valencian style, but tomatoes are rarely added. Going as far as Lisbon, this is the only reasonable dish.

Notes

1. In *Apol. des Hippias*, part 1, p 88 onwards, Sprengel attempts to rob Hippocrates of his *De Diaeta* books. Sprengel attributes them to a neo-Platonist from Alexandria. However, the very simplicity of the foodstuffs handled in the books indicates their antiquity.
2. An elegant example of the more recent medical works on the subject is Lud. Nonnii, *Diaeteticon, sive de re cibaria*, Antwerp, 1646, lib IV; a more comprehensive example is Jul. Alexandrini *Salubrium, sive de sanitate tuenda*. Cologne 1575, lib XVIII & XIX. There is a new edition of the latter book, which is the best of the dietetic cookbooks, including all the desirable aspects of contemporary lifestyles and scientific advances.
3. The comprehensive compilation of *Bergius über die Leckereien* offers ample evidence of this, without too much searching. From the Swedish, Halle, 1792.
4. I could give examples of cookery books which have been completely rewritten, with only the titles changed.
5. The following title of a new and extremely affected cookery book illustrates this point: The notebook, dedicated to the excellent cook who escaped from Parnassus, having been in the service of the goddesses Ceres, Diana and Pomona for many years. It has hitherto been shrouded in the greatest secrecy and its information disseminated by various ladies of Nuremberg who are skilled in the fine art of cookery. It explains how to prepare and cook one thousand, nine hundred and twenty eight dishes, both everday and rare dishes which are wholesome and tasty enough to please all tastes; soups, purees, pies, broths, vinegars, salads, sauces, essences, starters, side-dishes, eggs, fish, roast, baked, boiled and steamed, game, poultry, meat, also preserves, tarts and confectionery. It also explains when to buy all necessary ingredients and when to serve the dishes described. It has been compiled with untiring diligence and is now offered to the optional censure of those practised female artists who do not know it. All aspects of its contents, its teaching and instructions have been considerably expanded and this second edition is now printed for the public. Nürnberg, published by Wolffgang Moritz Endters, printed on the presses of Joh. Ernst Adelhülner, 1702.
6. 'Cur eget indignus quisquam te divite? quare / Templa ruunt antiqua Deum? cur, improbe, carae / Non aliquid patriae tanto emetiris avervo?' Horace.
7. 'laudas, insane, trilibrem / Mullum, in singula quem minuas pulmenta necesse est.' The last words of this verse demonstrate the iron will of convention, the inflexibility which was already beginning to penetrate the Roman style of cookery. Incidentally, I do not know whether some people wish to interpret *pulmentum* as the share of food offered to each individual guest, his portion. If we assume from the nature of Roman cookery in its state of degeneration that this fish was served chopped up, or in individual patties made from a puréed mixture, then Horace's description will give us a much clearer picture of the sheer waste of gluttony. Indeed the fish was not served in its natural shape. Apicius, lib IX, ch xiii (de Mullo): 'et si volueris in Formella piscem formabis', and Seneca *Epistles*, 95: 'torti distractique sine ullis ossibus mulli'.
8. *Apicii Coelii de obsoniis etc cum annot*. Mart. Lister. Amsterdam, 1709, lib II, ch i.
9. Liquamen; in this case the liquid is garum, rather like our soya. See Lister on Apicius.
10. I have inferred a change of object from the sense of the Latin, particularly from the plural *involuntantur*. The change is not expressed but is intended.

11. From the reading 'in omentum et singula involutantur folia lauri', Lister believes that the meatballs were wrapped in individual bay leaves. He overlooks the preceding 'in omentum'. This peritoneal membrane would be much more suitable for wrapping up the meatballs than the brittle bay leaves, which are only successful when combined with the caul fat. A similar, but simpler, dish remains common in Italy today.

12. *Satires*, II, 2.

13. *Deipnosophists*, lib I, xxx.

14. See particularly Pliny *Natural History*, lib IX, ch 54-56; the introduction of garos to the Italian coast in the same book, ch 17. Cicero in a letter to Atticus. – Qui ita sunt stulti, ut amissa republica piscinas suas fore salvas sperare videantur. [Garos was the fish originally used by the Greeks to make garum. The Romans adopted the method from them.]

15. I do not intend to imply that books of this kind are totally useless. A trained cook who is able to judge for himself and can distinguish between what is ridiculous and what is reasonable will be able to learn something from most of these books. *Das Bayerische Kochbuch* (Regensburg, published by Daisenberger) has a systematic layout and contains many useful household rules. One only has to read through the entry on leg of mutton to realise that it bears a certain similarity to the lapse of taste of the publisher of the Apician book. *Neubauers Kochbuch* (Munich, 1783) is less scientific in its approach but its instructions are more useful, following the French style. The cookery books of South Germany add lemon peel to everything while those of North Germany add almonds, raisins and rosewater. Before the revolution, the French had reduced themselves to consuming the utmost filth. Everything had the affected taste of fashion, and sometimes of worse things. My book refutes all this so I shall not trouble to criticise individual volumes.

16. War has already been declared on the traditional Bavarian style of cookery in the introduction to Neubauer's book. He says: 'anyone who wants to return to the traditional methods of cookery would do well to direct his efforts to a farmer's wedding celebration rather than at a fashionable dinner table.'

17. *Opera de Bartol. Scappi, cuoco secreto de Papa Pio V divisa etc. con il discorso funerale, che fu fatto nelle esequie di Papa Paolo III.*

18. Of these, the following cookery book, decorated with woodcuts by Jost Amman and Hanns Burgkmair, is a most splendid volume: *Ein new Kochbuch etc durch* (by) *M. Marxen Rumpolt, Churf. Meintzischen Mundkoch*, 1581, printed at Frankfurt on Main and published by M. Marx Rumpolts und Siegmundt Feyerabendts. The author of this book must have been very much in tune with the gourmets around him. There is very little mention of household necessities. He has a great deal in common with the aforementioned Scappi when it comes to the choice and arrangement of the dishes for all kinds of imperial and noble banquets. I intend to quote from this unusual book in due course. Before this, the translation of an Italian work was printed in Augsburg. Its title was: *Von der eerlichen, zierlichen, auch erlaubten Wolust des Leibes etc. durch – Bapt. Platina von Cremona etc., jetzt gründlich aus dem latein verdeutscht durch M. Stephanum Vigilium Vadimontanum. Im jar 1542.* [The honest, elegant and permissible bodily comforts etc, by Bapt. Platina di Cremona etc, now translated into German from the Latin by . . . in the year 1542.] [It has since been established that Platina was a pseudonym of Bartolomeo Sacchi.] An Italian method of carving accompanied this spread of the Italian cooking style. Books such as the *Trincier Büchlein* appeared on the subject. This explains how all sorts of foods should be sliced and served in the Italian style. Danzig, 1639.

19. The Italian novellas do mention flour pastes cooked in capon stock but this usage is very specific and certainly did not become widespread.

20. *Natural History*, lib XII, ch 7.

21. The following work is a good example of the type: *Almanac des Gourmands*, [by Grimod de la Reynière]. The early copies of this book were popular because of their liveliness. When it had been in circulation for a while, however, it became quite tiresome. There are also several poetic works which attempt to deal with

cookery. The following works are more useful: *Le cuisinier royal* (if I am not mistaken, an alternative title was *Le cuisinier impérial*), *ou l'art de faire la cuisine et la pâtisserie pour toutes les Fortunes*. This book has good intentions. [I refer to] the 8th edition, revised and corrected by A. Viard, homme de bouche, Paris, chez Barba 1814. Vegetables and herbs are used correctly. Meat stock is the basis of all dilutions. *Le pâtissier royal Parisien etc. composé par M. A.Carême*, de Paris etc, in two volumes, Paris, 1815. This book is also most instructive but gets itself lost in the idle amusements of an outrageously luxurious lifestyle. In the preface, the author explains his view thus: 'Si notre tourmente révolutionnaire a été funeste aux progräs de notre art pendant une dixaine d'années, les suivantes lui furent plus propices.' [For ten years the pain of our revolution had a morbid effect on the development of our art but, since then, circumstances have been more favourable.] The French style of cooking has also spread to England, at least to the dining tables of London. From London it has begun to displace the national dishes. We can see this in works such as: John Simpson, *A complete system of cookery etc*, third edition, London, 1813. The author is only an ordinary cook who has dedicated his book to various distinguished persons in order to appear to be a member of the fashionable circle himself. Apart from national dishes, the useful book *A new System of domestic Cookery, etc*, London, 1812, [by Maria Rundell] also contains a number of French dishes. *The recently published *Physiologie du goût* [of Brillat-Savarin] contains some important tips. It is an ingenious book.*

22. Cf *Hauschronik,* Hamburg, published by Perthes and Besser 1822, p 16.
23. This expression was used by Trajan, one of the great rulers of the Romans, see Pliny *Epistles*, no 43. lib X.
24. This was known to the ancient Greeks but its origins must lie in the rice-growing Indies.
25. *Le pâtissier royal Parisien, Discours préliminaire*, p xv.
26. More specifically the osmazome, which according to recent research is the most important and nourishing constituent of meat. [Anne Drayton explains that osmazome, the name given by the French chemist Jacques Thenard to what was in fact creatine, was a highly fashionable word in the early nineteenth century. Chambers defines creatine as 'a constant and characteristic constituent of the striped muscle of vertebrates.' Glutin is defined in the *Shorter Oxford Dictionary* as 'the viscid portion of gluten, the albuminous element of animal tissues, now called fibrin'.]
27. Carême, *loc cit* – 'et de ce bizarre galimatias ils masquaient des mets, qui n'avaient aucun rapport avec ces mauvais ingrédients. Voilà l'ennemi du bien; voilà véritablement le décor que les gourmands détestent, et que le bon goût du jour rejette et désavoue!'
28. See Alexander von Humboldt and other learned travellers on the farinaceous tubers and roots cultivated in America. Compare A. A. Cadet de Vaux, *Abhandlungen usw. aus dem Französischen*, Weimar, 1822, p 77 ff 'Vom Vegetationswasser der Kartoffeln' [the natural juices of potatoes].
29. Hippocrates, *De Diaeta*, lib III. αυτων τε των σιτων πολλυ διαψορα.
30. See Blumenbach (*Beiträge zur Naturgeschichte*) on the subject of certain deviant mummies.
31. See Raumer on the types of mineral coal.
32. *Allerneuestes Kochbuch*, Munich, 1783.
33. On page 83 of the excellent book, *Culinary Chemistry etc*, by Fredr. Accum, operative Chemist etc, London, published by R. Ackermann, 1821, there are instructions for roasting which some people might be inclined to follow just because they come from an Englishman. The advice here is to have the joint a good distance from the heat initially, and then to bring it gradually closer until it is cooked through. This rule is obviously at variance with mine. Starting on page 96 of the same book, this same author gives us a basic rule for grilling in which he cites the same reasons as I have given above for my method, to exhort the cook to expose the meat to a powerful heat at the outset so that its outer surface will seal itself, or form a crust, preventing evaporation. Now I cannot see why it should be less desirable to preserve the gelatinous materials and other tasty and nutritious

juices in the meat in the case of a spit roast than in the case of a grill. Incidentally I do not intend that the outer surface of the roast should be burnt from the start; it should just seal itself gently, forming a resistant skin.

34. In Hufeland's *Kunst*, there is a fine defence of soups as being able to prolong people's lives. The consumption of soups is also a very recent phenomenon. Soups were not yet common in sixteenth century Italy. They are still not part of English country cooking.

35. The German noun *Tunke* [sauce, gravy, dip] comes from the verb *eintunken* [to dip, or steep in; to sop]. In many German cookery books the sauce is erroneously referred to as *Brühe* [stock, broth]; *Brühe* comes, however, from the verb *brühen*, to boil or to scald; it signifies the bouillon and not the sauce.

36. The German *Sosse* comes from the French *sauce*; this comes from the Italian *salza* or direct from the Latin *salsum, salsa*, meaning something salted. Pliny gives *salsugo* and *salsilago* for brine; Apicius (lib IX) gives *in salso*, but the interpretation here is so tricky that no attempt has been made to explain it. Sauce as we understand it was known to the Romans as *jus*. During the Middle Ages, these Roman sauces were probably debased to simple brine, possibly mixed with oil and vinegar, and may have given rise to the modern European word *Salat* [salad] and to *salza*, sauce and *Sosse*.

37. Cato, *De Re Rustica*, ch 87, gives us a detailed account of his method of preparing amylon. Apicius mentions his amylum in connection with foods but does not tell us how it was prepared.

38. The following advertisement appeared in the supplement to the *Hamburgischer Korrespondent* on 15 June, 1822: 'Louise Meynier, lessons in mythology for the refined daughters of Germany. 2 Theile. 8. 1 Rthlr. Myths of the Greeks and Romans are presented in the most pleasant manner in this little course of instruction so that the young readers will acquire the knowledge thereof, so necessary to them in any refined circle, without the least danger to their moral outlook. Leipzig, April 1822. A. Wienbrack.' In other words: By reading these lessons, the young ladies are acquiring incomplete knowledge of an incomplete subject, and this very process is laying them prone to making fools of themselves in refined circles and of becoming the laughing stock of waggish fellows.

39. Whatever objections Sismondi and mankind may raise, it is to the credit of English taste that they have expelled a hostile population from the Highlands of Scotland and replaced the people with successful animal husbandry. This was the only way of assuring a sufficient supply of meat animals raised on pasture for English tables.

40. See *The Odyssey*, book 18, v. 43 and 118 ff.

41. See Apicius *De Arte Coquinaria*, Lib I, ch 8.

42. von Kotzebue, *Entdeckungsreise in die Südsee* etc, vol I, Weimar, 1821.

43. *Ibid* pp 10 and 11.

44. See Schubert's arguments against this theory in *Die Urwelt und die Fixsterne*, Dresden, 1822, p 537 ff.

45. *Clio*. Mungo Park found that the cultivation of maize was widespread in Central Africa. This leads to the conclusion that it was indigenous in the Old World, as well as in the New. The botanical varieties actually appear to be different in the new world. There is little information on the history of maize cultivation in Europe.

46. Pliny, *Natural History*, lib XVIII, ch 8 – 'Pulte autem, non pane, longo tempore vixisse Romanos manifestum.'

47. *De Diaeta*, II, x.

48. The German for yeast is *die Hefe*, but *der Hefen* is also used. By analogy, *die Hefe* is the correct form, likewise *die Hebung*, raising, and *das Hebende*, raising agent. The Italian *lievito* is derived in the same way from *levare*, to raise oneself, get up.

49. In the German edition of the writings of Cadet de Vaux, Weimar, 1822, the potato is recommended for baking bread. However, the writer uses a better method of separating the nutritional element of the potato from its juice than has been used in Germany to date.

50. See Heyne, *De originibus paneficii frugumque inventarum initiis*, in his *Opuscula*

Academica, vol I, p 330.
51. *De Diaeta,* III, 8. *Cf,* II, 8.
52. *Gazophylacium ling. Pers.,* Amsterdam, 1684, fol p 348 *ad vocem: riso.*
53. *Cauli neri,* a variety common in Central Italy.
54. *Solanum tuberosum esculentum,* Linn. Miller, from *Lycopersicon.*
55. *Cynara.* The globe variety, *hortensis,* is the most attractive, and the most popular in the North.
56. *Cynara-Cardunculus.* [The globe artichoke is *cynara scolymus.*]
57. *Cucurbita, pepo.*
58. *Cucurbita longa, folio molli, flore albo.*
59. *Pisum, sativum, hortense.* There are many varieties of varying degrees of sweetness. Details can be found in the reference works on horticulture, eg Lueder, Succow and others.
60. *Faba, major.* There are some very tasty, smaller varieties.
61. *Phaseolus [vulgaris].* Refer to the works of the horticulturalists, agriculturalists and botanists for the many varieties [of kidney bean].
62. *Cicer sativus,* the Spanish *garavanços,* a basic ingredient of [the dish] *Olla [podrida].*
63. *Apium dulce, degener, radice rapacca. Eppich* [celery]. Exhaustive details of the varieties and names of this important vegetable can be found in the scholarly notes to the newest edition of the famous Luise by J. H. Voss.
64. *Pastinaca sativa.*
65. *Daucus sativus, Carota.* Gardeners and cooks should be familiar with the varieties of carrots.
66. *Scorzonera, hispanica, latifolia sinuata.*
67. *Rapa (Brassica* Linn.)
68. *Rotunda, sativa, radice candida.* There are several different varieties.
69. *Napus sativa, radice alba.*
70. *Apium. Petroselinum latifolium.*
71. *Beta vulgaris, rubra radice.*
72. *Hortensis; alba vel pallescens.*
73. *Cucumis,* [German] *Kummerling, Kukumer. Sativus, vulgaris.*
74. *Asparagus.* See the accounts of gardeners for details of the numerous varieties of garden asparagus.
75. *Brassica - Botrytis - cauliflora.*
76. *Italica purpurea, broccoli dicta;* there is also a white variety which is not considered to be very good.
77. *Brassica oleracea.*
78. *Capitata alba.*
79. *Brassica, oleracea, capitata rubra.*
80. *Brassica Sabanda.* [In German] *Wersékohl.*
81. *Brassica Napus.* [According to Tom Stobart, kohlrabi belongs to one of the many forms of cabbage, *Brassica oleracea var. gongylodes,* but is sometimes elevated to a separate species, *Brassica caulorapa.*]
82. *Brassica peregrina, moschum olens.*
83. *Cauli neri.*
84. *Crithmum, s.* [or] *foeniculum maritimum minus.* Samphire.
85. *Allium.*
86. *Allium sativum.*
87. *Allium Scorodoprasum.*
88. *Allium Cepa.*
89. *Cepa vulgaris, floribus et tunicis purpurescentibus.*
90. *Cepa Ascalonica.*
91. *Cepa sectilis, juncifolio. – Allium schoenoprasum.*
92. *Porrum sativum commune capitatum.*
93. *Spinacia, oleracea. S. glabra.* Growers are again familiar with several varieties of spinach.
94. *Beta hortensis, alba.* Swiss variety.
95. *Acetosa:* there are many varieties. Or *Rumex* Linn.
96. *Endivia vulgaris, s.* [or] *Cichorium latifolium.* [Batavia endive or escarole.]

97. *Endivia crispa.*
98. *Lactuca.*
99. *Apium, Petroselinum, hortense.*
100. *Chaerophyllum.*
101. *Origanum. Majorana vulgaris.*
102. *Thymus vulg. erectus.*
103. *Ocymum, medium.*
104. *Angelica sativa.*
105. *Absynthium Ponticum.*
106. *Capparis spinosa.*
107. Saffron is obtained from the plant *Crocus sativus. Charthamus tinctorius* may be used as a substitute.
108. *Lycopersicon (Solanum* Linn.) *esculentum.* [Rumohr calls them *Liebesäpfel* (love apples) and *pomi d'oro.*]
109. *Mentha.*
110. *Glabra* and *candicans.*
111. *Salvia.*
112. *Ruta, hortensis.*
113. *Sambucus, nigra.* [European elder.]
114. *Anethum. [graveolens].*
115. *Erysimum vernum.* [Tom Stobart gives *Lepidium sativum* for garden cress, the cress of mustard and cress.]
116. *Nasturtium aquaticum majus et amarum (Cardamine).*
117. *Campanula, radice esculenta, Rapunculus.*
118. *Cochlearia, officinalis.* [Tom Stobart gives *Tropaeolum majus* for Indian Cress.]
119. *Poterium, Pimpinella sanguisorba.*
120. *Borrago officinalis.*
121. *Cuminum.*
122. *Coriandrum sativum.*
123. *Anethum vulgare. Finocchio dolce.*
124. *Sinapis nigra.*
125. *Capsicum.*
126. *Capsicum minimum.*
127. *Amomum Zingiber.*
128. *Caryophyllus aromaticus.*
129. *Tellina Garum.*
130. *Herbar. Amboin.* Amsterdam. 1741-50.
131. *loc cit*
132. *De la vida del picaro Guzman de Alfarache etc*, lib III, ch VII, Milan, 1603, a.p. 559.
133. His cookery book, as already mentioned.
134. This copperplate, like those mentioned subsequently, was ruined during the engraving process and the artist therefore insisted that it be omitted.
135. *Jugendspiegel* [Mirror of Youth] *etc*, by Christoph Achatius Hagerius, Francomont. Misn. etc, Hamburg, 1643. Fourth, fifth and sixth chapters in Part One.
136. Joh. v. Müller's general history offers an excellent discussion of this subject.
137. 'Alles, was ihr die Jahrszeit gibt, das bringt sie bei Zeiten / Dir auf den Tisch und weiss mit jeglichem Tage die Speisen / Klug zu wechseln.' Goethe. [She offers you the fruits of each season as they appear and knows the secret of daily variety.]
138. I am happy to recommend the 'fonda do'l Oso' to all gentlefolk. K.
139. Cf. *P. Virgilii M. Moretum*, ed. Heyn, IV. p 226-7. Anyone reading the account of the preparation of *Gaspacho* in this text will not fail to notice the elegant little poem which is attributed to Virgil. In it, a farming man wakes up, lights the lamp and stokes the fire ready to make a fresh loaf of bread. He then picks garlic and other herbs from the garden, cleans them and pounds them in a stone mortar with oil, vinegar and other ingredients, and takes the resultant purée, with the bread, to his work in the fields.

Index

This index, compiled by Marcus Bell, does not repeat the headings of the numerous chapters in the book; it is assumed that the reader will have prior acquaintance with the extensive Table of Contents at the front of the book.